China Governance System Research Series

More information about this series at http://www.springer.com/series/16158

Changhong Pei · Zhen Wang · Jingfang Sun

The Basic Income Distribution System of China

中国社会科学出版社
CHINA SOCIAL SCIENCES PRESS

Springer

Changhong Pei
Institute of Economics
Chinese Academy of Social Sciences
Beijing, China

Zhen Wang
Institute of Economics
Chinese Academy of Social Sciences
Beijing, China

Jingfang Sun
Institute of Economics
Chinese Academy of Social Sciences
Beijing, China

Translated by Yanqing Li

ISSN 2662-3048 ISSN 2662-3056 (electronic)
China Governance System Research Series
ISBN 978-981-15-3460-7 ISBN 978-981-15-3461-4 (eBook)
https://doi.org/10.1007/978-981-15-3461-4

Jointly published with China Social Sciences Press
The printed edition is not for sale in China Mainland. Customers from China Mainland please order the print book from: China Social Sciences Press.

This Springer imprint is published by the registered company Springer Nature Singapore Pte Ltd.
The registered company address is: 152 Beach Road, #21-01/04 Gateway East, Singapore 189721, Singapore

Series Preface

Since the Reform and Opening-up, China's economy and society have soared in development and much has been achieved in building socialism with Chinese characteristics. The achievements, collectively called "the China model", "the China miracle", or "the China path", have enjoyed worldwide recognition and acclamation although at the same time been questioned, twisted, and even attacked. Unfortunately, the acclamation is mostly out of recognition of China's success in economic development, but not from in-depth analysis, understanding, or applause of the systematic factors lying behind the success. Lack of understanding of China's systems is only one of the reasons, and the other, more important reason is that most people would not let go the "Western-centrism" that they deem modern. In addition, we are equally to blame because, for a long time, we have not explored and studied our socialist system with Chinese characteristics sufficiently and are thus not fully aware of and confident in it. As a matter a fact, the sustained rapid growth with the accompanying huge achievements for nearly 40 years cannot be an accident, but a result of historical continuity. There are reasons why China has successes, and the reasons are the "China theory" and the "China system". Put in other words, the achievements China has made in reforms and development are rooted in progressions of the system. As remarked by General Secretary Xi Jinping in his speech on the ceremony to celebrate the 95th anniversary of the founding of the Communist Party of China (CPC), "we must firmly believe that the socialist system with Chinese characteristics guarantees the progressive advancements of modern China fundamentally and that it is a characteristically Chinese, advantageous, strong, self-correcting and advanced system."[1]

In the practice of revolution and socialist modernization in China and on the winding road to the great revival of the Chinese nation, CPC has led the Chinese people to find a socialist path, a theoretical paradigm and a system with Chinese characteristics through arduous and complex explorations. The socialist path with Chinese characteristics is the way to realize modernization, the socialist theoretic

[1]Xi, Jinping, *Speech on 95th Anniversary of Founding of Communist Party of China*, People's Publishing House, 2016, p. 13.

paradigm with Chinese characteristics, the guide for actions, and the socialist system with Chinese characteristics, the fundamental guarantee, which are all integrated together in the great practice of socialism with Chinese characteristics. The socialist theoretic paradigm with Chinese characteristics must be eventually manifested in practice and implemented in the establishment of institutions. The results and experiences of the practices of socialism with Chinese characteristics need rules and regulations to be protected and consolidated. The Reform and Opening-up and the sustainable development of socialism with Chinese characteristics must be grounded on a system of institutions with Chinese characteristics that is comprehensive, scientific, and effective.

The modern system of China's institutions is formed through history. Our confidence in it is rooted in our rich heritage of history, culture, traditions, and practices, which collectively form unique characteristics. Unique national conditions, historical rises and falls, and cultural traditions have made China's unique system. The richness of China's history and culture is manifested in the following two aspects most prominently. The first is the global vision. China has tolerated, digested, and integrated numerous cultural factors of various nations along the history, which has continuously re-energized its own culture. The second is a love for family and country. The Chinese bear the traditional gene that seeks unification and opposes separation of China, which has united all the Chinese with a deep love for the country and a strong bond among the nation. These historical and cultural traditions have shaped the modern system in China deeply. The Chinese have struggled in pursuit of a prosperous country, a strong nation, and a happy people since the recent history, and have walked a walk with Chinese characteristics of revolutions, establishments, and development driven by reforms and opening-ups and formed a whole system of politics, economics, culture, and society step by step. As pointed out sharply by General Secretary Xi Jinping, "China's pathway of socialism with Chinese characteristics was found through the great practices for more than 30 years of the Reform and Opening-up, through the explorations for more than 60 years since the establishment the People's Republic of China, through in-depth conclusions of the development course of more than 170 years of recent history, and through inheriting and passing on the Chinese civilization of more than 5000 years, and thus is deeply rooted in history and widely supported in reality."[2] These remarks by General Secretary Xi Jinping offer clear and in-depth description on the historical heritage and practical foundation of China's system.

The modern system of institutions in China has been continuously perfected in practice. The leaders of the first generation in the Central Committee of CPC with Comrade Mao Zedong as the core led the party and the people of all ethnic groups in China to complete the new democratic revolution and the socialist transformation, establish the basic system of socialism, succeed in the social transformation that was the deepest and greatest in China's history, and lay foundations in politics and institutions for China's further development. The leaders of the second

[2] *Series of Major Speeches by General Secretary Xi Jinping*, Xuexi Press and People's Publishing House, 2014, p. 30.

generation with Comrade Deng Xiaoping as the core led the party and the people of all ethnic groups in China to draw in-depth conclusions, both positive and negative, of the building of China's socialism, make the historic decision that the major tasks of the party and the country transition to the track of economic development, start the Reform and Opening-up, and push for further development and perfection of China's system. Comrade Deng Xiaoping paid close attention to the construction of the socialist system with Chinese characteristics. In fact, he proposed the goal for the system construction as early as 1992: "it will probably take us another 30 years to have a comprehensive and mature system from all aspects, and the principles and policies in this system will be more fixed."[3]

In the recent period of nearly 40 years, we established a basic economic system and allocation system with public ownership in dominance and mutual development of various types of ownership under the guidance of CPC's "one center, two basics points" and in the great practice of the Reform and Opening-up; we established the law system with Chinese characteristics that met the demands of the socialist market economy; we further perfected the basic political system that was centered on the National People's Congress in cooperation with and seeking consultation from multiple parties under the leadership of CPC together with autonomy of ethnical regions and grass-root units; and based on all these, we established, step by step, various detailed regulations of economic, political, cultural, and social institutions, together with the institutions of the National Congress of CPC (NCCPC), democratic centralism, tenure of leaders and cadres, selection and appointment of talents, and monitoring in the party. All these institutions are connected and coordinated with each other and have formed an entire web of systems in modern China.

Since the 18th NCCPC, the Central Committee with Comrade Xi Jinping as the core has continuously pushed for innovations in practices, theories, and systems. The 3rd Plenary Session of the 18th NCCPC specified in particular to comprehensively deepen the reform, perfect, and develop the socialist system with Chinese characteristics, and promote the modernization of national governance. It signaled that the building of the system had been promoted to the importance of modernizing national governance. Detailed measures include actively exploring an effective self-monitoring mechanism in long-term rule, deepening the reform on national monitoring and supervision, establishing a supervision committee, drafting and perfecting the law of supervision, establishing an anti-corruption working system under the uniform leadership of CPC, releasing "Regulations of Self-Monitoring of the Communist Party of China", integrating the comprehensively strict management of the party with comprehensive deepening of the reform and comprehensive rule of law, and strengthening the self-cleaning, self-perfection, self-revolution, and self-improvement of CPC. Major progress has been made in strengthening the system building of power monitoring, and the integration of rule of law inside CPC and rule of law nationally has become a prominent character of China's governance.

[3] *Selected Works of Deng Xiaoping*, vol. 3, People's Publishing House, 1993, p. 372.

The confidence in China's system is not an unfounded illusion. It is grounded on the great achievements of the Reform and Opening-up through nearly 40 years and has withstood time. Meanwhile, compared to the system in the Western developed countries, the China system has increasingly shown unique advantages and strong livelihood. The world is faced with unprecedented changes and turbulence, especially since the global financial crisis in 2008, the developed countries in the West have been challenged with economic stagflation, terrorism and refugees, which, all intertwined together, have hindered these countries from development and trapped them in various dangers. Neoliberalism is refused in practice and capitalist politics and social governance are faced with unseen risks and are widely questioned. Socialism with Chinese characteristics, increasingly showing its advantages, has challenged the Western capitalism as a new system and been recognized and valued by more and more people worldwide. General Secretary Xi Jinping has also summarized these comprehensively: "Our system may effectively guarantee that people enjoy a wider range of and more solid rights and freedom and participate in the governance of the country and society in a variety of ways, may effectively lubricate the political relationships in the country, develop vigorous relationships among parties, ethnical groups, religions, classes and people outside and inside China, strengthen the bond of the Chinese nation, and form a stable and harmonious political pattern, may make achievements in major tasks with forces joined together and effectively promote the emancipation and development of the social forces of production, all modernization causes and continuous improvement of people's lives, and may effectively protect our country's independence, autonomy, sovereignty, security and interest of development and protect the Chinese people and the Chinese nation."[4]

The establishment and operation of China's comprehensive and scientific system is the greatest achievement of socialism with Chinese characteristics, is the source of our confidence, and is the definitive symbol of the great revival of the Chinese nation. The establishment and perfection of the system cannot be done overnight, and we must keep pushing for the modernization of the system with no delay. Meanwhile, system belongs to the superstructure of a society, and the building of it must follow the basic principles of the relations between the forces and means of production and the reciprocal impacts between the base and the superstructure. Currently, the macro-level system of the party and the country is only starting to diffuse to the intermediate- and micro-level institutions and there is much space for improvement in how different rules and regulations match and cooperate with each other. Arduous investigation and in-depth research must be performed on a series of major issues on the socialist path with Chinese characteristics in order to perfect and develop it. This is why the China Social Sciences Press organized distinguished domestic scholars to complete the work of *China Governance System Research Series*. The aim was to offer in-depth study and discussion on the major issues concerning the socialist system with Chinese characteristics, such as historical

[4]Xi, Jinping, Speech on the 60th Anniversary Marking the Founding of the National People's Congress, *People's Daily*, p. 2, September 6, 2014.

evolution, practical foundations, basic contents, internal logics, characteristics and advantages, future goals, and steps to take. The series is helpful for us to find where to make further efforts in the process of building the socialist system with Chinese characteristics that is comprehensive, scientific, and effective so that we are more confident in the system.

I expect that the series will become a window for readers, domestic and overseas, to learn and understand China's system.

Beijing, China
December 2016

Zhao Jianying
President, China Social Sciences Press

Introduction

Income distribution system is one of the core systems of an economy, and also a primary standard to judge the nature of an economy. The criticism of Marxist economics writers about capitalism is firstly based on the unequal distribution system of capitalism. In the imagination of future society, income distribution is one of the cores of the new system. According to the imagination of classical Marxist writers, final distribution system of communist society is "from each according to his abilities, to each according to his needs", however, since the influence of old systems still exists and productivity is not fully developed, the principle of "to each according to his work" should still be followed at the first stage of communism. In the ensuing socialist practice, public ownership of the means of production and the income distribution principle "to each according to his work" become the main symbols of the socialist system.

During the socialist construction practice in China, it was explored for a long time about which distribution system to be implemented. In the planned economy period, the principle of "to each according to his work" was once criticized as bourgeois right. Reform and opening, as it were, was started accompanying the recovery of "to each according to his work" principle. After the reform targets of socialist market economy system were established, two major theoretical problems had to be solved in the construction of distribution system, one was the relationship between the principles of "to each according to his work" and "distribution according to productive factors/contribution"; the other was treatment of efficiency and fairness in the distribution system. In practical explorations, a distribution system has been developed gradually in which "to each according to his work" is dominant, and distribution types according to productive factors/contribution, etc., coexist; the relationship between efficiency and fairness also experiences the transition from giving priority to efficiency with due consideration to fairness to considering efficiency and fairness in both primary distribution and redistribution, with more emphasis on fairness in redistribution.

With respect to the researches on income distribution system at the primary stage of socialism, on the one hand, the income distribution theories and system explorations made by classical Marxist writers and in international socialist practices should be summarized and evaluated systematically, at the same time, Western economics and income distribution theories and systems in Western developed countries should be analyzed and judged; on the other hand, the explorations in Chinese socialist construction practice should be summarized and analyzed systematically.

Since the 18th CPC National Congress, the exploration of basic socialist distribution system has become an important content of "Chinese Dream" to complete the building of a moderately prosperous society in all respects, bring about a great rejuvenation of the Chinese nation; it is also an important content to innovate and develop socialist political economics with Chinese characteristics theoretically. The key to construct socialist political economics with Chinese characteristics is to stick closely to the development pulse of the era, to the development practice of contemporary China on the basis of adhering to basic position and method of Marxian. The same applies to the exploration of basic socialist distribution system, which should be understood and grasped against the background of economic development in China entering new normal state, and new features emerging in social structure. These new features include economic growth entering decrease section, rapid demographic transition and aging of population, normalized mass population movements, continuous emerging of new technologies and new business modes and so on.

Facing these new features and new trends, central government puts forward the concept of sharing economy in the construction of basic distribution system, this is a major theoretical innovation of socialist political economics with Chinese characteristics. Adhering to the coexistence of distribution according to work and distribution according to factors/contribution, sharing economy reinterprets income distribution from the viewpoint of sharing development results by members of the society, breaks through binary opposition of efficiency and fairness, emphasizes the complementarity and compatibility of efficiency and fairness, and puts forward new policy implications.

Firstly, deepen the research on distribution according to work and distribution according to factors. Distribution according to work is a fundamental distribution principle of socialism. In traditional socialist concept, distribution according to work is opposite to distribution according to factors, distribution according to factors is a capitalist distribution principle. With the development of modern science and technology, especially the development of modern information technology and mobile technology, new industrial organization mode and employment pattern emerge, the relationship between capital and labor also changes. Especially in China where public ownership of the means of production has become dominant, capital contribution, labor value, return of other factors are combined together, the barrier between distribution according to work and distribution according to factors must be broken up, both of them are the ways of socialism to realize sharing economy. In the modern information economy characterized by new technologies such as information technology and mobile technology, new representation forms of the relationship between capital and labor appear, for example, a large number of employments without definite employers or informal employments. These new business modes and employment patterns mix distribution according to work and distribution according to factors together. Such a new situation requires further study on basic representation forms of income distribution. These new distribution forms should be included in the concept of sharing economy.

Next, emphasize coordination and unity of efficiency and fairness. It is thought in traditional economics that, efficiency and fairness are opposite, giving priority to efficiency means decrease of fairness, and emphasizing fairness means decrease of efficiency. Such a viewpoint should be further analyzed in the framework of socialist political economics with Chinese characteristics under new economic conditions. Human capital is dominant in modern economy, and investment in human capital becomes the main factor to judge whether an economy is competitive. For the investment in people and people-oriented development concept, on the one hand, large- scale investment in human capital increases efficiency, on the other hand, investment in human capital itself is the main way to eliminate poverty, realize inclusive development. The concept of sharing economy not only shares development results, but also shares development opportunities. From this viewpoint, the concept of sharing economy emphasizes more on the unity of efficiency and fairness.

Thirdly, sharing economy also requires new innovative social security concept. Social security system is main institutional arrangement for income redistribution. Traditional social security is firstly a social "safety net" to rescue competition losers and people falling into poverty. Such "passive" social security concept is not adaptive to modern social risk features. Starting with the concept of sharing economy, innovation and development are required for the concept of social security. Affordability and sustainability of social security should be considered to enhance the ability of individuals, families and the society to cope with risks from the viewpoint of eliminating vulnerability of social members; the ability of themselves to cope with risks should be enhanced, rather than only passive provision of income compensation.

Socialism is a dynamic process, rather than a static concept. The same applies to basic socialist distribution system. Distribution system has been improved continuously in the explorations from classical Marxist writers to international socialist construction practices, then to the exploration in Chinese socialist construction. Income distribution system has been developed at the primary stage of socialism in China since the reform and opening. To adapt to the new phase of economic development, a new concept of sharing economy has been developed for the basic income distribution system since the 18th CPC National Congress. This is a major theoretical innovation of socialist political economics with Chinese characteristics. This book provides a systematic and comprehensive analysis of the evolution and development of basic socialist distribution as well as the development, features and policy implications of sharing economy concept under the theme of the basic socialist distribution system. Of course, basic socialist distribution system is a very large topic, and our research is preliminary, some conclusions still need to be further discussed. It's wonderful if this book arouses the interest of readers, sheds light on any further research.

September 2016 Changhong Pei

Contents

Chapter 1
The Theoretical and Institutional Evolution of Marxist Political Economy on Distribution

Socialism is a dynamic process both in theory and practice, it is developed continuously as time goes on. In the history of the theory of socialism, income distribution system is also a dynamic, constantly developing process advancing with times. In this process, the theory and institutional practice of socialist income distribution system are also enriched and developed continuously. Classical Marxist writers only put forward some basic principles for social income distribution system in the future. In the socialist construction practice later, what kind of basic distribution system to be built has been explored continuously. Especially in the practice of socialism with Chinese characteristics, new explorations have been made on basic distribution system under the guidance of basic principles of Marxism, which has become an important component of socialist political economics with Chinese characteristics.

1 Basic Thought of Classical Marxist Writers on Income Distribution

1.1 Marx's Basic Principle of Income Distribution

In Marxist classics, basic principle of distribution starts from analyzing the capitalist relations of production. Different from previous bourgeois economists who studied distribution as the starting point of political economy, a basic viewpoint of Marxist Political Economy is to understand the distribution and relation of distribution from production and relations of production. In the four links of production, distribution, exchange and consumption, production plays a decisive role. Production not only decides the content of distribution, but also decides the form of distribution. Marx gave a special explanation for this in the introduction of Critique of Political Economy, "the structure of distribution completely depends on the structure of production, distribution itself is a product of production, not only in respect of object, but also in respect of form. In respect of object, only production results may be distributed;

C. Pei et al., *The Basic Income Distribution System of China*, China Governance System Research Series, https://doi.org/10.1007/978-981-15-3461-4_1

in respect of form, certain form participating in production decides specific form of distribution, and decides the form participating in distribution.[1] "production not only dominates production itself relative to other factors, but also dominates other factors. Process always restarts from production. Exchange and consumption cannot play a dominant role, this is self-evident. This also applies to distribution when distribution of product is concerned. When factors of production are concerned, distribution itself is a factor of production. Therefore, certain production decides certain consumption, distribution, exchange and certain relations of these different factors."[2] "Certain relation of distribution is only an manifestation of the historically specified relations of production."[3]

So understanding and analysis of the relation of distribution under different social systems firstly requires analysis of the relations of production on which relation of distribution is based. With respect to relation of distribution in capitalist society, workers could only obtain the wages to subsist due to private possession of the means of production, surplus value created by labor is possessed by bourgeoisie. Such deprivation of labor by capital comprises basic characteristic of capitalist society. Such deprivation is not only unfair, but also leads to economic crisis of capitalism from the perspective of movement process of social production, and finally leads to death of capitalism. This is a logic illuminated by Marx repeatedly in Das Kapital. The source of exploitation of working class by bourgeoisie is private possession of means of production, bourgeoisie occupies the surplus value of working class free of charge based on its occupation of the means of production. Therefore, assumption of future society is firstly the revolution of relations of production, "elimination of private ownership" becomes a banner of communists.

1.2 Two Stages of Communism

Then, what's the social form after "elimination of private ownership" and social possession of means of production is realized? Classical Marxist writers had envisaged this. These assumptions originated logically from analysis of the operating logic of capitalism. The uppermost characteristic of this new society is social possession of means of production, separation of labor from means of production caused by private possession of means of production disappears. In a capitalist society, private possession of means of production leads to the separation of labor from means of production, and this is the precondition of bourgeoisie to exploit working class. In new social form, due to social possession of means of labor, unpaid occupation of the fruits of labor of other people by some people based on their occupation of means of production disappears. Such change in the relations of production is reflected directly on relation of distribution.

[1] Selected Works of Marx and Engels (1995), p. 13.

[2] Ibid., p. 17.

[3] Marx and Engels (1974), p. 997.

Assumption of the relation of distribution in future society corresponds to the division of development process in future society. According to the understanding of Marx, future communist society which features joint occupation of means of production may be divided into two stages according to its development process: at the first stage (or socialist stage) "such communist society we mention here is not developed on its own basis, quite opposite, it is just generated from capitalist society, so it has the traces of the old society from which it was born in all aspects, including economy, morality and spirit".[4] While at advanced stage of communism "after the situation in which people have to obey work division slavishly disappears, and thus opposition between mental and physical labor also disappears; after labor is not merely a means of life, but itself becomes the first need of life; after growth of productive forces with all-round development of the individual, giving full play to all sources of social wealth".[5] Distribution mode at these two stages varies greatly due to development level of productive forces, traces of old society and other reasons. Understanding of these two differences is the key to understand basic distribution system in socialist construction practice later.

1.3 "Distribution According to Work" at the First Stage of Communism

At the first stage of communism, the distribution principle assumed by classical Marxist writers is "distribution according to work". "Distribution according to work" refers to the distribution of remaining output aggregate according to the labor input provided by members of society after necessary deductions of aggregate social product, these deductions include compensation for the consumed means of production, and guarantee fund to cope with various social risks, as well as overheads etc. With respect to distribution according to labor input provided, on the one hand, because joint occupation of means of production has been realized, members of society "could not provide anything other than their labor, on the other hand, except personal means of subsistence, nothing may become personal property",[6] so distribution may be made only according to the labor provided by each member of society.

Distribution according to work admits the income gap between people, although source of such gap is also "an unequal right", yet it is mainly the difference in different operational capability of each worker as well as the difference in family burden of different workers, rather than "class difference" generated by the difference in occupation of means of production in capitalist society.

[4]Critique of the Gotha Programme (1965), p. 12.

[5]Ibid., p. 14.

[6]Critique of the Gotha Programme (1965), p. 13.

Whereas productive forces determine the relations of production, relations of production determine the relation of distribution, such difference "is inevitable at the first stage of communist society in the form just generated from capitalist society after long labor pain".[7] According to the statement of Marx "rights can never go beyond social economic structure as well as social cultural development restricted by economic structure".[8]

Distribution according to work is not the most "ideal" distribution mode in communist society, because "the same principle prevailing in exchange of commodity equivalents also prevails here, i.e., certain quantity of labor in one form may be exchanged with equivalent labor in another form", "here equal rights are still bourgeois rights by principle".[9] With respect to the use of such distribution mode still with the traces of capitalist society, fundamental cause lies in the development level of productive forces not "extremely abundant". That is to say, the distribution mode of distribution according to work is transitional, staged and temporary. Once social productive forces are highly developed, material products are extremely abundant, people's communist consciousness reaches a certain height, then social possession of means of production will surely surpass distribution according to work in term of relation of distribution.

1.4 "Distribution According to Needs" at the Advanced Stage of Communism

After entering the advanced stage of communism, work division disappears, the difference between physical labor and mental labor disappears, labor becomes primary need, productive forces are highly developed, all sources of social wealth are given full play, "only then, can we go beyond the narrow insight of bourgeois right completely, can the society write on its banner: from each according to his ability, to each according to his needs". This is an assumption of Marx for the distribution mode at the advanced stage of communism. "From each according to his ability, to each according to his needs" is a fundamental feature at the advanced stage of communism, its basic meaning is that each worker does his best to work for the society, work for the public interests voluntarily, without any quota or remuneration, give full play to his intelligence; while the society distributes consumer goods according to the needs of everyone.[10]

According to the understanding of classical Marxist writers, the most important difference between communist society and other social forms is that "the differences in people's brains and intelligence should not cause the difference between their stomach and physical needs at all", the meaning behind this sentence is that, in a

[7]Critique of the Gotha Programme (1965), p. 14.

[8]Ibid.

[9]Ibid., p. 13.

[10]Zhou (1986).

communist society, "payment according to capability" is not allowed, "distribution according to needs" should prevail, "the difference in labor will not lead to any inequality, any privilege in aspects of occupation and consumption".[11] That is to say, any distribution mode that links the distribution of consumer goods with "labor" "contribution" "capability" is not communist. And this is why distribution according to work is still a distribution mode in the framework of bourgeois right.

The precondition for understanding "distribution according to needs" is firstly highly developed productive forces and highly developed communist consciousness of people; while institutional condition is social possession of the means of production. These two conditions are non-dispensable. If productive forces are not very developed, even if institutional condition is met, "distribution according to needs" may only be low standard ration system for workers, or could only meet basic survival needs of the members of society; if productive forces are highly developed, institutional condition is not met, i.e. social possession of the means of production is not realized, it is also very difficult to realize "distribution according to needs". "Distribution according to needs" is the basis to realize human freedom and full development, and is also one of the symbols of communist society. If distribution according to work is transitional, then "distribution according to needs" is one of the ultimate ideals of communism.

2 The Exploration of Soviet Union on Income Distribution System in Socialist Construction

Soviet Union is the first country that turned the theory of socialism into reality. For how to construct socialism, except theoretical discourse of classical Marxist writers, there was no ready-made socialist system and income distribution mode under socialist system for reference at that time. Under such conditions, the Communist Party of the Soviet Union (Bolshevik) represented by Lenin and Stalin explored how to construct socialism, and established the principle of distribution according to work and its realization form under the planned economy. One of the main features of Soviet socialist system is completely planned economy. With respect to ownership of the means of production, ownership by the whole people and collective ownership were established in this planned economic model, basic principle of "from each according to his ability, to each according to his work" was established in distribution mode.

[11] Marx and Engels (1960), p. 637.

2.1 *Theory Development of Lenin, Stalin Concerning Distribution According to Work*

1. Confirm distribution according to work as the distribution principle of socialism (the first stage of communism)
   Soviet Socialist Republic explored what kind of communist social system to be built at the beginning of its establishment. The practice of war communism shows that, it is impossible to realize the principles of communism immediately while breaking away from actual development of social productive forces. The implementation of a new economic policy is the exploration of Lenin on how to construct socialism in a backward country. In these explorations, Lenin, Stalin and Communist Party of the Soviet Union (Bolshevik) thought the basic distribution system of socialism should be distribution according to work. The practical meaning of distribution according to work is the distribution according to quality and quantity of the work provided by each member of society, "more pay for more work, less pay for less work, no work no pay".

   In the State and Revolution, Lenin divided communism into two stages when he analyzed the implementation process of communism: socialist stage and advanced stage of communism. Two main features of socialist stage are public ownership of the means of production and distribution according to work: "human being could only transit from capitalism directly to socialism, i.e. transit to public ownership of the means of production and distribution of products according to the work done by everyone."[12] However, Lenin also recognized that distribution according to work was still "unfair", distribution was made still according to "work" rather than needs. Lenin thought of two reasons for this: firstly, people do not have communist quality and consciousness, "after overthrowing capitalism, people will learn to work for the society without any rights norms immediately", this cannot be realized; secondly, lack of economic conditions, i.e. underdeveloped productive forces, "the abolishment of capitalism cannot create economic premise for such change immediately".[13]

   While Stalin included distribution according to work into the socialist formula directly, regarded it as one of the standards of socialist society, "from each according to his ability, to each according to his work" is the socialist formula of Marxism at the first stage of communism, i.e. the formula at the first stage of communist society".[14] "From each according to his ability, to each according to his needs" cannot be implemented immediately, because "class has not been completely wiped out" "work has not become primary need of people from means of survival, become voluntary work for social welfare".[15]

---

[12]The Tasks of the Proletariat in Our Revolution (1984), p. 178.

[13]The State and Revolution (1984), pp. 90–91.

[14]Conversation with a German writer, Emil Ludwig (1979), p. 308.

[15]Ibid.

2. Adhere to distribution according to work, state supervision and anti-equalitarianism
Lenin and Stalin developed the theory of distribution, continued the analysis of Marx on distribution according to work, also continued the transitional and temporary viewpoints of Marx on distribution according to work. However, facing complicated reality of socialist construction, Lenin and Stalin had to fully consider realistic conditions to realize distribution according to work, and consider the impact of distribution according to work on socialist production. In order to realize the principle of distribution according to work successfully in reality, two realistic policy issues have to be fully considered: firstly, the state supervision required for distribution according to work; secondly, distribution according to work and equalitarianism.
To promote the policy of distribution according to work, quality and quantity of the work provided by workers should firstly be measured and recorded for linking with the society products to be obtained. But in a socialist society, due to the difference of work ability between members of society, the difference between mental labor and physical labor, and due to "narrow insight of bourgeois right" "narrow insight like Shylock, haggling over every ounce ruthlessly, reluctant to work half an hour more than others, reluctant to get less remuneration than others",[16] big difference still exists in the quality and quantity of work provided by different members of society. Under such conditions, "before 'advanced' stage of communism comes, socialists require the society and sate to supervise the quantity of work and consumption strictly".[17] Of course, nature of such supervision is different from the supervision of capitalist on workers in a capitalist society. In a socialist society, social occupation of the means of production has been realized, exploitation of people by some persons who own the means of production has been eliminated, the basis of exploitation has been eliminated. Therefore, such supervision has lost the meaning of exploitation, but becomes the supervision only required for production process.
Supervision of workers, from the viewpoint of distribution according to work, not only realizes principle of equity on distribution of products according to the differences in capacity and contribution, but is also an instrument to motivate workers to work harder. At this point, equalitarianism is incompatible with distribution according to work. "Equalitarianism argues for average labor remuneration regardless of work quantity and quality, and regardless of the proficiency and labor productivity of workers. Equalitarianism is a concept of petite bourgeoisie for socialism, it thinks socialism means completely identical consumption, living conditions, tastes and needs. It brings tremendous hazard to production".[18] Lenin recognized this clearly in early phase: in a backward agricultural country like Russia, at the very beginning of socialism, if "distribution of grain in

[16]The State and Revolution (1984), p. 92.
[17]Ibid., p. 93.
[18]Prepared by the Institute of Economics (1959), p. 525.

the principle of equal distribution will generate equalitarianism. This is often detrimental to increase in production".

2.2 *The Distribution System and Distribution Pattern in the Planned Economic Period of the Soviet Union*

(I) Wage and wage system under the planned economy

Socialist economic system in the Soviet Union is a typical planned economic system, an economy of ownership by the whole people and collective ownership has been established in term of ownership structure, and complete plan control has been basically realized in the arrangement of production. Correspondingly, distribution system according to work is adopted in term of distribution. With respect to specific realization mode of distribution according to work, as assumed by Marx, distribution according to work is the distribution mode at the first stage of communism, workers "get a certificate from society, which proves how much labor provided by him (deducting the labor provided by him for social fund), and he may take this certificate to get a portion of means of subsistence from social stock equivalent to the quantity of labor provided by him".[19] This is an assumption of "labor note".

In case public ownership of the means of production has been realized, such "labor note" evolves into wage in socialist system. According to the institutional arrangement in the Soviet period, since labor trade has been eliminated under socialism, wage of workers is not the price of labor, but the voucher for distributing means of subsistence to workers specified in compliance with "economic law of distribution according to work".[20]

In fact, under the planned economy, wage together with the system of distribution according to work that specifies wage is not only the voucher for distributing means of subsistence to workers, but also "one of the most important economic instruments", such economic instrument is to encourage labor, as an instrument to motivate workers to work harder, link the distribution gains with labor contribution, "in a socialist society, such economic instrument may be used to encourage honest attitude toward labor, promote each worker to care for his labor result from individual material benefits. Therefore, wage is a powerful factor to increase labor productivity, it may combine individual material benefits of workers with national benefits (of all people) properly".[21]

The difference in wage embodies personal income difference within working class, while such difference in wage income is also an inherent requirement of distribution according to work. However, since public ownership of the means

[19] Critique of the Gotha Programme (1965), p. 12.

[20] Prepared by the Institute of Economics (1959), pp. 526–527.

[21] Prepared by the Institute of Economics (1959), p. 527.

of production has been realized, such difference is merely the difference in means of subsistence. In actual wage system, "as required by the economic law of distribution according to work, wage policy of a socialist country is established in the principle of fully differential labor remuneration".[22] Those workers with higher work ability, better labor proficiency may obtain more wages. Of course, under planned economic conditions, sector gap also exists in wage income. In the Soviet period, "higher wages are specified for workers in heavy industry sector such as metallurgical industry, coal industry, petroleum industry, machinery manufacturing industry, because the labor of major sectors of the national economy needs to be encouraged economically".[23]

In the form of wage, at the beginning of socialism, because equalitarianism tendency still exists and starting from the consciousness of socialism objecting income gap, in the 1920s, "equalitarianism and pay by the hour system was dominant in socialist enterprises of the Soviet Union".[24] such equalitarianism tendency is unfavorable to production development. In the practice of socialist construction, it has been recognized gradually that equalitarianism is not distribution according to work, nor a characteristic of socialism. Stalin thought "all people receive the same wage, equivalent quantity of meat, equivalent quantity of bread, traditional clothes, receive the same and equivalent quantity of products—such socialism is unknown to Marxism".[25] Therefore, in state-owned enterprise wage system later, the form of piece-wage has been adopted extensively. "the form of piece-wage intends to promote workers to care more about their labor result from material benefits".[26]

To use wage scale system as an incentive for workers, reasonable wage registration form should be formulated, each type of work, each kind of labor should be evaluated reasonably. Therefore, very complicated wage scale table, technical grade table were developed in the planned economic period of the Soviet Union, corresponding wage scales were set according to proficiency, technical level etc. of the workers.

(II) Wage growth and distribution pattern

In socialist construction period, wage growth is always a problem to be faced. In the framework of socialist planned economy, aggregate social product, after removing the compensation for consumed means of production, the remaining additions (i.e. V+M in the formula of aggregate social product) are the means of subsistence available for distribution after deducting the accumulation part; while in the means of subsistence, product consumption for common needs of society should also be deducted, such as public service fund, social welfare fund, education fund and other accumulations, the remaining is consumption fund available for distribution.

---

[22]Ibid., p. 528.

[23]Ibid.

[24]Prepared by Trifonov and Shirokorad (1994), p. 409.

[25]Conversation with a German writer, Emil Ludwig (1979), p. 308.

[26]Prepared by the Institute of Economics (1959), p. 530.

According to the theory of planned economy, since scheduled production has been realized under socialist planned economy, economic crisis caused by inherent conflicts between accumulation and consumption in capitalist economy has been eliminated. In actual operation process of planned economy, reasonable distribution is required between accumulation and consumption as well as between public spending deduction and means of subsistence available for distribution. In this process, an important problem is how to deal with wage growth, i.e. the so-called how to deal with the relationship between "construction" and "dining". At this point, Soviet Union developed two principles in socialist construction gradually, the first is large proportion of invisible income in real income of workers; the second is lower growth of wage than the growth of labor productivity.

Actual continuous wage growth is closely related to socialist distribution system. Under the planned economy of the Soviet Union, wage of workers is not only embodied in the income released in the form of currency, but also embodied in all inclusive social public products, social welfare and social security. In this aspect, the first is provision of public housing; the second is very low tax and stable price; the third is universal social insurance; and the fourth is public services provided in the form of physical object including education, medical care. As it were, such real income provided in non-monetary form is one of the main features of socialism under the planned economy. In the Soviet period, "real income of workers and staff is approximately one third more than their wages (in the form of currency)".[27]

At early stage of socialist construction in the Soviet Union, too high wage growth once occurred, beyond labor productivity, due to insufficient recognition of socialist construction rules, thus production growth became slower. With recognition on the laws governing socialist construction, the principle of wage growth no more than labor productivity has been established gradually. But in actual economical operation, for a variety of reasons, the growth of wage exceeded the growth of labor productivity in some major production sectors of the Soviet Union. During the period of 1966–1980, in material production sector, average wage growth was 262%, labor productivity growth was 259%; and wage growth was 1/3 faster than labor productivity growth in 1982.[28] This was one of the main reasons that led to slow economic growth at a later stage of the Soviet Union.

Soviet Union is the first country that carried out socialist construction, made many initiative explorations on distribution system in socialist construction process. To sum up, firstly, it theoretically determined distribution according to work as the only distribution principle at socialist stage, which would be transited to "distribution according to needs" gradually with the development of productive forces and the increase of workers' communist consciousness; secondly, basic principle of personal income distribution in the form of wage

[27]Prepared by the Institute of Economics (1959), p. 537.

[28]Liang (1986).

was determined in practice; thirdly, the relationship between accumulation and consumption, between economic growth and wage growth should be treated well in primary distribution. However, some problems exist in planned economy features and associated distribution mode in the Soviet period, such problems are summarized, firstly, in personal income distribution, how could distribution according to work deal with the problems between equalitarianism and wage as material incentive for workers; secondly, in primary distribution, how to deal with the relationship between "construction" and "dining".

Nevertheless, the exploration of Soviet Union on distribution system under socialist system is of initiative significance, and becomes a blueprint for socialist countries including China to extract experience later.

3 Exploration of Socialist Distribution System After the Founding of the PRC

After the founding of the PRC, how to construct socialism, how to determine the distribution principle and distribution system in the socialist system, also experienced a continuous exploration process. This exploration process on distribution system may be roughly divided into two stages: the first stage is the planned economic period from 1949 to the end of the 1970s, the second stage is from the end of the 1970s and since the reform and opening up. The theory and institutional characteristics of basic distribution system at the first stage of China are analyzed in this section.

3.1 Proportional Relation Between Accumulation and Consumption and the Development of Pooling Principle

A main feature of socialist construction in the Soviet Union was strictly planned economic system in which "regulations" were dominant. In term of basic distribution system, this feature allowed resources to be centralized for construction in a planned manner, so as to achieve fast economic growth in a period. This is the Soviet model of fast development of heavy industry. But a drawback of this model is shortage of consumer goods and overall slow income growth of workers. At a later stage of the Soviet Union, people's living standard increased slowly even stagnant, closely related to poor treatment of the relationship between accumulation and consumption.

At an early stage of the founding of the PRC, Mao Zedong had profound recognition on poor treatment of the relationship between accumulation and consumption and subsequent problems in the Soviet Union, and enhanced it to how to deal with the relationship among the interests of state, collective and individual, as well as the relationship between long-term interests and short-term interests. In his On the Ten

Major Relationships, Mao Zedong proposed to give considerations to all these three aspects with reference to the lessons of Soviet Union, and particularly pointed out, "with increase in labor productivity of workers, their labor conditions and collective welfare should be improved gradually. With the development of entire national economy, wages should also be adjusted properly".[29] With respect to the conflict of interests among state, collective and individual, "the relationship among national tax revenue, accumulation of cooperatives and personal income of peasants must be treated properly, their conflicts should be regulated frequently. The state needs accumulation, cooperatives also need accumulation, but should not be excessive. We should allow peasants to increase their personal income from additional production year after year in normal years".[30] The basic principle to handle the relations between the three is pooling, "our tax policy, commodity price policy, wage policy and cooperatives income distribution policy should ensure the capital accumulation required for socialist construction, and guarantee gradual improvement of the people's life".[31]

As basic principle to deal with the relations of distribution between accumulation and consumption, between state and collective, between individuals, although pooling has been theoretically established, yet not implemented successfully in practice, but repeated over and over again. From early stage of the founding of the PRC to the end of the 1970s, proportion of accumulation in national income was up to 43.9% (in 1959), and down to merely 10.4% (in 1964).[32]

In the Gross National Product calculated using expenditure approach, if capital formation is regarded as accumulation, final consumption is regarded as consumption, the change trend of proportion of accumulation in the period of 1952–1979 as shown in Fig. 1 fluctuates drastically. This also reflects uncertainty to determine the proportional relation between accumulation and consumption in a planned manner under planned economic conditions.

3.2 *Distribution According to Work and Wage Scale System*

The second feature of basic distribution system in Soviet Union is the determination of distribution principle according to work for individual consumer goods, and its institutionalization as wage scale system. In socialist construction of the Soviet Union, in addition to the distribution standard of consumer goods, another important role of wage is a method, tool and means to increase productivity. The thought of wage (distribution) as material incentive was highlighted at a later stage with the decline in economic growth of Soviet Union: "utilize wage in the best way, take it as one of the factors to increase labor productivity, as one of the factors to stabilize

[29] *Collected Works of Mao Zedong* (1999), p. 28.

[30] *Collected Works of Mao Zedong* (1999), p. 221.

[31] *Resolution concerning Political Report at the Eighth National Congress of the Communist Party of China*, Sept. 1956.

[32] Yu and Zhao (1993).

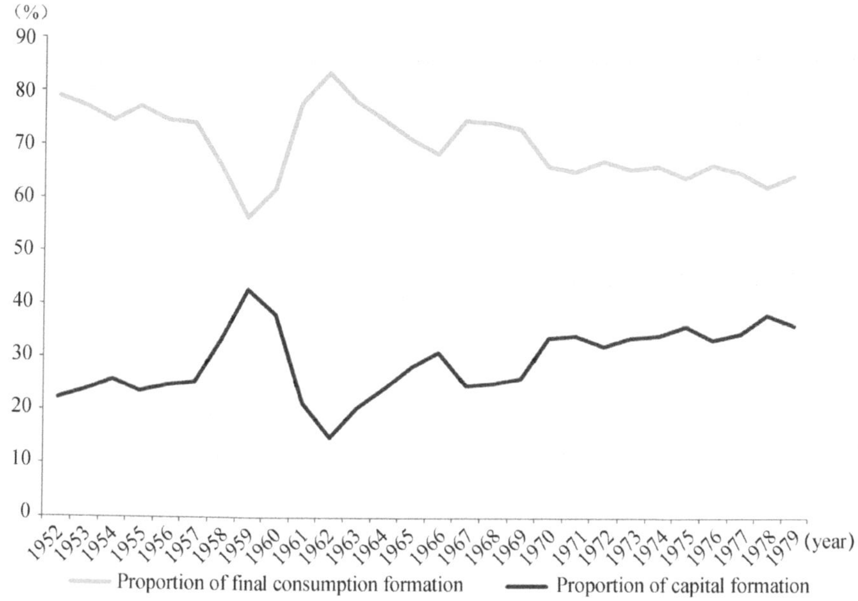

Fig. 1 Proportions of capitals formation and final consumption in gross domestic product calculated using expenditure approach (1952–1979). *Data source* Compilation of Statistics in 60 Years of the PRC. *Note* Gross Domestic Product calculated using income approach = final consumption + capital formation + net exports of goods and services. Gross Domestic Product and national income are calculated using different methods, so the proportion of accumulation in national income is somewhat different from the proportion of capital formation calculated using expenditure approach

labor force and prevent labor migration, as one of the factors to increase skills for further socialist competition and shock worker movement, rational production and better organization of labor. Wage is not only an issue of welfare level, but also an issue of labor organization."[33]

After its founding, the PRC mainly took reference from the planned economy socialism of the Soviet Union in aspect of building a socialist system, it also established the principle of "distribution according to work" in aspect of personal income distribution. In specific distribution mode, China also established wage scale system as Soviet Union gradually. Before the founding of the PRC in 1949, Communist Party of China implemented supply system for distribution of individual consumer goods, and implemented salary system for some technical workers at the base. In the period after founding of the PRC to 1955, a mixed system of supply system and partial wage system was implemented for state personnel and Party workers; in August 1955, the State Council decided to implement a new wage system to unify the standard of treatment for state personnel, thus wage scale system was implemented, from Scale 1 for chairman of the central committee to the lowest Scale 30 for odd-jobmen. In June 1956, the State Council issued a decision on wage reform, divided wage standard all

[33] Prepared by Trifonov and Shirokorad (1994), p. 405.

over China into 11 categories of districts. At the same time, in this reform, a system was also determined to specify wage standard using currency directly.[34] Wages were kept unchanged in nearly 30 years after this reform, only a few wage adjustments were made for employees of different categories or different grades.

3.3 Opposite Material Incentive and Practical Equalitarianism in Distribution Field

In addition to distribution standard of individual consumer goods, "distribution according to work" that was realized in the form of wage scale system under the planned economy also played a major role of material incentive for workers. But this tended to enlarge the income gap between workers, thus was criticized. The voice against distribution according to work as material incentive was also one of the focus issues of Soviet distribution system in dispute all along.[35] Theoretical basis against distribution according to work as incentives mainly came from temporary and transitional nature of distribution according to work. Marx assumed communism in the future at two stages, distribution principle at the first stage is distribution according to work, but distribution according to work is only a temporary distribution mode for transition to advanced stage. As analyzed by Marx in Critique of the Gotha Programme, rules of commodity exchange still prevail in distribution according to work, which embodies bourgeois right; distribution according to work is adopted at socialist stage just because conditions are not ready, once conditions are ready, "distribution according to needs" should be implemented immediately.

The viewpoint against distribution according to work as material incentive thinks that distribution according to work should not be sanctified and solidified, it should be a transitional distribution mode for "distribution according to needs". As a means of material incentive, distribution according to work also violates fundamental viewpoint of Marxism, and could really give play to its "incentive role" for workers. After the founding of the PRC, although distribution according to work was admitted by Mao Zedong in his thinking and viewpoint of socialist distribution system, yet Mao thought distribution according to work could only exist in a short time, should transit to "distribution according to needs" as soon as possible. Mao Zedong also opposed distribution according to work and wage scale system as material incentives for workers, Mao thought material incentives should not be one-sided, absolute, what may be relied on should be communist consciousness and political education, politics in command. In his talk on reading the Textbook of Socialist Political Economy of the Soviet Union, Mao Zedong pointed out that "material incentives are one-sided and absolutized in the Textbook, priority is not given to consciousness raising, this is a very big mistake in principle. Take eight-grade wage scale as an example, they could

---

[34] How the Wage System was Established in the PRC, published in *the Nanjing Daily*, Mar. 14, 2012, A23.

[35] Prepared by Trifonov and Shirokorad (1994), p. 405.

not explain why different labor situations exist in the wage of workers at the same grade. For example, among Grade Five workers, some work well, some work poorly, and some workers do a roughly good job. Material incentives are the same, why such difference exists? Following their reasoning, this doesn't make sense".[36] For incentives of material benefit, Mao Zedong thought "material benefit is an important principle, but not the only principle, nor could it be regarded as decisive action power".[37] Starting from this, Mao Zedong thought certain leeway should be left for the implementation of distribution according to work, "'thorough implementation of distribution according to work' will lead to danger of individualism".[38]

In 1975, Mao Zedong said for this "All in all, China is a socialist country. Similar to capitalism before liberation. Now eight-grade wage scale, distribution according to work, currency exchange are implemented, as near as make no difference from the old society. The difference is the change of ownership. Chairman Mao pointed out that: commodity system is implemented in China now, wage system is also unequal, eight-grade wage scale exists, and so on. These could only be restricted under proletarian dictatorship".[39] Under the guidance of this thought, such bourgeois right was explained as follows in the Socialist Political Economics published in the mid 1970s, "must be restricted under proletarian dictatorship, we should narrow grade difference gradually, criticize the ideas of bourgeois right, carry forward the spirit of communism, create material and spiritual conditions, and supersede distribution according to work with distribution according to needs gradually. Otherwise, distribution according to work will be sanctified and solidified, bourgeois right and the inequality caused by it will be consolidated, expanded and intensified, that will surely lead to polarization of rich and poor, growing income disparity, capitalism and the bourgeoisie will be developed faster".[40]

A consequence of opposition to material incentive role of distribution according to work, and emphasizing politics in command is the prevailing equalitarianism in reality, getting an equal share regardless of the work done, this influences labor productivity severely. Although Mao Zedong repeated anti-equalitarianism, "our wage system, opposes to equalitarianism, and opposes to excessive disparity",[41] at that time, Socialist Political Economics also pointed out particularly "absolute equalitarianism is the embodiment of petite bourgeoisie's equality concept in distribution issue, is the product of handicraft and small-scale peasant economy", "we should also oppose to absolute equalitarianism on the distribution of individual consumer goods".[42] However, under the development level of productive forces at that time, and under historical conditions at that time, the material incentive role of distribution according to work was needed, the so-called politics in command could not play a

[36]Prepared by Chinese History Society (2000), pp. 280–281.

[37]Ibid., p. 281.

[38]Ibid., p. 285.

[39]People's Daily, Feb. 22, 1975, A1.

[40]Prepared by the Writing Group of Socialist Political Economics (1975), p. 303.

[41]Prepared by Chinese History Society (2000), p. 285.

[42]Prepared by writing group of Socialist Political Economics (1975), p. 306.

role to promote production. On the contrary, the practice of relying on politics in command, ideological education to develop production, not only brought equalitarianism, getting an equal share regardless of the work done, "no difference for doing more or less", but material benefits were also immobilized, lifelong and hereditary, social mobility and occupational mobility were seriously limited.

4 Exploration of the Socialist Income Distribution System Since the Reform and Opening-Up

4.1 Re-establish Distribution According to Work as the Socialist Distribution Principle

Although the exploration of the socialist distribution system after the founding of the People's Republic of China adhered to distribution according to work, it over-emphasized the transitional and temporal nature of distribution according to work, emphasized that distribution according to work can lead to extreme wealth polarization and acknowledged distribution according to work to the level of "capitalism restoration".

Deng Xiaoping having first-hand experience knew this clearly. In the middle of the 1970s, after his return to the national leadership, Deng Xiaoping proposed to insist on the principle of distribution according to work and specially emphasize material incentive principle of distribution according to work. "Until now, we haven't resorted much to so-called material incentives. But people's contributions do differ. Shouldn't there, therefore, be differences in remuneration? All are workers, but some people have greater technical competence than others. Shouldn't they be upgraded and given a higher wage? Shouldn't the pay for technical personnel be raised also? It may appear that all are equal if everyone makes 40 or 50 Yuan a month, no matter whether his contribution is great or small, his technical competence high or low, his ability strong or weak, and his job heavy or light. However, in fact this practice does not conform to the principle, "to each according to his work", so how can it encourage people's initiative?"[43] The viewpoint emphasized the connection between capability, contribution, and distribution in the distribution system and the material incentive principle of distribution according to work.

Since the reform and opening-up, economic construction had been taken as the central task, which actually started with the discussions on distribution according to work. The academia held four theoretical symposiums on the issue of distribution according to work in 1977–1978 and re-established the influence of material incentives on motivating workers. "Distribution according to work can promote the development of social production and the creation of new labor productivity". No matter for workers or managements, rewardable or punishable actions should all be

[43] Selected Works of Deng Xiaoping (1994), p. 30.

accounted for and fair.[44] In 1978, the Political Research Office of the State Council drafted the article of "Implement the Socialist Principle of Distribution according to Work" and Deng Xiaoping believed that "it's a good article, and it explains why the principle discussed is socialist, not capitalist". He emphasized that the so-called distribution according to work "calls for distribution according to the quantity and quality of an individual's work. In accordance with this principle, a person's grade on the pay scale is determined mainly by his performance on the job, his technical level and his actual contribution. Political attitude should also be taken into account, but it must be made clear that a good political attitude should find expression mainly in a good performance in socialist labour and a greater contribution to society. If, in handling distribution, we judged mainly on the basis of a person's politics rather than on the basis of his work, that would mean we were following the principle "to each according to his politics" rather than "to each according to his work". In short, distribution should be made only according to a person's work, not according to his politics or his seniority."[45]

Another creation on the issue of distribution during this period was the theory that allows some individuals and regions to get rich first. Adhering to the material incentive principle of distribution according to work and distribution by the quality and quantity of work would inevitably create income gaps and the phenomena of some individuals getting rich first. On how to deal with the problem, in his speech of "Emancipate the Mind, Seek Truth From Facts and Unite As One In Looking to the Future", Deng Xiaoping proposed "in economic policy, I think we should allow some regions and enterprises and some workers and peasants to earn more and enjoy more benefits sooner than others, in accordance with their hard work and greater contributions to society."[46] He believed the regions and individuals getting rich first can promote the achievement of common prosperity with other regions, entities, and individuals through demonstration and promotion effects. "This will help the whole national economy to advance wave upon wave and help the people of all our nationalities to become prosperous in a comparatively short period."[47]

The principle of distribution according to work can have different specific realization forms. Grade wage was a realization form and distribution by work-points in rural collective economy was another form. However, actual practice had proved that both these forms were not beneficial for production development and could easily lead to equalitarianism like everyone eating from a big pot. In the late 1970s' and early 1980s, the villages first broke the old realization form of collective economy by implementing the household contract responsibility system to directly link the production result to work contribution to greatly improve the rural productivity and to evidently increase the peasant income levels. On the basis of rural reform, "Decisions on the Reform of Economic System" was passed at the Third Plenary Session of the 12th Central Committee of the Communist Party of China (CPC) to implement

---

[44] Implement the Socialist Principle of Distribution according to Work, *People's Daily*, May 5, 1978.

[45] Selected Works of Deng Xiaoping (1994), p. 101.

[46] Selected Works of Deng Xiaoping (1994), p. 152.

[47] Ibid.

economic system reform in cities. In distribution aspect, on the basis of implementing the principle of distribution according to work, the decisions include: 1. To closely link the wages and bonuses of the company workers and the enterprise economic performances, which broke the limitations of the unified grade wage system and linked the personal work with enterprise performance; 2. "Within the companies, to increase wage difference in ladders to fully realize rewards for good hard work and punish idle work and laziness, different incomes according to workload, and the difference between brain labor and manual labor, complex work and simple work, skilled labor and unskilled labor", and heavy work and non-heavy work[48]; and 3. To allow and encourage some regions, companies, and individuals to get rich first through hard work. The propositions of these reform measures adhered to distribution according to work in the distribution system and however broke the grade wage system in specific distribution forms. In the grade wage system, the wages of workers were linked to the pre-set grades, not work results. Thus the motivation orientation for workers was to improve grades. Increasing the income difference between regions, companies, and individuals in a company and linking personal income with work results would fully realize the incentive effects of distribution according to work, which is a characteristic of the distribution system reform during this period.

4.2 Distribution According to Work Playing Dominant Role with the Existence of Multiple Distribution Forms

Since the start of the reform and opening-up, China had had the imminent issue of determining the historical stages and the forms of objectives of its socialist construction. The economic regime determined by the 12th National Congress of the CPC was planned commodity economy, among which the distribution system was distribution according to work. The specific distribution form in rural villages was the household contract responsibility system and the one in cities was gradually eliminating the grade wage system and linking distribution to work results, enterprise performance, etc. From the 12th to the 13th National Congress of the CPC, China was determined to be in the socialist preliminary stage and the theory of socialism with Chinese characteristics was proposed.

On distribution form, in addition to distribution according to work, the coexistence of multiple distribution forms was acknowledged. The precondition of the acknowledgement of the coexistence of multiple distribution forms was the coexistence of multiple forms of ownerships and private economy with the public ownership playing the dominate role. The coexistence of multiple forms of ownerships was determined by the productivity development level in the preliminary socialist stage and would evidently produce multiple distribution forms. For example, "when companies issued bonds to raise funds, there would be income of interests by creditor's rights. With the appearance of share economy, there would be income by shareholding. A part of risk

[48] *Decisions on the Reform of Economic System*, Central Committee of the CPC, 1984.

compensation would be included in the income of enterprise operators. Private companies hired a certain number of labor force and it would bring the company owners a part of non-labor income." The report of the 13th National Congress of the CPC proposed that "it is permitted as long as it is legal". "Our distribution policy should not only be beneficial for well operated companies and honest working individuals to get rich first and reasonably increase the income difference, but also prevent the extreme wealth polarization and persist in the direction of common prosperity". "For overly high individual income and illegal profiteering, effective adjustment measures and strict legal actions should be taken respectively".[49] This was the acknowledgement of the basic distribution system of China of the coexistence of multiple distribution forms with distribution according to work playing the leading role.

The 14th National Congress and the Third Plenary Session of the 14th Central Committee of the CPC established the objective of China's economic system reform was to establish socialist market economic system and to make markets the foundation for resources allocation. In the socialist market economic conditions, the basic principle of income distribution was adhering to the system of the coexistence of multiple distribution forms with distribution according to work playing the leading role reflecting the principles of efficiency prioritization and giving consideration of equitability simultaneously,[50] and encouraging some regions and individuals to get rich first requiring the realization of common prosperity at the same time.

On the issue of income distribution, another important problem during the period was the overly fast increase of wages and "wages eroding profits" leading to inflation. Due to the system with planned economy playing the leading role at the time, the state-owned companies had actual soft constraints of the budgets and un-determined factors in establishing the macro-plans to cause the phenomena of too much wages and bonuses and overly fast growth of gross payroll resulting in macro-inflation.[51] It reflected that the existence of inner contradiction in implementing distribution according to work under planned economic conditions as follows: distribution demanded to link wages to work results, which linked wages to profits directly impacting the national macro-control of wages under the existing soft constraints of the budgets in the planned economic conditions.[52] For this situation, the 13th National Congress of the CPC proposed "to strictly prevent consumption inflation and to ensure the growth rate of social consumption funds less or equal to the growth rate of the assignable national income and the growth rate of the average wages and bonuses of employee less or equal to the growth rate of labor productivity".[53] For the soft constraints of the budgets behind overly high growth rate of the

[49] *Report of the 13th National Congress of the CPC*, 1987.

[50] *Decisions on the Establishment of Socialist Market Economic System by Central Committee of the CPC*, 1993.

[51] Liu et al. (1985).

[52] Dai and Li (1988).

[53] *Report of the 13th National Congress of the CPC*, 1987.

gross payroll, the 13th National Congress proposed for the companies to form self-constraining mechanism through deepening reform.[54] The Third Plenary Session of the 14th Central Committee of the CPC also proposed the growth rate of the gross payroll of the employee of the state-owned companies less than the growth rate of enterprise economic benefit and the growth rate of the average wage of the employee less than the growth rate of enterprise labor productivity.[55] The issue of the overly rapid growth of wages in the state-owned companies and the overly high gross payroll is currently an important issue resulting in China's uneven income distribution.

Another break-through in the income distribution domain during this period was starting to explicitly propose to establish the corresponding social security system for the socialist market economic system to increase secondary distribution dynamics. In the planned economic system, employees were affiliated with the companies so that the companies operated more like small societies and the labor insurances became enterprise benefits. To establish socialist market economic system, the companies took different burdens of the enterprise benefits, which affected their competitions in the markets. At the same time, from the aspect of the personal income distribution of the employee, some companies carried overly heavy burden due to the great number of old employee affecting the enterprise benefits and the income of the employee in the current period, which was unfair. Therefore, the Third Plenary Session of the 14th Central Committee of the CPC proposed to "establish multi-level social security system including social insurance, social relief, social welfare, veteran benefit and replacement, social mutual and personal saving accumulation security."[56]

4.3 Distribution According to Work and Distribution According to Productive Factors

In the exploration of the basic distribution theories and systems since the reform and opening-up, the acknowledgement of distribution according to productive factors was a great theoretical creation and leap. Before the 14th National Congress of the CPC, although the coexistence of multiple distribution factors was acknowledged, distribution according to productive factors had not been proposed explicitly. It is mainly due to classical Marxism authors' theoretical criticism on distribution according to productive factors under the capitalist regime. According to the statements of the classical Marxism authors, under the capitalist regime, distribution of capital, land, and labor was respectively realized through profit, land rent, and wage, which reflected the exploitation of capital to labor. However, what needed to be clarified was that the ideal socialism faced by the classical Marxism authors was the socialism on the

[54] Ibid.

[55] *Decisions on the Establishment of Socialist Market Economic System by Central Committee of the CPC*, 1993.

[56] *Decisions on the Establishment of Socialist Market Economic System by Central Committee of the CPC*, 1993.

basis of highly developed productivity and production material commonly owned by the whole society. Under such socialist regime, commodity currency relations would disappear and only personal labor could be used as distribution measures.

However, the construction of China's socialism was implemented on the basis of un-developed productivity and the basic national condition during the preliminary stage of socialism demanded to develop multiple ownership economy with the public ownership playing the leading role to motivate the largest group of people. The diversity of the ownership and property right structure determined the diversity of distribution forms and the necessity of distribution according to productive factors.[57] Distribution according to productive factors was acknowledged and clarified in the 15th and 16th National Congresses of the CPC as follows: "to combine distribution according to work and distribution according to productive factors, adhere to efficiency prioritization and giving consideration of equitability simultaneously to effectively optimize resources allocation, promote economic development, and maintain social stability"[58] and "to establish the principle of distribution according to the contribution of the productive factors including labor, capital, technical, management, etc. and improve the distribution system of the coexistence of multiple distribution forms with distribution according to work playing the leading role".[59]

The coexistence of multiple distribution forms with distribution according to labor playing the leading role and combining distribution according to work and distribution according to productive factors were the main characteristics of the distribution system during this period. The basis for combining distribution according to work and distribution according to productive factors was the coexistence of multiple ownership and multiple property right structure and its objective is to motivate the extensive masses to make contributions to the socialist modern construction. However, undoubtedly, distribution according to work and distribution according to productive factors could both increase the income difference and might cause some people to be caught in poverty due to various reasons. Therefore, the basic distribution system during the period determined the policies of "protecting legal incomes, striking illegal incomes, and limiting overly high incomes". At the same time, it emphasized to establish and improve the corresponding social security system with economic development level.[60]

4.4 Scientific Outlook on Development and Sharing Economy Idea

Since the reform and opening-up, the main theoretical clues of China's distribution system had been opposing to equalitarianism, re-establishment of the leading

---

[57] Wei (1999).

[58] *Report of the 15th National Congress of the CPC*, 1997.

[59] *Report of the 16th National Congress of the CPC*, 2002.

[60] *Report of the 16th National Congress of the CPC*, 2002.

role of distribution according to work, establishment of material incentive function of distribution according to work, and acknowledgement of distribution according to productive factors. The main objective of the exploration of these theories and systems was to motivate the masses to increase the development of productivity and achieve rapid economic growth. However, undoubtedly, the distribution thinking oriented with "efficiency prioritization" brought gradually increased income difference reflected by Gini coefficient, which increased from 0.2 in 1980s to 0.491 in 2008.[61] The negative influence of the overly large income difference began to appear. Under the condition, the focus of China's income distribution policy since the 16th National Congress of the CPC was to timely adjust the distribution policy and emphasize more on equitability on the basis of maintaining economic efficiency. The basic distribution theory for the period was mainly the proposition of scientific outlook of development and development fruits shared by the people and the idea developed into the new idea of sharing economy after the 18th National Congress of the CPC.

No matter the scientific outlook of development or the sharing economy, their theoretical foundation was still the socialist common prosperity theory proposed by Deng Xiaoping. He stated many times his ideology that people getting rich first drive others to follow to achieve common prosperity at last. The common prosperity is one of the basic characteristic of socialism in that "the essence of socialism is liberation and development of the productive forces, elimination of exploitation and polarization, and the ultimate achievement of prosperity for all."[62] The scientific outlook of development proposed by the 17th National Congress of the CPC demanded development fruits to be shared by the people to enrich the connotation of common prosperity. The report of the 17th National Congress of the CPC put the income distribution system reform and increasing the income of urban and rural residents together and proposed that reasonable income distribution system is the important embodiment of social equality. On specific distribution policies, it proposed "to deal with the relations of efficiency and equality for both primary distribution and redistribution with more focus on the equality of redistribution".[63] The report of the 18th National Congress of the CPC re-stated this principle. The Fifth Plenary Session of the 18th Central Committee of the CPC proposed sharing economy idea, a new creation and development of socialist basic distribution theories and systems, to include sharing economy into the overall objective of fully building moderately prosperous society. This is the new exploration to construct socialist political economics with Chinese characteristics. New explorations on income distribution under the scientific outlook of development and new sharing economy idea will be analyzed in details in the following chapters of the book.

---

[61]National Statistics Bureau first Published the Values of China's Gini Coefficient from 2003 to 2012, January 18, 2013, http://politics.people.com.cn/n/2013/0118/c1001-20253603.html, downloaded on June 20, 2016.

[62]Selected Works of Deng Xiaoping 1993, p. 373.

[63]*Report of the 17th National Congress of the CPC*, 2007.

References

Collected Works of Mao Zedong, Volume 7, People's Publishing House, 1999 Edition.

Critique of the Gotha Programme, translated by Central Compilation and Translation Bureau of Marx, Engels, Lenin and Stalin Works, People's Publishing House, 1965 Edition.

Dai Yuanchen, Li Hanming, Erosion of Profit by Wage—Potential Risks in China's Economic System Reform, *Economic Research Journal*, 6th Issue, 1988.

Karl Marx and Frederick Engels, Volume 3, People's Publishing House, 1960 Edition.

Karl Marx and Frederick Engels, Volume 25, People's Publishing House, 1974 Edition.

Liang Huaying, Exploration of Soviet Union in the Relationship between Labor Productivity Growth and Wage Growth, *Journal of Tianjin University of Finance and Economics*, 1st Issue, 1986.

Liu Guoguang et al, Commentary on Reform of Economic System and Macroeconomic Management—"International Seminar on Macroeconomic Management", *Economic Research Journal*, 12th Issue, 1985.

Prepared by Institute of Economics, Soviet Academy of Sciences, *Political Economy Textbook (Volume II)*, People's Publishing House, 1959 Edition.

Prepared by writing group of Socialist Political Economics, *Socialist Political Economics* (Preprint 2nd edition for Comments), 1975.

Prepared by Trifonov, Shirokorad, *History of Socialist Political Economy*, translated by Li Jingqi, Xu Yunqing et al, the Commercial Press, 1994 Edition.

Prepared by Chinese History Society, the People's Republic of China, *Comments and Talks of Mao Zedong on Socialist Political Economics (Abridged Edition)*, 2000.

Selected Works of Deng Xiaoping Volume 3, People's Publishing House, 1993 Edition.

Selected Works of Deng Xiaoping Volume 2, People's Publishing House, 1994 Edition.

Selected Works of Marx and Engels, Volume 2, People's Publishing House, 1995 Edition.

Talks with German writer Emil Ludwig, *Selected Works of Stalin*, Volume 2, People's Publishing House, 1979 Edition.

The State and Revolution, *The Collected Works of Lenin*, Volume 31, People's Publishing House, 1984 Edition.

The Tasks of the Proletariat in Our Revolution, *The Collected Works of Lenin*, Volume 29, People's Publishing House, 1984 Edition.

Wei Xinghua, Theoretical Issues Concerning the Combination of Distribution According to Work and Distribution According to Productive Factors, *Practice and Theory of Sezs*, 3rd Issue, 1999.

Yu Junwen, Zhao Yanrong, Study the Theory of Mao Zedong for Accumulation and Consumption, *Economic Review*, 12th Issue, 1993.

Zhou Chengqi, Historical Investigation on "From Each According to His Ability, to Each According to His Work" and "From Each According to His Ability, to Each According to His Needs", *Journal of Anqing Normal University*, 3rd Issue, 1986.

Chapter 2
Theoretical Review on Income Distribution in Western Economics

This chapter collected and reviewed the theories of distribution and distribution systems from different schools of western economics. According to tradition and time characteristics, western economics was divided into classical school, new classical school, and schools after the World War Two. The development of economics has distinctive staging characteristics and constraints endowed by resources. Therefore, theories of income distribution from different schools in different stages were reviewed from the aspect of the stages of economic development.

1 Income Distribution Ideology of Classical Economics

The representatives of the school of classical economics mainly include William Petty, Adam Smith, and David Ricardo. Among them, William Petty (M.D., 1623–1687) lived in the UK in the middle of the 17th century. Adam Smith (1723–1790) lived in the UK in the middle of the 18th century and the publication of his master work "Wealth of Nations" marked the founding of classical economics and that economics became an independent subject. David Ricardo (1772–1823) lived in the UK from the late 18th century to the early 19th century, considered consummator of classical economics. The UK lived by the three representatives of classical economics went through bourgeois revolution and industrial revolution. In the 17th century, workshop handicraft was quite common and haring a large number of labors to specialize in handicraft production was the main form of industrial production in the UK at the time. Between the bourgeois revolution and industrial revolution, workshop handicraft fully developed. It is during this period that Adam Smith lived in and it became the social background for his "Wealth of Nations". In the middle and late 18th century, gradually appearing advanced technology, like the creations of Spinning Jenny and steam engine, drove the industrial revolution to transform workshop handicraft into modern industry. It is during this time that David Ricardo lived and experienced the transformation of the economic development structures. The objective of the economic research of the three representatives was to reveal the sources

C. Pei et al., *The Basic Income Distribution System of China*, China Governance System Research Series, https://doi.org/10.1007/978-981-15-3461-4_2

Table 1 Growth rates of total output and output per capita in UK in the 17th–18th century

	Duration (years)	Grow rate every 10 years (%)		Times (compared with 100 years ago)	
		Total output	Output P.C.	Total output	Output P.C.
England and Welsh, Total Output Index, Price of 1800					
1695/1715–1765/1785	70	5.0	1.9	1.6	1.2
1765/1785–1785/1805	20	16.1	6.2	4.4	1.8
UK, Gross National Income, Price of 1865 and 1885					
1801/1811–1851/1861/1871	55	28.4	12.7	12.2	3.3
UK, Gross National Income, Price of 1913–1914					
1855/1864–1920/1924	62.5	23.0	11.1	7.9	2.9

Data source Simon Kuznets, *Economic Growth in Countries*, 1999 Edition, Commercial Press, p. 13

of national wealth growth and their economic theories were compatible with the production situation in the UK at the time. The UK was the first capitalist country and the starting place of industrial revolution. There was no referential experience in how to accumulate national wealth, most of which was carried out through comparison and research of the UK and other countries at the time. William Petty reached the conclusion through comparison from many aspects with different countries that "it is feasible and achievable for the subjects of the UK to gasp the global trade in the entire commence".[1] Therefore, we should first gather information of the economic background of the UK at the time and then elaborate on the distribution theories of the three representatives.

1.1 Economic Structure During the 17th and 18th Century

The late 18th century is considered the start of the modern economy of the UK and Simon Kuznets defined the exact time period to be 1765–1785. According to Table 1, for the time of nearly 70 years before the time period, the growth rates of the total output value and output value per capita in the UK were relatively low and it was difficult for output value per capita to double in a century. Later on, the economy in the UK grew relatively fast. The growth speed during 1765/1785–1785/1805 increased significantly with the potential for output value per capita to double in a century and the growth speed after the 19th century increased further more.

Right before the UK entering modern economics, its gross national product per capita was 227 USD (calculated for the year of 1965).[2] According to the current

[1] Petty (1978), p. 87.

[2] Simon Kuznets, *Economic Growth in Countries*, 1999 Edition, Commercial Press, p. 31.

classification of the U.N. on the development levels of countries, the UK was a low-income country at the time. This is why the research of three representatives of classical economics all focused on how to increase national wealth.

When the feudal system dominated the UK, agriculture was the main department in its national economy. The agricultural population kept dropping with the gradual collapse of the manorial system. In 1700, 66% of the rural populations were agricultural and the rest 34% were non-agricultural. The urban population only accounted for 17% of the total population and the rural population accounted for 83%. The rural non-agricultural population accounted for 28% of the total population.[3] Assuming the population distribution and industrial distribution were consistent, the percentage of the sum of urban population and non-agricultural rural population in the total population would be 45%, working in industry, and the rest 55% would be rural agricultural population. It shows that industry and agriculture had close status at the time. In 1801, the urban population increased to 27.5% and rural non-agricultural population increased to 36.25%.[4] The sum of them accounted for 63.75% of the population and the rural agricultural population accounted for 36.25%. Comparison with the previous numbers shows that the agricultural population kept decreasing and the industrial population kept increasing. This shows that the industry went through great development during the period in between.

From the aspect of factors and components needed for economic growth, land, labor, and capital were undoubtedly important growth sources. William Petty pointed out in his *A Treatise of Taxes and Contributions* that land is the mother of wealth and labor is the father. It shows that productive factors are crucial for national development.

The enclosure movement provided a large amount of labor for the development of workshop handicraft in the UK It made small farmers lose their lands to flow from agriculture into industry. Its starting reasons were that the wool price increased due to the rapid development of the textile industry in the UK and that cultivated lands were turned into pastures through enclosures to produce more wool. In addition, small pieces of cultivated lands were gathered together to realize collective cultivation, which increased agricultural productivity and created surplus labor resulting in some peasants unemployed. Although there was no specific data to reflect the number of peasants who lost their lands through enclosure movement, the existing literature does show that the number is great. "There are many newly enclosed manors, were taken and are currently owned by 4–5 rich owners from the hands of 20–30 tenant peasants and similar 20–30 smaller land owners and residents. In addition, there were many other families dependent on them to make a living. All of them were driven from the lands they previously occupied."[5] In 1698, it was mentioned by the Scotland Congress that the number of beggars in Scotland was estimated to be no less than 200,000.[6] Adam Smith pointed out in discussing labor wages that "common

---

[3]Gao (1994).

[4]Gao (1994).

[5]Marx, *Capital*, Volume 1, 1953 Edition, People's Publishing House, p. 801.

[6]Ibid., p. 797.

labor wages are determined by the contracts signed by labor and capital. … It is not difficult … to estimate which of the two parties has the upper hand. The number of owners is limited, easy to unite. … In addition, in disputes, owners always last longer than labor."[7] There were large amounts of cheap labor in the UK at the time, this was showed from the facts of enclosures, the number of beggars, and the status of labor and capital. It was an important beneficial factor for the economic development of the UK The theories of values of William Petty, Adam Smith, and David Ricardo all emphasize the importance of labor for wealth creation.

1.2 William Petty's Theory of Distribution

William Petty lived in a period close to feudal society, although some large-scale handicraft workshops emerged at that time, yet agriculture was still dominant. William Petty's theory of distribution mainly discussed the distribution of wages and land rents, profit was not listed separately. "land rent is regarded as a normal form of general value surplus, … And profit is mingled ambiguously with wage."[8] In light of this, we review the theories of wages and land rent separately as follows.

Firstly, determinants of wages. William Petty believed wages to be determined by the "things eaten for survival, labor and carrying on the family line".[9] This shows that, wages are determined by daily living expenditure of the workers for consumption, yet consumption is only limited to "things to eat", i.e. food consumption, other consumptions are not mentioned, consumption could only meet the requirements for survival, labor and carrying on the family line. When most or even all of the income is used for food consumption, this income is an extremely low income. William Petty's discussion also proved this. He thought: "law should enable workers to obtain only appropriate means of livelihood. Because, if you give double wage to a worker, then actual work done by the worker is only equal to half of the work that he could actually do in case the wage is not doubled. This means loss of products created by equivalent quantity of work for the society."[10] That is to say, in order to expand output, the wages paid to workers should only meet their necessary expenditures. Such way of wage determination was closely linked with numerous cheap workers in Britain at that time. William Petty suggested to specify wage level by law. Adam Smith mentioned in The Wealth of Nations that, the union of workers was banned by law, any group aimed at increasing labor price was prohibited. However, Adam Smith also mentioned, insufficient number of workers would lead to competition among employers, who would give higher price to hire workers.[11] It may be seen that, supply and demand structure in labor market is an important wage influencing

[7] Adam Smith, *Wealth of Nations*, Volume 1, Commercial Publishing House, p. 61.

[8] Marx and Engels (1974), p. 883.

[9] William Petty, *Political Anatomy of Ireland*, the Commercial Press, 1964 Edition, p. 57.

[10] Petty (1978), p. 85.

[11] Smith (2009), Volume I, p. 63.

factor. Besides the characteristics of labor market, development stage of Britain at that time also influenced the determination of wages. Although the economic level of Britain was relatively high at that time, yet it was only a country of low income level, the principal issue of economic development was to increase national wealth. When high wages were paid to the workers, workers would reduce their works, thus reduce output, unfavorable to the increase of national wealth.

Secondly, the source of land rent. Land rent is the remaining value of agricultural products after deducting wages, seeds and other expenses. Enclosure movement concentrated lands in the hands of the wealthy few, it became a common phenomenon to cultivate land by paying rental to the land owner, or land owner hired labors for cultivation and obtained income from land. "Land is the mother of wealth"[12] just originated from this, the difference in rents of different lands comes from the difference of lands themselves. Firstly, land rent is different due to different geographic locations of lands, secondly, land rent is different due to the difference in land fertility. Marx thought that, William Petty explained the source of differential land rents better than Adam Smith.[13]

1.3 Adam Smith's Theory of Distribution

Adam Smith's theory of distribution originated from the discussions on commodity price components. The source and determination of wage, profit and land rent as components of commodity price were discussed separately after natural price and market price of commodity were discussed.

Firstly, the theory of wages. Adam Smith made clear the purpose and main theme from the very beginning, and described the source of wages, "labor product constitutes natural remuneration or natural wage of labor". However, in case land becomes private, could realize capital accumulation, the wage of workers is merely a part of labor product. Firstly, the deduction of land rent. "once land becomes a private property, landlord will require workers to give him certain share of almost all articles produced or acquired from land. Therefore, land rent of the landlord becomes the first item to be deducted from labor product on the land." Secondly, the deduction of profit. "in any industry or manufacturing sector, most workers need advancement from their employer for raw materials, wages and cost of living before completion of the works. The employer shares their labor products, in other words, shares the added value of labor on raw materials, while this shared portion is his profit."[14]

Adam Smith discussed the determinants of wages from the aspects of minimum wage and the relationship between supply and demand in labor market, defined minimum wage from the viewpoint of cost of living. "wage of the people who live on labor must be enough to at least maintain their life… To support family members, the

---

[12]Petty (1978), p. 66.

[13]Marx and Engels (1972), pp. 384–385.

[14]Smith (2009), p. 60.

earned income of an ordinary working couple even at the lowest level must be slightly higher than the cost to maintain their own life."[15] Adam Smith positioned such wage as "minimum wage in compliance with general standards of humanity". However, at that time, the wage of British workers exceeded the amount for maintaining family life of the workers. Adam Smith described that the labor wage across the UK was not the minimum wage in compliance with the standards of humanity from the aspect of inconsistent changes of labor wage with cost of living and food price in actual life. Since the price of grain and many other things dropped sharply, "even poor workers now feel unsatisfied with previous clothing, food, shelter conditions, ... We are convinced that, the currency price and real price of labor have increased."[16]

Whether labor wage should be increased from the minimum wage in compliance with general standards of humanity is closely linked with economic development. Adam Smith mentioned that, the demand for workers is a derived demand, "the demand for wage workers increases with the increase of national wealth". The increased demand for workers will bring about rise in wages. "if, every year, employment opportunities are higher than the previous year, ... workers are insufficient, employers will hire workers at a higher price competitively." In addition, "it is not the existing huge national wealth, but the continuously increasing national wealth that boosts labor wages."[17] This shows that, rapid economic development could create more employment opportunities, demand for workers will also increase inevitably; when the supply of workers becomes insufficient, increase in labor wages becomes inevitable.

Various servants, workers and employees were called "underclass" by Adam Smith, they accounted for the largest part. Poor quality of life of such population may be seen from high mortality rate of their infants, means of livelihood still restricted their reproduction and health status.[18] This suggests that, although Adam Smith saw the impact of labor supply and demand relationship on labor wages, yet there were a large number of workers brought by enclosure movement at that time in Britain, even the wage in Britain at that time was higher than minimum wage, it is difficult to increase significantly. Because adequate labor remuneration improved children provision conditions, would increase labor supply soon, this would decrease labor remuneration. In such repetitions, labor supply would be maintained at certain level, and thus labor keeping would also be maintained at certain level, which was a low wage level.

Next, the theory of profit. While describing the source of wage, Adam Smith also described the source of profit, as mentioned above, the employer shared a part of the added value produced by workers, the shared portion is the employer's profit. This means that, profit comes from the added value of product, while this part of added value comes from production of workers. Nevertheless, the achievement of profit has its own reason, Adam Smith thought, for the employer, profit was used to "repay

[15] Smith (2009), pp. 62–63.
[16] Ibid., p. 72.
[17] Smith (2009), pp. 63–64.
[18] Ibid., pp. 72–74.

all capital of his advancement for raw materials and wages. If sales income of labor product is no more than the capital of his advancement, he will not be interested in hiring workers".[19] Profit is the precondition of investment, and the level of profit influences the amount of investment. "profit is entirely different from wage, they are controlled by two completely different principles, … Profit is completely controlled by the value of investment capital, the level of profit is in proportion to the size of capital."[20]

Since capital has strong liquidity, profit margin will tend to average profit margin gradually, and profit margin will show downtrend. The only goal of investment is profit, the higher the profit is, the higher the investment becomes. "the intention of private profit is the only motive to determine capital purposes. … seeking higher profit in whichever purpose".[21] Capital could not cope with all businesses when facing the achievement of new territory or development of new industry, "it should only be invested in those industries offering maximum profit. A part of the capital invested in other industries previously has to be taken back, and transferred to more advantageous new industry".[22] Such flow of capital keeps the profits in different industries at certain level, approaching average profit. But Adam Smith also emphasized the change of profit was too quick to capture. The decrease of profit margin was deemed inevitable by Adam Smith, "a natural result of business prosperity, or a natural result of the capital invested more than ever".[23] Adam Smith attributed the decrease of return on capital to "huge capital used and numerous rich competitors", in the meantime, "people with mass production capital usually could not hire the required number of workers, … Thus, labor wage is raised and capital profit is reduced".[24]

Finally, the theory of land rent. The same as the source of capital, land rent also originates from the added value of workers' product, as a part of it. The source of land rent is the privatization of land, land becomes a private property. To use a land, rental should be paid to landlord, the owner of land; land rent serves as the cost of land use. "To determine the conditions of tenancy agreement, landlords try to enable the portion of tenants from land product to only compensate the provision of seeds, payment of wages, purchase and maintenance of farm animals and agricultural capital of other farm implements, and provide ordinary profit of local agricultural capital." This means that, "as the cost of using land, land rent is a monopoly price".[25] On these grounds, Adam Smith discussed the source of land rent from phenomenon to cause and then to nature in three aspects, firstly, deduction of the added value of labor product, secondly, as the cost of using land, thirdly, monopoly price brought by private land ownership.

---

[19]Smith (2009), p. 42.

[20]Ibid., p. 42.

[21]Ibid., p. 354.

[22]Smith (2009), p. 87.

[23]Ibid., p. 85.

[24]Ibid., p. 84.

[25]Ibid., pp. 140–141.

1.4 David Ricardo's Theory of Distribution

David Ricardo's theory of distribution carried on Adam Smith's theory of distribution, still discussed the distribution problems in aspects of wage, profit and land rent, yet developed and emphasized them particularly to some extent.

Firstly, the theory of wages. David Ricardo had basically consistent viewpoints with Adam Smith in aspects of the source of wages and natural price of wages, also thought of wages as a part of labor product, and labor was also a commodity. Labor "like all other tradable things that may be increased/decreased quantitatively, has its natural price and market price. The natural price of labor is the price that enables workers to roughtly subsist and continue their descendants without increase or decrease".[26] This natural price of wage is determined by food and other necessities, "the strength of workers to maintain themselves and their families to keep their clans, does not depend on how much currency they earn in the name of wage, but depends on how many food necessities and habitual hedonic products that may be purchased by this amount of currency. Therefore, natural price of labor depends on the price of food necessities, habitual hedonic products required to maintain workers themselves and their families. If price of food necessities increases, natural price of labor also increases; and if price of food necessities decreases, natural price of labor also decreases".[27] With respect to the determination of natural price of labor, the definition given by David Ricardo is consistent with that given by Adam Smith, it is only enough to maintain basic needs of workers and their families to subsist, continue offspring, and guarantee labor supply according to the replacement level. The determinants of wage price still come from the price of necessities. This also reflected abundant British workers at that time, they had no bargaining power, became wage acceptors for survival.

In the theory of wages, Adam Smith thought wage would increase with the rapid growth of national income, but David Ricardo thought currency wage might increase, but actual wage of workers would tend to decrease. Natural price of labor is the foundation of wage, while market price of labor is linked with labor supply and demand, and fluctuates with the changes of supply and demand. The same as that mentioned by Adam Smith, abundant wage will bring about increase of population, while the increase of population increases labor supply, thus wage falls back to natural wage level. David Ricardo placed more attention on actual wage when he analyzed wages, in the analysis of long-term trend of wages, David Ricardo thought "with social progress, wages dominated by the ratio of supply to demand often tend to decrease".[28]

Next, the theory of profit. The value of commodity is determined by the labor required to produce commodity, and "it is unnecessary for the manufacturers of various goods to sacrifice a part of product to pay land rent. All value of their

---

[26] *The Works and Correspondence of David Ricardo*, Volume 1, the Commercial Press, 1981 Edition, p. 77.

[27] Ricardo (2014), p. 45.

[28] Ricardo (2014), p. 49.

commodities is only divided into two parts, one is capital profit, the other is labor wage".[29] After explaining the source of profit, David Ricardo studied the relationship between profit and wage. Which includes three aspects: firstly, despite the changes of labor productivity, and subsequent changes of product quantity and price of single commodity, work day of certain size always embodies the same quantity of product of value. Secondly, wage and profit change in reverse directions. The core lies in the change of labor productivity. When labor productivity increases, labor wage will decrease, thus profit will increase. Thirdly, the increase or decrease of profit is always the result of corresponding decrease or increase of labor value, never for any other reason. Marx pointed out that, "David Ricardo is the first man who formulated the above-mentioned three rules strictly".[30]

David Ricardo also thought of profit decrease as an inevitable trend. "The natural trend of profit is decrease. In case of social progress and increase of wealth, labor must be added to get additional necessary food." under the action of the above-mentioned three rules, the increase of wage inevitably causes the decrease of profit. David Ricardo also mentioned, new improvement and discovery would offset the decrease of profit. "fortunately, the machines for producing necessities are often improved, and there are new discoveries in agricultural science, so such trend of profit may be suppressed; such improvement and discoveries allow us to reduce a part of necessary labor, reduce the price of labor necessities."[31] This means that, affected by industrial revolution, David Ricardo found out the role of mechanical progress in economic development, technological advance increases labor productivity, decreases the price of necessities, and decreases actual wage, thus keeps and even expands profit, this is helpful to increase national wealth.

Finally, the theory of land rent. David Ricardo thought of the theory of land rent more important than the theory of wage and profit, in his representative work, on the Principles of Political Economy and Taxation, the theory of land rent is arranged ahead of the theory of wages and the theory of value. He thought that, if the theory of land rent is not explained first, "the impact of wealth increase on profit and wage cannot be understood, nor the impact of taxes on different social classes be explored satisfactorily; this is particularly the case when taxable commodity is a product obtained directly from ground".[32] David Ricardo did not think of land rent as the source of commodity value, on the contrary, in his opinion, the existence of land rent was not the reason of relative increase in the price of agricultural products, but the result of relative increase in the price of agricultural products. "the reason of expensive relative value of primary product is merely the investment in additional labor required for the production of final portion, not the payment of land rent. It is the investment in labor required for producing grain on a land without rent that dominates the value of grain, in other words, the labor required to produce grain

---

[29]Ricardo (2014), p. 56.

[30]Marx (1953), p. 566.

[31]Ricardo (2014), p. 64.

[32]*The Works and Correspondence of David Ricardo*, Volume 1, the Commercial Press, 1997 Edition, p. 3.

relying on the capital part without paying rent. The reason of expensive grain is not the payment of land rent; on the contrary, the reason of paying land rent is because grain is expensive. Even if landlord waives all land rents, grain price will not drop".[33] This reflects that land rent is the result of land difference, with the increase demand for agricultural products, more and more poor lands are reclaimed continuously, and more labor is required for production of agricultural products on the worst land. The value of agricultural products is thus determined by the value of agricultural products produced on the worst land, in this way, good land will earn land rent.

2 The Neoclassical Theory of Distribution

2.1 *Marshall's Theory of Distribution*

Marshall was called the representative figure of neoclassical school of economics, his representative work was the Principles of Economics published in 1890. Marshall (1842–1924) lived in Britain from the second half of the 19th century to the beginning of the 20th century. During this period, marginal revolution in economics occurred, the theory of margin was developed rapidly, and the theory of distribution was also developed with the theory of margin. Stigler thought "the theory of distribution did not exist in the 1870s. Most British economists later than Adam Smith put forward discussions on land rent, wage and profit, yet they only depicted the incomes of three most important social classes in contemporary England hardly with any important exceptions. … The fundamental defect lies in its lack of a price theory of production services".[34] Although researchers of the theory of margin may determine distribution shares according to marginal utility theory, yet the theory was not developed smoothly, until the theory of marginal productivity appeared in the 1890s. Marshall's economics originated from David Ricardo and Moeller, plus new content, he erected an economic framework, and provided instruments for economic analysis, "as far as the logic of analysis methods used by economists is concerned, no matter they research international trade, unemployment, profit, currency or any other issues, they basically always use the same illustration, such illustration does not change with their specific topics".[35]

Marshall lived in an era when British economy was being developed rapidly. Simon Kuznets defined that modern British economy started from 1765–1785, in the century of 1801–1901 thereafter, growth rate of UK GDP was about 30% per 10 years (see Table 2), far higher than the economic growth rate in the 17th–18th century as shown in Table 1. However, poverty did not disappear in Britain at that time, Marshall turned to the research on economics just because of this. "he was driven by an ethical

[33]Ricardo (2014), p. 32.

[34]Stigler (2008), p. 2.

[35]Schumpeter (2013), p. 114.

Table 2 Growth rate of GDP, population and GDP per capita in Britain in the 19th century

	Duration (year)	Growth rate per 10 years (%)		
		GDP	Population	GDP per capita
1801/1811–1831/1841	30	32.1	15.4	14.5
1831/1841–1861/1871	30	23.8	12.2	10.3
1861/1871–1891/1901	30	38.6	12.4	23.3

Data source Simon Kuznets: *Economic Growth of Nations*, the Commercial Press, 1999 Edition, p. 47

thought of charitable motive. He saw the hardship and humiliation of British poor, wished to help them to alleviate their disasters."[36] This shows that, poverty was still serious in Britain at that time, poverty still existed, and even widespread.

Just as evaluated by Schumpeter on Marshall, the logic of economic analysis will be determined according to a series of illustrations and instruments put forward by Marshall. The theory of distribution is not an exception, distribution of the factors is also under this logic.

For distribution of the factors, Marshall thought, "the distribution of national income to labor, capital and land is in proportion to people's need for their services. But such need is not total need, but marginal need. The so-called marginal need refers to the need at one point, at this point, no matter people purchase slightly more services of certain factor (or service deliverables), or use their additional funds to purchase the services of other factors (or service deliverables), there is no difference to them".[37] This means that, the income share that a factor could achieve depends on the marginal need for the product or service derived from this factor, labor, capital and land are all determined in this way.

Demand curve of manufacturers for factors is determined according to the substitution relation between factors and the theory of marginal productivity. Cost of the factors of production depends on supply price. Demand and supply determine equilibrium price of the factors jointly. This determination process is completely under the framework of Marshall's equilibrium price theory. From the perspective of factor price determination process, Marshall considered the distribution of national income based on factors.

The theory of wages. Wage serves as a compensation for labor, its price is also determined by the equilibrium between supply and demand. "demand and supply play the same role on wage, without difference, just as two edges of scissors, two columns of archway. Wage tends to be equal to pure labor product, marginal productivity of labor determines the demand price of labor, from another point of view, wage tends to be closely related to cultivation, training and the cost for keeping efficient labor energy (although indirect and complicated)."[38] Although Marshall's theory of

[36] Ibid., p. 107.

[37] Marshall, *Principles of Economics*, Volume II, the Commercial Press, 1965 Edition, p. 208.

[38] Marshall, *Principles of Economics*, Volume II, the Commercial Press, 1965 Edition, pp. 204–205.

wages did not resemble classical school any more, which determined wages based on maintaining the demand for necessities, even affected by the relation between supply and demand, wages only fluctuated around the established wage level; however, the source of Marshall to determine wages is still similar to classical school, only the content of necessities is added, there are more abundant necessities, which is reflected on labor supply curve in the form of factor supply cost.

How to determine the scope of necessities is closely linked with the level of economic development. For workers in underdeveloped countries, "because working class in most countries could consume the least luxuries, and their customary necessities are not many. The increase of their remuneration will lead to the increase of their number greatly, so their remuneration will drop rapidly to original level only for subsisting. In most parts of the world, wage is almost specified according to the so-called iron law or brazen law, this law fixes wage on a cost to foster and maintain a working class of very poor efficiency".[39] Such situation means that, labor supply is perfectly elastic, supply of workers is unlimited, without scarcity. Number of workers is determined within certain scope through reproduction, so quantity of labor is always in a state of unlimited supply. For workers in developed countries, besides the above-mentioned a basket of necessities hardly with any luxuries, they also need necessities to maintain or increase efficiency. This part of necessities increases the wages of workers in developed countries.

2.2 Keynesian Theory of Distribution

John Maynard Keynes (1883–1946) was born in London, UK, he published his representative work, *The General Theory of Employment, Interest, and Money* (hereinafter referred to as *The General Theory*) in 1936, thus established the theoretical system of modern macroeconomics. This is not to say no macroeconomics before Keynes. The sum of microeconomy was macroeconomy before Keynes, under the action of market regulation, optimal choice of individuals will inevitably bring about optimal choice of the society, they are consistent, not disjointed. However, in the era when Keynes lived, UK economy declined. UK made huge achievements in Victorian Era (1837–1901), yet declined gradually thereafter, things got worse with the outbreak of World War I. The changes of growth rate per 10 years shown in Table 3 reflected this reality clearly. Although single manufacturer still carried out production and investment in the precondition of market optimization, yet the growth rate of national wealth decreased greatly, economic crisis and unemployment problem became evident. On this background, Keynes broke up the consistency between individual optimum and social optimum in the General Theory, he pointed out that, individual optimum did not necessarily mean social optimum. As the most revolutionary aspect in Keynes' General Theory, he pointed out clearly and firmly that, with respect to the output and

[39]Marshall, *Principles of Economics*, Volume II, the Commercial Press, 1965 Edition, p. 203.

Table 3 Growth rate of UK GDP, population and GDP per capita before and after World War I

	Duration (year)	Growth rate per 10 years (%)		
		GDP	Population	GDP per capita
1855/1864–1885/1894	30	35.4	12.5	20.4
1885/1894–1905/1914	20	23.8	11.1	13.4
1885/1994–1925/1929 (excluding Ireland)	37.5	14.0	8.4	5.2

Data source Simon Kuznets: *Economic Growth of Nations*, the Commercial Press, 1999 Edition, p. 47

employment level, we couldn't see "invisible hand" guiding self-interested behavior to social optimum spontaneously in practice.[40] Keynes focused on the analysis of macroscopic variables, researched social gross output (income), how to increase gross output became the research priority of General Theory. The status of income distribution also became a part of the content influencing gross output, and the impact of unfair wealth distribution on the growth of gross output was also discussed.

In the view of classical school, savings is helpful, may bring about investment, thus means increase of national wealth, while consumption will bring about more consumption, means loss of wealth. Although Sismondi pointed out that "equal result on consumption always expands manufacturer's market; while unequal result always diminishes the market",[41] consumption also influenced gross output, but this did not become mainstream view at that time. Keynes started with the relationship between aggregate supply and aggregate demand, discussed the factors that influence aggregate demand, thus included consumption into macroeconomic theory, which became an important factor influencing gross output.

The theory of effective demand is a basic theory of Keynes for income and employment analysis. Keynes thought of effective demand as the intersection point of aggregate demand curve and aggregate supply curve, where supply price was equal to demand price. Judging from demand, effective demand refers to affordable demand; when judging from supply, effective demand could enable enterprise to realize profit maximization. This is often the case in short term when aggregate supply function is given, gross output and employment depend on aggregate demand. In the view of Keynes, aggregate demand includes two aspects, one is investment, the other is consumption. This is entirely different from the view of orthodox classical school, consumption becomes an important factor influencing output and employment. Consumption depends on income and propensity to consume. Keynes analyzed the factors influencing propensity to consume from objective and subjective views, "subjective factors … including those psychological characteristics of human nature as well as those social conventions and institutions. Although these factors are not unchangeable, but … could hardly be changed significantly in a short time. … Generally speaking, regard subjective factors as given, and assume: propensity to consume

[40] Yang (1999).

[41] Sismondi (2009), p. 211.

only depends on the change of objective factors".[42] Among objective factors, change in fiscal policy is an important one, "if fiscal policy is intentionally used as a means of relatively average income distribution, then, it will influence more on increasing propensity to consume".[43] This shows that, income distribution is one of the important factors that influence consumption and further influences gross output, and it may be changed to achieve good effect. Keynes pointed out in the General Theory that, unequal distribution of income would decrease propensity to consume. He also thought that, "significant drawbacks of the economic society in which we live: firstly, it cannot provide full employment; secondly, it distributes wealth and income in unprincipled and inequitable manner. The theory in this book has obvious effect on the first drawback. However, it's also related to the second drawback in two important aspects".[44] Mrs. Robinson further explained the influence of income distribution on output and sufficient employment. She thought "main idea of Keynesian Theory is in this way: unequal distribution of income has developed long-term trend of demand for commodities lagged behind industrial production energy".[45]

Keynes emphasized that, unequal distribution of income will bring adverse impact on the growth of gross output i.e. national income, but he did not give detailed description of how to realize equal distribution of income. Just as Gao Hongye said in the Translator's Guide "ultimate goal of this book is to put forward the countermeasures or policies to solve capitalist crisis and unemployment problems", Keynes set his foothold of solving such problems on investment, after analyzing the theory of consumption, he thought it's difficult to change the value of propensity to consume, hence he put forward "our setpoint is: employment quantity could increase only with the increase of investment".[46]

Keynes also thought the factor income distribution in microscopic field to be determined by market, the theory of margin determined factor remuneration. Based on the disjunction between micro and macro, in the chapter of price theory, Keynes mentioned "the correct bisection method recommended by me should differentiate two aspects: on the one hand, the theory of single industry or manufacturer as well as the remuneration and distribution of given quantity of resources on different usage; on the other hand, output and employment quantity of the whole society". This shows that, although Keynes proposed government intervention in economy, yet government intervention is very limited, factor compensation and distribution as well as microscopic individual behaviors are determined by market.

[42] Keynes (1999), pp. 96–97.

[43] Ibid., p. 100.

[44] Keynes (1999), p. 386.

[45] Robinson (1963), p. 4.

[46] Keynes (1999), p. 117.

3 Theoretical Study of Western Economics on Income Distribution After World War II

3.1 The Theory of Distribution of Structuralist School

With independence of a large number of developing countries after World War II, the difference of economic level and economic structure between developing countries and developed countries, promoted the booming of structuralism. Structuralism spreaded far and wide since it was used by Chenery in 1965. Structuralism contributed to the establishment of development economics discipline for research on economic growth and development issues in developing countries. Lewis, Myrdal and others obtained the Nobel Prize in Economics, further promoted the development of development economics. Structuralism thinks that, all countries have similar development path and characteristics, the process of development and growth is identifiable and regular, the core of research is how to promote economic structural transition.[47] Although neoclassical school had many questions about structuralism, yet economic growth and development became overriding consideration in developing countries after World War II, the research core of structuralism fitted this well, developing countries adopted the policy claims of structuralists to a great degree, this established dominant position of structuralism at the same time.

Representative figures of structuralism include Hirschman, Lewis, Myrdal, they all emphasized the difference between development and growth. "in more than two decades from the end of World War II to the mid and late 1960s, developing countries experienced unprecedented economic growth, yet the distribution of interests brought by economic growth was unbalanced. In most developing countries, inequitable distribution deteriorated, unemployment problem became increasingly serious, the difference between urban and rural areas was intensified continuously, absolute poverty increased with the increase of wealth. Hence, the voice of growth not equal to development rose gradually."[48] We explain the distribution ideology of a representative figure, Gunnar Myrdal, below.

Firstly, the theoretical basis of his distribution ideology—"Circular and Cumulative Causation" theory. Myrdal put forward this theory when he studied discrimination issues in America. In his book An American Dilemma: the Negro Problem and Modern Democracy, he pointed out that, "the discrimination of white people against negros and low material and cultural level of negros are two factors that interact as both cause and effect, white people's prejudice and discrimination lead to low material and cultural level of negros; while poverty and ineducation of negros intensify white people's discrimination against them in turn". "there is not only upward circular and cumulative motion, but also downward circular and cumulative motion

[47]Hu (1992).

[48]Saatchi (1988).

in 'circular and cumulative causation' between things."[49] "Circular and cumulative causation" means spontaneous growing income disparity in social economy. Such growing income disparity will inevitably participate in circular and cumulative motion, and thus influence economic development. Myrdal thought, in the cumulative process of economic changes, non-economic factors were main instruments of circular causation. This was also his basis to reprehend and criticize neoclassical school, because they neglected these non-economic factors.[50]

Next, Myrdal's theory of distribution. Myrdal put forward his theory of distribution under the theoretical frame of "circular and cumulative causation". With respect to the relationship between equality and economic development, Myrdal pointed out that "inequality and its worsening trend become a complex of restrictions and barriers to development, therefore, it's urgent to reverse this trend, and create greater equality, as a condition of accelerated development".[51] He explained general reason of "greater equality in underdeveloped countries is almost a condition of faster development"[52] from four groups of relationship, namely, income equality and savings, low income and labor productivity, social equality and economic equality as well as social justice and national cohesion. In the view of Myrdal, distribution should not be performed completely in accordance with the theory of margin of neoclassical school of economics, but should realize equal distribution, reverse the downward cumulative process. He mentioned, downward cumulative process may be reversed by national policy, this policy should "point directly at the equality in wider region: the echo effect caused by market forces has been offset, while those that cause diffusion effect are supported".[53]

Then, sources of inequality. Firstly, power. When discussing the equal slogan and unequal reality in underdeveloped countries, Myrdal pointed out that, "the policy statement of all underdeveloped countries agrees with greater equality. ... However, in almost all underdeveloped countries, economic inequality seems to expand ... Explanation of this contradiction must be linked with the distribution of power in underdeveloped countries".[54] Almost all political power is controlled by the privileged, the public is political object rather than subject. Secondly, land. Extremely low land productivity, labor productivity and underemployment exist commonly in most underdeveloped countries, determinants of these behavior patterns lie in institutional factors. "various institutions, especially those in economic and social stratifications, above all, the institutions related to land ownership and use right provide foundation for these behavior patterns, these institutions are very important to determine the use of land."[55] Agricultural laborers have no land or only have a small part of land, so they have no incentive to increase labor input and labor intensity, "tenancy system is the

[49]Jiang et al. (2003), p. 230.

[50]Trautwein (2010).

[51]Myrdal (1991), p. 44.

[52]Ibid., p. 48.

[53]Trautwein (2010).

[54]Myrdal (1991), pp. 53–54.

[55]Ibid., p. 77.

origin of complicated restrictions and barriers in South Asia, these restrictions and barriers have prevented any attempt to improve technology, increase labor efficiency and output effectively".[56] Myrdal pointed out that, "in order to create a new environment, in which workers may obtain opportunities, feel incentives and give greater play to their strengths, 'land reform' including leasehold reform must be implemented".[57] Thirdly, education. He thought, in underdeveloped countries, "education monopoly together with the monopoly of land ownership is the most fundamental foundation of inequality, the poorer the country is, the stronger the foundation becomes, the same is true even in education to the general public".[58] Screening mechanism exists in education commonly and is rooted deeply, so "even if a school is very excellent, those children from poor families will encounter severe problems after they enter the school, adhere to study and complete their schoolwork".[59] Myrdal thought, education program should include three stages, firstly, primary education, secondly, secondary and higher education, thirdly, adult education. To link these three stages together, he put forward five requirements, firstly, education quality must be guaranteed in the expansion of education coverage; secondly, priority should be given to primary education; thirdly, only fewer students may enter secondary and higher education, so as to reduce school noncompletion due to stay down, drop out and low marks; fourthly, technical, occupational and professional training should be added in secondary education and higher education; fifthly, adult education should be developed to avoid adults only with primary education becoming illiterate again.[60]

3.2 *Neoclassical School's Theory of Distribution*

Although structuralism became dominant after World War II, yet neoclassical school never stopped criticizing. Neoclassicism made a comeback in the 1960s, became dominant again. Mainly because the effect of policies based on structuralist theory was not ideal in practice, including unsatisfactory plan implementation, severe urban unemployment during expansion of industrial scale, drawbacks in trade policy of import substitution were revealed.[61] On the contrary, newly industrialized countries in East Asia under policy guidance of free market economy ranked first on economic growth rate, and the problems such as unemployment, difference between urban and rural areas were basically eliminated.[62] Comparing the results of two policies, neoclassical school became dominant again. There were many representative figures of neoclassical school in this phase, although they had slightly different propositions,

[56]Myrdal (1991), p. 90.
[57]Ibid., p. 89.
[58]Myrdal (1991), p. 173.
[59]Ibid., p. 173.
[60]Ibid., pp. 176–178.
[61]Hu (1992).
[62]Saatchi (1988).

yet basically proposed free trade and free market. Thus their theories of distribution also continued the theory of margin put forward by Marshall at previous stage, and discussed how to determine factor income on this basis. We will not repeat it here, but discuss the development theory of neoclassical school, describe the rationality of existence of inequality and its change process, thus provide theoretical basis to promote free market, free trade policies in developing countries where inequality exists commonly.

The conflict between development and equality, production and distribution is one aspect in which structuralism disproves neoclassical school. Myrdal wrote: "a preconception almost self-evident to them is, these extremely poor countries are insufficient to think and pay the cost of equality reform in aspect of social justice. Social justice must be sacrificed to achieve economic development."[63] And according to the "circular and cumulative causation" put forward by Myrdal, it is difficult to realize equality, inequality will become more and more prominent. With respect to the blame from structuralism, neoclassical school discussed economic growth vs income distribution in long-term economic development process. In which Kuznets inverted U-curve was most prominent, it explained the links between economic growth and income distribution at different development stages.

Kuznets explained the relationship between economic growth and income distribution at different development stages in his *Economic Growth and Income Inequality*.[64] Kuznets used historical data of some developed countries such as UK, USA and Germany to analyze the changes of income inequality at different per capita income levels. And then compared the data of a developing country India and a developed country USA. According to these studies, Kuznets obtained inverted U-curve between growth and distribution. Long-term trend of income distribution is "expansion before diminishing". At early stage of economic development, income distribution expands continuously; after economic development reaches certain degree, income distribution will diminish with further economic development. From cross-section view, the degree of income distribution inequality in developing countries is higher than that in developed countries, this also suggests the relationship between growth and income distribution. After this view was put forward, the attention of innumerable scholars was aroused to verify it. Judging from the results, pros and cons coexist.

3.3 Neoliberalism's Theory of Distribution

Both classical school and neoclassical school advocate free, neoliberalism also advocates free, the reason of difference from classic and neoclassical lies in the addition of sociology, politics, jurisprudence, ethics and moral science etc. into neoliberalism. Although merging many fields, yet different from multiobjective of structuralism,

---

[63]Myrdal (1991), p. 45.

[64]Kuznets (1955), 45 (1), pp. 1–28.

neoliberalism still involves single objective, ultimate purpose of adding these fields is only to create better environment for free competition, give full play to optimal capability of free competition. The representative figure of neoliberalism F. A. Hayek and the representative figure of structuralism Myrdal won Nobel Prize in Economics simultaneously in 1974. The fact that two economists with completely different viewpoints won Nobel Prize simultaneously reveals the continuous growth of different schools after World War II, in which the decline of one means the growth of another, and also shows more complicated and diversified economic development environment due to different development modes in different countries after the War.

Firstly, F. A. Hayek emphasized free competition market. Everyone is different, each participant in the market has special information, all information is decentralized, and nobody could obtain all of such information. This reality enables market allocation of resources to achieve higher efficiency. F. A. Hayek wrote in his speech for Nobel Prize in Economics: "why market order is superior, and why this order will supersede any other type of order as usual (as long as not suppressed by government power), really lies in its resource allocation using knowledge of many specific facts, such knowledge exists dispersedly among innumerable people, cannot be mastered by anyone."[65] While advocating free competition market, F. A. Hayek criticized structuralism in five aspects, i.e. technological advance, economic efficiency, democratic politics, rule of law and individual freedom of choice.

Next, F. A. Hayek's distribution ideology. under theoretical background of emphasizing free market competition, F. A. Hayek's theory of income distribution also follows the theory of margin, market itself determines factor income distribution. With respect to the relationship between equality and freedom, F. A. Hayek emphasized more on equality of opportunity. He thought "exactly similar to a competition in all important aspects, that is to say, a competition that depends in part on workmanship, in part on opportunities. … We are fully justified in demanding fair play in market competition, and fully justified in demanding no cheat, yet if we demand fair competition result for each participant, then such demand will become extremely ridiculous".[66] As can be seen, F. A. Hayek advocated equality of opportunity, process justice. But in the meantime, he also mentioned limited "equality of opportunity". He pointed out that, "although equality of opportunity is very attractive, yet once this concept is extended to be applicable to outside the scope of convenience provided by government due to some other reasons, then the proposition of equality of opportunity will become a totally illusory ideal".[67] This is consistent with neoliberalism in creating an environment for free competition. Offering the same opportunity to everyone as far as possible is also a part of free competition, resources are allocated through competition under the same opportunity condition, so resources are allocated optimally. At the same time, individualism is also respected, freedom of choice is given to everyone. It may be seen from the above-mentioned expressions of F. A. Hayek that, it is difficult to create equal opportunity environment in natural market,

[65]Hayek (1981), p. 73.

[66]Hayek (2000), pp. 128–129.

[67]Ibid., p. 148.

although it's also difficult for government to provide absolute equality of opportunity, yet government could still promote equality of opportunity to certain degree. This also embodies the difference between neoliberalism and classical school, government should create environment for free competition, but should not intervene the freedom of market itself.

References

Adam Smith, *The Wealth of Nations*, the Commercial Press, 2009 Edition.
David Ricardo, *Principles of Political Economy and Taxation*, Shanghai Joint Publishing Press, 2014 Edition.
F. A. Hayek, *Law, Legislation, and Liberty* Volume 2, Encyclopedia of China Publishing House, 2000 Edition.
F. A. Hayek, the Use of Knowledge in Society, published in *The Proceedings of Modern Foreign Economics*, Second Collection, the Commercial Press, 1981 Edition.
Gao Debu, Coordinated Development of Industrialization and Urbanization—Case study of British Economic History, *Social Science Front*, 4th Issue, 1994.
Gunnar Myrdal, *The Challenge of World Poverty—A World Anti-Poverty Program in Outline*, Beijing Institute of Economics Press, 1991 Edition.
Hans Michael Trautwein, Cumulative Processes and Polarizing Development: Myrdal's Contribution, *Review of the History of Economic Thought*, 1st Issue, 2010.
Hu Jian, Discussion on Structuralism and Neoclassicism Thoughts in Development Economics, *Economic Science*, 2nd Issue, 1992.
Jiang Ziqiang et al, *General History of Economic Thought* Volume 4, Zhejiang University Press, 2003 Edition.
Joseph schumpeter, *Ten Great Economists: From Marx to Keynes*, the Commercial Press, 2013 Edition.
Karl Marx and Frederick Engels, Volume 26, Book 1, People's Publishing House, 1972 Edition.
Karl Marx and Frederick Engels, Volume 25, People's Publishing House, 1974 Edition.
Keynes, *The General Theory of Employment Interest and Money*, the Commercial Press, 1999 Edition.
Kuznets, Simon, Economic Growth and Income Inequality, *The American Economic Review*, 1955, 45 (1), pp. 1–28.
Marx, *Das Kapital* Volume 1, People's Publishing House, 1953 Edition.
Robinson, *Marx, Marshall and Keynes*, the Commercial Press, 1963 Edition.
Saatchi, Prosperity and Depression of Structuralism, Neoclassicism and Development Economics, *The Journal of World Economy*, 7th Issue, 1988.
Sismondi, *New Principles of Political Economy*, the Commercial Press, 2009 Edition.
Stigler, *Production and Distribution Theories*, Huaxia Publishing House, 2008 Edition.
William Petty, *Political Arithmetic*, the Commercial Press, 1978 Edition.
William Petty, *Treatise on Taxes and Contributions, Verbum Sapienti, Quantulumcunque Concerning Money*, the Commercial Press, 1978 Edition.
Yang Chunxue, Significant Development of Economics in the 20th Century, *Economic Perspectives*, 10th Issue, 1999.

Chapter 3
Primary Distribution and Macro Distribution Patterns of National Income

With the gradual deepening of reform and opening up, China's economy has been developed quickly since the establishment of socialist market economy system in 1994, but in the meantime, income distribution has also been deteriorated continuously. The ceaselessly widened income gap has become the focus of people of all walks of life. This chapter firstly describes the necessity to reform low efficiency distribution system, and reviews the evolution of income distribution system since 1994. Then, analyzes overall change trend of resident income distribution status since the reform and opening up according to Gini coefficient and social structure, and discusses the reason of large resident income gap. We may find from the reasons of yawning income gap of residents that, yawning income gap is mainly reflected between urban and rural, regional and industrial fields, as well as a bit low share of labor remuneration. In view of this, urban and rural, regional and industrial income gaps as well as labor remuneration change trend are analyzed in two sections below.

1 The Evolution of Income Distribution System

1.1 The Necessity to Reform Low Efficiency Distribution System

If systems are divided according to process justice and outcome justice, distribution system was centered at outcome justice before reform and opening up. Under the background of heavy industry priority development strategy, labor migration between urban and rural areas is restricted strictly. Under a series of systems such as household registration system, food stamp system, employment system, security system, systems of outcome justice were developed in urban area and rural area respectively, at the same time, huge income gap appeared between urban and rural areas. However, taking outcome justice as the center of distribution system does not meet economic development rules when the level of economic development is lagged behind and

C. Pei et al., *The Basic Income Distribution System of China*, China Governance System Research Series, https://doi.org/10.1007/978-981-15-3461-4_3

material basis is weak. Just as Marx pointed out in the *Critique of the Gotha Programme*, at the first stage of communist society, workers with equal social status could achieve fair distribution only based on the same dimension "labor", i.e. "from each according to his ability, to each according to his work"; "from each according to his ability, to each according to his needs" may be achieved only at the second stage of communist society where abundant materials are available. Before reform and opening up, outcome justice oriented distribution decreased workers' enthusiasm. In collective labor of the People's Commune "swarming for headlong mass action", "the same outcome regardless of doing more or less, well or badly", hence "hitchhiking" became a common phenomenon. In addition, the strategy of heavy industry priority development turned most agricultural output income to industry, living standard of peasants was poor. As mentioned in the Decision of the CCCPC on Some Major Issues Concerning Quickening Agricultural Development passed at the Fourth Plenary Session of the Eleventh Central Committee, "from 1957 to 1978, … Although both output per unit area and total grain output increased, national average per capita grain in 1978 was roughly equivalent to 1975 only, average per capita annual income of agricultural population in China was only slightly more than seventy Yuan, the income of nearly one fourth of production team members was below fifty Yuan, average accumulation of each production team was less than ten thousand Yuan, even simple reproduction could not be maintained in some places". The Great Famine also reflected the decrease of agricultural output from side. Grain output decreased by 15% in both 1959 and 1960 than previous year, while grain output in 1961 only maintained the level in 1960.[1] That is to say, regardless of the output, peasants could only obtain basic grain ration, they could hardly make a living in the Great Famine, this also promoted hitchhiking behavior of peasants.

The Third Plenary Session of the Eleventh Central Committee of the CPC shifted the focus of work to "economic construction", and changed the distribution system gradually. At the early stage of reform, main work was rural reform. With respect to equalitarianism in distribution, the distribution principle, from each according to his ability, to each according to his work, was particularly emphasized in twenty-five agricultural policies in the Decision of the CCCPC on Some Major Issues Concerning Quickening Agricultural Development, remuneration should be paid according to labor quantity and quality, necessary reward and punishment system should be established to correct equalitarianism uncompromisingly. Such distribution system embodied the relationship between labor productivity and income to certain degree, could increase labor enthusiasm and labor productivity. From the Third Plenary Session of the Eleventh Central Committee of the CPC to Deng Xiaoping's Southern Tour Talks in 1992, China's economy experienced rapid development in these 14 years. The development results in coastal areas demonstrated the correctness of basic line. Thereafter, Report of the 14th National Congress of CPC summarized the development practice in these 14 years, and put forward main tasks of reform and construction in the 1990s, distribution system was also an important part of the

[1] Lin et al. (2010, p. 53).

reform. With the continuous development of economy, reform of the income distribution system was also deepened continuously, the system of income distribution was erected gradually. We review the income distribution system since the 14th Party Congress from different angles.

1.2 Development of Primary Distribution System

In primary distribution system, microcosmic subject was detailed gradually, priority was given to efficiency. It was defined in the Third Plenary Session of the Fourteenth Central Committee of the CPC that "personal income distribution should insist on a system in which distribution according to work should be subject, multiple distribution modes should coexist" this distribution system is closely linked to market economic system reform. At that time, basic policy of market economic system was "we should keep the public sector remaining dominant and allow diverse sectors of the economy to develop side by side". Now that individual economy, private economy, foreign trade economy are supplementary to the ownership by the whole people and collective ownership, corresponding distribution system should also allow multiple distribution modes while distribution according to work is the subject. With respect to individual income, giving priority to efficiency became important principle. under this principle, competitive mechanism should be introduced to break up equalitarianism, more pay for more work, a gap should be opened reasonably. Here, outcome justice was no longer a distribution principle, process justice was emphasized, and incentive system was introduced, the link between income and efficiency was intensified. However, here "multiple distribution modes" were detailed in a very limited way, only capital and other factors of production that belonged to individuals were allowed to participate in income distribution.

It was mentioned in the 15th National Congress of CPC Report "to combine distribution to each according to work with distribution according to productive factors, insist on priority to efficiency with due consideration to fairness, favorable to optimize allocation of resources, and promote social development". Other factors of production were included in the scope of income distribution, the content of factors of production was further detailed in the ensuing Fifth Plenary Session of the Fifteenth Central Committee of the CPC, besides previous capital, technology was also regarded as an important factor of production. It's noteworthy that, capital and technology were not only permitted to participate in distribution, but also were encouraged to participate in distribution. During this period, labor intensive industries were leading industries, capital and technology belonged to scarce resources, capital investment could obtain high rate of return and also promote economic growth. In the meantime, developing factor market, and promoting reasonable flow of the factors of production were also put on the agenda.

The 16th National Congress of CPC Report further improved "the distribution system in which distribution to each according to work is dominant, multiple distribution modes coexist", "establish the principle in which factors of production including labor, capital, technology and management should participate in distribution according to their contributions". Compared with the 15th National Congress of CPC, the content of factors of production was further expanded, management was listed separately as a special labor form, may participate in income distribution. With the continuous development of economy, enterprise development becomes more and more modern, corporate governance becomes increasingly important, and the requirements for management capability also become higher and higher. The impact of full-time management personnel on enterprise development becomes increasingly apparent. What's more different from previous, the factors "participate in distribution according to their contributions". Distribution principle of the compensations for factors is defined here, contribution of factors becomes main basis to obtain income. With the deepening of reform, based on "developing factor market" passed at the 15th National Congress of CPC, the 16th National Congress of CPC further put forward "give play to fundamental role of market in resource allocation to a larger extent. … Promote reform and opening up and steady development of capital market. To develop property right, land, labor force and technology markets". This means that, market will play a more and more important role in resource allocation, under market allocation, efficiency will also become increasingly important for factor remuneration. "In primary distribution, we should pay more attention to efficiency" was also emphasized for income distribution in the 16th National Congress of CPC. The 16th National Congress of CPC differentiated primary distribution from redistribution, made previous "we should give priority to efficiency with due consideration to fairness" more explicit. In primary distribution, efficiency was the most important; in the redistribution, fairness became main object to be considered. Although primary distribution was separated from redistribution, yet the 17th National Congress of CPC Report emphasized it again, "both primary distribution and redistribution should deal with the relationship between efficiency and fairness". Although priority was given to efficiency in primary distribution, yet process justice was promoted to reduce discrimination, and realize equal pay for equal work in the process of distribution. After "We should establish the principle that labor, capital, technology, managerial expertise and other production factors participate in the distribution of income in accordance with their respective contributions" was put forward at the 16th National Congress of CPC, corresponding systems were required to be completed at the 17th National Congress of CPC and the 18th National Congress of CPC for improving the mechanism of factors participating in primary distribution according to their respective contributions. The principle, systems, mechanism for factors to participate in primary distribution were established correspondingly.

While primary distribution system was detailed and marketized continuously, minimum wage system was also introduced gradually. Although original intention of minimum wage system was to guarantee workers' rights and interests, yet it was implemented mainly by influencing primary distribution. Therefore, evolution of minimum wage system is discussed in this part. In 1993, the Ministry of Labor and Social Security issued *Regulations on Enterprise Minimum Wage*, China started to implement minimum wage system in cities, but the provisions were mainly set down by the provinces, autonomous regions or municipalities directly under the

Central Government respectively, no mandatory restrictions. In the *Labor Law of the People's Republic of China* publicized in 1994, "specific standard of minimum wage should be specified by the people's governments of provinces, autonomous regions or municipalities directly under the Central Government, and reported to the State Council for archiving". The former Ministry of Labor and Social Security promulgated *Minimum Wage System* in Jan. 2004, this marked official introduction of minimum wage system into labor market. According to the provisions, minimum wage standard "refers to the minimum labor remuneration to be paid by the employer according to law in case workers have provided normal labor in legal working hours or in the work time under the labor contract signed according to law". Minimum wage standard may be divided into monthly minimum wage standard and hourly minimum wage standard, "monthly minimum wage standard is applicable to full-time workers, hourly minimum wage standard is applicable to part-time workers". Minimum wage standard was not unified in the whole country, but determined by the provinces, autonomous regions or municipalities directly under the Central Government respectively, so different standards existed in different administrative regions. In the meantime, adjustment time of minimum wage was also set, "minimum wage standard should be adjusted at least once per two years". Minimum wage system had been established in all 31 provinces (autonomous regions, municipalities directly under the Central Government), and monthly minimum wage standard in respective regions had been issued and executed by the end of 2004[2] (Su et al. 2006).

1.3 The Evolution of Redistribution System

Redistribution scope has been expanded gradually, and more attention has been paid to fairness. China is a country with a large population, the scale of poor population was very huge at the early stage of reform. In 1978, poor population below absolute poverty line was up to 250 million in China, accounting for 25% of national population, poor rural population in China dropped to 125 million in 1985.[3] Although poor population decreased greatly, yet the task of poverty alleviation was still arduous. *Seven-Year Priority Poverty Alleviation Program* was issued in 1994, aimed to reduce poverty by adding investment in rural and poor populations. It was also emphasized in the Fifth Plenary Session of the Fourteenth Central Committee of the CPC to intensify poverty alleviation. Reform of urban social security system ran in parallel to rural poverty alleviation. It was mentioned in the Fifth Plenary Session of the Fourteenth Central Committee of the CPC that, "during the 'Ninth Five-Year Plan', the reform of pension, unemployment and medical insurance system should be quickened to take initial shape of a multi-level social security system that combines social insurance, social relief, social welfare, veteran benefit and placement & social mutual aid and personal savings accumulation guarantee together". Since

[2]Su et al. (2006).

[3]Lin (2004).

state-owned enterprises encountered many difficulties in production operation, their management system and operational mechanism were not adaptive to socialist market economy, the reform of state-owned enterprises became an important content in the Suggestions of the Central Committee of the Communist Party of China on Formulating the "Ninth Five-Year Plan" and 2010 Perspective Goal for National Economic and Social Development. under the planned economic system, social welfare of the staff in state-owned enterprises was paid by the state, local government and enterprises jointly, in a mode of wide and full coverage. With the reform of state-owned enterprises, some of the staff in state-owned enterprises will be laid off, they could no longer obtain original social welfare. In this case, the establishment and formation of urban social security system was put forward together with the reform of state-owned enterprises.

With deepening of the reform of state-owned enterprises and popularization in the whole country, as mentioned in the Decision of the CCCPC on Some Major Issues Concerning the Reform and Development of State-Owned Enterprises, "we should encourage laid-off workers to seek employment in non-public economic units, organize themselves for employment or engaging in individual operation, so that the laid-off workers who need reemployment may find new jobs". According to statistics, in the five years from 1998 to 2002, cumulative total number of workers laid off from state-owned enterprises was 27.145 million.[4] Reemployment of the laid-off workers became first issue of the Chinese government at that time. Laid-off workers were in unemployed status before reemployment, urban poverty issues were also aggravated. The "Tenth 5-Year Plan" passed at the Fifth Plenary Session of the Fifteenth Central Committee of the CPC, defined "include basic life security of the workers laid off from state-owned enterprises into unemployment insurance on the basis of pilot. Strengthen and consummate minimum living standard security system for urban residents, increase standard of urban poor relief subsidies gradually". Minimum living standard security system became a main system to cut down urban poverty. On the other hand, urban social security system should also be further developed quickly, more pertinent contents have been put forward for capital source, service and management style.

After urban social security system framework was basically established, rural poverty and social security system became critical to further reform. Decision of the CCCPC on Some Major Issues Concerning the Improvement of Socialist Market Economy System with reference to the experience of urban minimum living standard security system was passed at the Third Plenary Session of the Sixteenth Central Committee of the CPC, it put forward "explore to establish rural minimum living standard security system if conditions permit". *The Seven-Year Priority Poverty Alleviation Program* was basically completed in 2000, rural poor population was 32.09 million.[5] Rural poverty alleviation went from plane to point, targeted poverty alleviation was more needed. Minimum living standard security system was a targeted

[4]Calculated according to relevant data of *China Labor and Social Security Yearbook* in 2003.
[5]National Bureau of Statistics (2010).

poverty alleviation, plus urban implementation experience, it was explored gradually in rural areas. It's also helpful to balance urban and rural poverty alleviation systems. After the 16th National Congress of CPC explored rural minimum living standard security system, the 17th National Congress of CPC put forward "explore the establishment of rural pension insurance system". Rural social security system was further improved to provide a foundation of full coverage.

Social security system has been established in both urban and rural areas respectively, basically realized full coverage, but difference still exists between urban and rural areas, between systems, and between regions. From a national perspective, social security system was fragmented. The 18th National Congress of CPC proposed to establish a social security system covering urban and rural residents comprehensively, and to integrate basic pension insurance and medical insurance systems of urban and rural residents gradually, so as to realize national pooling of basic pension.

1.4 The System for Regulating Income Gap

Income gap should be regulated by means of policy and market. Firstly, the regulation of personal income distribution pattern. The Third Plenary Session of the Fourteenth Central Committee of the CPC paid more attention to personal income growth, break/abandon equalitarian, "adhere to the policy that encourages some people in some regions to become rich through honest work and legal operations before others, advocate people who become rich early to drive and assist those who become rich later, so as to realize common prosperity step by step". Protecting legitimate income becomes a more important role for the income gap between members of society, in the meantime, illegal income should be banned. "Preventing excessive expansion of income distribution gap" was put forward in the "Tenth 5-Year Plan" passed at the Fifth Plenary Session of the Fifteenth Central Committee of the CPC, national tax was utilized to regulate the gap, individual income tax became an important means to regulate income gap, aimed to regulate over high income. In the Third Plenary Session of the Sixteenth Central Committee of the CPC, in addition to regulating high income, increasing the income level of low income earners also became an important aspect. Gradual establishment of olive-shaped income distribution structure became dominant in regulating personal income distribution pattern. In the 17th National Congress of CPC, besides increasing the income of low income earners, the role of minimum wage system and increasing poverty alleviation standard were more emphasized. In the Opinions on the Deepening of Income Distribution System Reform after the 18th National Congress of CPC, expansion of middle-income group was deemed as an important aspect to bridge the income gap, and develop "olive-shaped" distribution structure gradually.

Secondly, urban-rural income gap should be regulated. Although economy was developed rapidly and continuously after the reform and opening up, the income of both urban and rural residents was increased greatly, yet in the meantime, urban-rural income gap was enlarged. The central government put forward a series of policy suggestions to narrow the urban-rural income gap. It was mentioned in the Third Plenary Session of the Fourteenth Central Committee of the CPC that "township and village enterprises are important pillars of rural economy". And liquidity was promoted in rural-urban labor market, "we should allow peasants to work or engage in business in small towns, develop rural tertiary industry, and promote transfer of surplus rural labor". Peasants were no longer confined in agriculture, but may work in small towns and rural non-agricultural industries, get relatively high income from industry. In the Third Plenary Session of the Fifteenth Central Committee of the CPC, "allow" was changed to encourage, "we should organize peasants to go out for work, the state should use more rural labor force when investing in the construction of infrastructures, so as to increase cash income of the peasants". Peasants were no longer prohibited from going out for work, instead, surplus rural labor should be guided actively to go out for work. With rapid development of urban industry, scale of rural migrant workers increased gradually. With respect to the discriminated and inferior status of rural migrant workers in urban employment, it was put forward in the Third Plenary Session of the Sixteenth Central Committee of the CPC to further "unify urban and rural labor market gradually, form equal employment system for urban and rural workers, create more employment opportunities for peasants". Transfer training of rural surplus labor was emphasized at the 17th National Congress of CPC, national rural policy was also required to be improved and implemented to safeguard the rights and interests of workers according to law; to enhance the protection for legal rights and interests of rural migrant workers while increasing non-agricultural employability of rural migrant workers. With respect to the backward technical level of rural migrant workers, free professional education and skills training system was provided for rural migrant workers especially after the 18th National Congress of CPC, so as to enhance employability of rural migrant workers. This shows that, a unified labor market for urban and rural areas has been established gradually, urban-rural mobility of labor force has become more smooth, rural migrant workers could get higher income from urban labor market than farming in rural areas, so as to narrow the urban-rural income gap.

Thirdly, regional income gap should be regulated. Encouraging some regions to get rich first is Step 1 in the two-step strategy, thereafter rich people helping the poor is Step 2 in the two-step strategy. Although it experienced 14 years from the reform and opening up to the 14th National Congress of CPC, economy was developed tremendously in these 14 years, yet China was still a low-income country at that time, development remained a priority, Step 1 in the two-step strategy was not completed yet. Here regional unbalance was permitted. In view of this, in the Third Plenary Session of the Fourteenth Central Committee of the CPC, starting from overall development, "coastal area should be developed first and continue to play its advantages, this is an overall situation, inland should take consideration of this overall situation". Although more importance should be attached to support inland development, so as to narrow the gap actively during the "Ninth Five-Year Plan", yet priority was still given to the development of coastal area. "implementing Western Development Strategy to quicken the development of central and western regions" was put forward at the Fifth Plenary Session of the Fifteenth Central Committee of the CPC to narrow regional income gap. Quickening infrastructure construction became the breakthrough point to promote Western Development. While promoting the Western Development, the leading role of eastern coastal areas in national economic development should still be played. "resultant regional development pattern" was put forward in the Fifth Plenary Session of the Sixteenth Central Committee of the CPC, western, central and eastern coastal areas had different development priorities. Regional coordinated development was restricted by administrative segregation to certain degree, it was proposed to "improve market mechanism, break up the restrictions of administrative divisions, promote free mobility of the factors of production between regions, and guide industrial transfer". Breaking up the regional restrictions of factor market was favorable to form a unified factor market. With respect to the regional gap, it was proposed at the 17th National Congress of CPC to give play to comparative advantage, promote harmonious development between regions. In addition to the barriers between regions, central and western regions also lack of funds and other factors, the 18th National Congress of CPC implemented a system of narrowing income gap in microscopic field. For example, promote employment equity, improve vocational skills. Promote the development of central and western regions via changes in microenvironment.

Fourthly, industry income gap should be regulated. With the deepening of the reform in state-owned enterprises, industry income gap also became increasingly apparent, the gap between monopoly industry and competitive industry was widened continuously. "strengthening the supervision and management of income distribution in monopoly industry" was put forward in the "Tenth 5-Year Plan" at the Fifth Plenary Session of the Fifteenth Central Committee of the CPC. Thereafter, supervision of income in monopoly industry has always been emphasized.

1.5 Adjustment of Macro Distribution Pattern

Macro income distribution pattern became an important content of income distribution. It was proposed at the 14th National Congress of CPC to "make overall plans and take the interests of the state, collective, individual into consideration together, sort out the distribution relationship between state and enterprises, between central and local governments, realize payment of the tax plus a percentage of profits to the state and tax sharing system gradually". This shows that, the central government concerns the relationship between government, enterprise and household sector in macro distribution pattern, as well as the relationship between central and local governments. With the reform of tax sharing system, tax revenue distribution pattern between central and local governments was determined gradually. However, there was no clear institutional arrangement for the relationship between government, enterprise and household sector. Until the 17th National Congress of CPC Report, adjustment of macro distribution pattern became a part of deepening the reform of income distribution system. It was proposed in the 17th National Congress of CPC Report to "increase the proportion of resident income in distribution of national income gradually, and increase the proportion of labor remuneration in primary distribution". On this basis, the 18th National Congress of CPC intensified fiscal transfer payment of government to increase the proportion of resident income, and enhance the regulation role of redistribution.

It may be seen from the above-mentioned review that, after the 14th National Congress of CPC, China's income distribution system changed from plan to market, from outcome justice to process justice gradually. Efficiency in primary distribution was mainly dominated by market, remuneration of factors was determined by contribution of factors. The scope of redistribution was expanded gradually, urban and rural areas were unified gradually, social security and social assistance system was also established and improved gradually. For the income gaps, personal income gap, urban-rural income gap, regional income gap and industry income gap were regulated pertinently, including: establish unified labor market, establish unified factor market, improve taxation system, and strengthen supervision. In the national income, with the continuous development of economy, the proportion of resident income and the proportion of labor remuneration becomes a main content of income distribution system in recent years, is of great significance to increase resident income.

2 Overall Trend of Resident Income Distribution Status Since the Reform and Opening Up

In this section, change trend of resident income distribution since the reform and opening up is analyzed as a whole. Gini coefficient and relevant social structure indicators are used for analysis. Gini coefficient and its variations, especially the underlying reasons are analyzed and explained.

2.1 The Change Trend of Gini Coefficient

Gini coefficient is a comprehensive indicator to evaluate the income distribution structure among residents. When the income of everyone is the same, it's absolutely fair, Gini coefficient is 0; when all incomes are centralized in the hands of one person, it's absolutely unfair, Gini coefficient is 1. These are two extreme cases, in real economic society, Gini coefficient is between 0 and 1, the larger the Gini coefficient is, the larger the resident income gap becomes, and it's more unfair. It is generally believed that, when Gini coefficient is less than 0.2, resident income is absolutely average; between 0.2 and 0.3, resident income is relatively average; between 0.3 and 0.4, it's relatively reasonable; between 0.4 and 0.5, resident income gap is too large; if above 0.5, great income disparity exists.

Gini coefficient reflects overall income gap. The change of Gini coefficient depends on relatively income change of all residents, it is a comprehensive indicator. The change of Gini coefficient might be inconsistent with the change of one group compared with another group. For example, as a whole, income of low income group increases, and income of high income group is regulated effectively, middle-income group is widened, this will enable income distribution structure to be more fair, Gini coefficient decreases. However, in the meantime, a part of group falls into poverty because of illnesses, their income is worsened compared with original income level. Overall Gini coefficient cannot reflect such situation, unless calculation is made for special groups. In addition, although Gini coefficient may be used to measure income gap, and judge income distribution status according to general standard, yet Gini coefficient cannot reflect the source of excessive income gap and features among groups, so a lot of researches were conducted to break down Gini coefficient, discuss the income gap between different groups, and compare with the overall income gap, so as to judge from which group the income gap comes.

According to the estimate of World Bank, at the early stage of reform and opening up, China's Gini coefficient in 1981 was merely 0.2911, and dropped to 0.2764 in 1984, relatively average. Although relatively fair at that time, yet the level of economic development of China was relatively backward at that time, it was a low income developing country. Although income level of everyone was relatively average, yet the income of everyone was very low, and economic products were insufficient, urban residents got household goods from ration system, they used tickets to purchase goods. under the concept of common prosperity, in some regions where necessary conditions were satisfied, some people became rich, other regions were developed slowly. In this way, income gap was widened continuously. In 1987, it was restored to the level in 1981, up to 0.2985; in 1990, Gini coefficient was 0.3243, income distribution was relatively reasonable. Thereafter it climbed steadily, up to 0.3923 in 1999, still in relatively reasonable section, but approaching the international warning line. It exceeded the internationally recognized warning line in 2002, up to 0.4259. The Gini coefficient released by National Bureau of Statistics of China was 0.479 in 2003. This shows that, from 1984 to 2002, China's Gini coefficient climbed continuously, experienced three stages successively, i.e. relatively equal, relatively reasonable and too wide income gap.

In 2013, National Bureau of Statistics of China publicized the Gini coefficient since 2003, thereafter Gini coefficient became a routine indicator in annual statistical reports on national economy and social development. Although this indicator was different from the result of Gini coefficient in other social surveys, yet the data publicized by the Bureau of Statistics had relatively high authority. Firstly, because coverage of the data from Bureau of Statistics is the most extensive. Due to restrictions of labor force and financial resources, social surveys conducted by academic groups might only be sampling surveys, and sample size is far less than the quantity of Bureau of Statistics. Secondly, because statistical data are publicized year after year. For the same reason, most surveys conducted by academic groups have timeframes, cannot be done every year, data continuity is relatively poor. In view of this, we analyze Gini coefficient trend from 2003 to 2014 according to the data publicized by National

Bureau of Statistics of China in 2013. The Gini coefficient in 2003 publicized by National Bureau of Statistics of China is 0.479, continues the Gini coefficient growth trend publicized by the World Bank. Although two groups of data are different in aspects of statistical data and statistical standard, yet their data structures show China's Gini coefficient a bit high, exceeding the international warning line 0.4. From 2003 to 2008, Gini coefficient still increases slightly, up to 0.491 in 2008. the difference from the judgment standard of income disparity 0.5 is extremely small. Gini coefficient shows a downtrend since 2009, downward continually for 7 years, although slightly, it dropped to 0.462 in 2015. Within the range of comparable data, Gini coefficient in 2015 was already lower than the level in 2003 (Fig. 1).

Continuous decrease of Gini coefficient shows the decrease of income gap at overall income level. Although the judgment of downtrend was unclear when Gini coefficient started to decrease in 2009, yet decrease for continuous 7 years shows downtrend in this period as a whole. In another aspect, no further increase of Gini coefficient, and no further deterioration of income gap since 2009 is a generally accepted fact.

However, it is noteworthy that, Gini coefficient is still relatively high, above the international warning line even in 2015. According to the judgment standard of Gini coefficient, China is still a country with excessive income gap. From international comparison, China's Gini coefficient is also a bit high. World development indicators data in 2016 show that, there were only 20 countries whose Gini coefficient exceeded China in 2010, among which, except Georgia, Israel and Vietnam, other countries were African or Latin American countries, this means that China's income gap is high in the world.

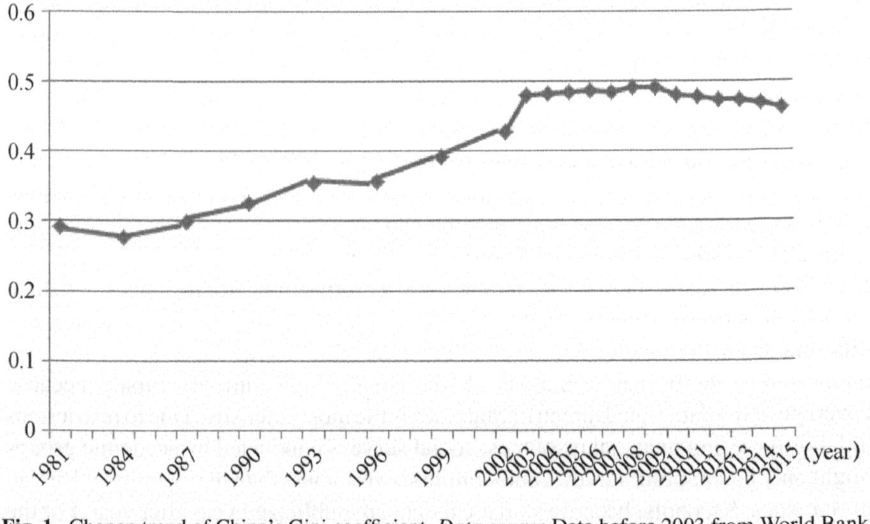

Fig. 1 Change trend of China's Gini coefficient. *Data source* Data before 2003 from World Bank 2016 WDI, data of 2003 and later from National Bureau of Statistics of China

2.2 Change Trend of Social Structure

Social structure refers to the composition and relationship pattern of members of the society who possess certain resources and opportunities in a country or region, including a number of important substructures such as demographics, family structure, social organization structure, urban and rural structure, regional structure, employment structure, income distribution structure, pattern of consumption and social class structure. Social structure has complexity, integrity, hierarchy, relative stability and other important features. An ideal modern social structure should have fairness, rationality, openness and other important features. Wherein employment structure and income distribution structure are more prominently related to income distribution. This also becomes an important content of sociological research.

Many indexes are used to measure social structure from different perspectives, international socio-economic index is an important indicator for measurement. This method gives weighted score according to average educational level and average income level of each occupational group, and even considering other individual characteristics and family characteristics of the employed. "socio-economic index" refers to the sequence and score ranked according to comprehensive socio-economic factors of people, it is an objective status rather than subjective status, although this index is very strongly correlated with occupational subjective reputational measures index. Yet generally speaking, this index is calculated according to "Standard International Occupational Prestige Scale", based on generally accepted values as far as possible.

As a general rule, social structure may be divided into olive-shaped (or spindle-shaped), pyramid-shaped and dumbbell-shaped. Wherein olive-shaped social structure has two small ends and one big middle part, is considered as a relatively reasonable and stable social structure by the academic world and society. From a single perspective of income, olive-shaped social structure means dominant middle-income group, small scale low income group and high income group. Pyramid-shaped social structure has big bottom, big middle part and small upper part, is generally thought of as a transitional social structure. Dumbbell-shaped social structure is reverse to olive-shaped social structure, shows two big ends and small middle part. Dumbbell-shaped social structure is very unstable, large difference exists between social groups, and social mobility is also relatively poor.

China's socio-economic index calculated according to the Standard International Occupational Prestige Scale is shown in Fig. 2. We can see the very unique social structure of China. In 2000, groups with very low occupational prestige accounted for over 60% of total working population, the remaining nearly 40% of working population was sporadically distributed on occupational prestige axis, groups on each score were very small. Such social structure is called "inverted T-shaped". Peasants were dominant in the group with occupational prestige score 23. This also embodied the difference between urban and rural areas in China. Both income level and occupational status of peasants were at the lowest level. Ten years later, the same method was used to calculate the data in 2010. The result showed that, China's

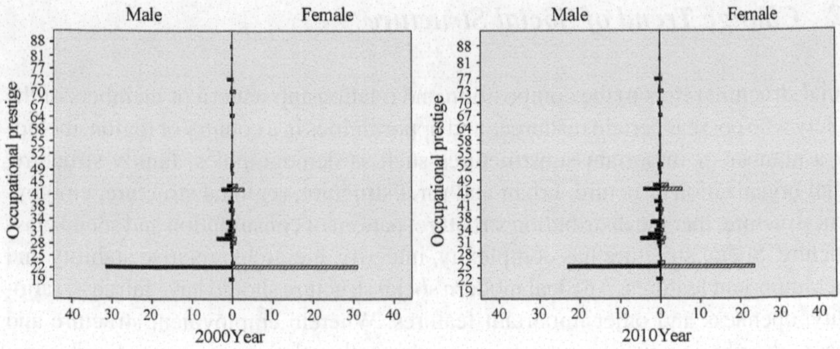

Fig. 2 Transition of social hierarchy in China (2000–2010). *Data source* Li Qiang, Wang Hao: Four worlds of social hierarchy in China, *Social Science Front*, 9th issue, 2014

socioeconomic status structure was still "inverted T-shaped" in 2010 as a whole, groups with low scores accounted for a half of total working population. Different from that in 2000, underlying group decreased, scale of middle group expanded. In other words, in these ten years, some underlying groups entered middle group, expanded the middle group, a flow from bottom up existed in the social structure.

Both the social structure plotted based on socio-economic index and the income distribution structure reflected by Gini coefficient embody large income gap in China.

2.3 The Reason of Large Resident Income Gap

With gradual improvement of marketization level, factor allocation and income distribution are determined by market to a larger extent, differences between individuals become prominent. After reform and opening up, market degree of labor market and factor market increases gradually, especially after the reform of state-owned enterprises, non-public economy, private economy, foreign funded economy have been developed rapidly, further promote market degree of factor market. Labor remuneration is main income source of residents. In case marketization is improved, marginal output of labor determines labor remuneration, the higher the marginal output is, the higher the labor remuneration becomes. Marginal output is determined by human capital of workers themselves to a great degree. This means that, the difference of human capital between individuals leads to different marginal productivity, then brings about difference in labor remuneration. In the process of breaking up a communal pot and factor marketization, income difference caused by individual characteristics is gradually revealed, and further leads to the widening of income gap.

Blocking of factor mobility intensifies the income gap between different groups. Although market degree of factor allocation and income distribution process is improved continuously, yet free factor mobility is still restricted, unified factor market has not been developed. Compared with capital, free mobility of labor force is more difficult. Barriers to entry exist in the labor mobility between urban and rural areas, between regions, and between industries. Labor mobility between urban and rural areas is confined to the restriction of household registration system, has been discriminated for a long time. Blind flow of rural residents was controlled from 1989 to 1991, rural labor mobility was encouraged after 1992, but after the reform of state-owned enterprises, from 1995 to 2000, for reemployment of laid-off workers, some provinces and cities issued various regulations and policies to restrict rural labor force and external labor force from going to urban areas for work. Even after wages of rural migrant workers increased greatly in 2003, rural migrant workers were still strongly discriminated when entering public sector. Capital mobility is higher than labor, and favorable terms have been given by local authorities one after another to attract investments, but barriers against capital mobility also existed. Price of capital factor cannot be determined completely by market due to government control and monopoly on the capital market, so capital factor could get price or gains above its marginal output easily.[6] With respect to the resource compensation, inequality and injustice became more prominent in resource compensation distribution due to incomplete systems. In Ordos region, there were 7,000 billionaires. They became rich mainly by selling resources, for example, by selling coal. This mainly exploited policy loopholes, even violated laws and regulations, might be linked with bribery corruption.[7]

Factor distribution structure inclined to capital. Since the reform and opening up, China has been developed quickly, taking comparative advantage of labor force. However, in the process of development, capital was seriously scarce compared with labor, thus return on capital was high. High investment rate and high rate of return became main features in the process of rapid economic development. In the labor relations, capital was dominant, held the right to speak, labor was weak, capital could obtain relatively high remuneration, the portion for distribution of labor remuneration was relatively low. And capital monopoly led to capital income concentrated in the hands of a few people. under dual effect of small share of labor distribution and centralized capital income, income gap between residents was widened.

Incomplete legal systems, unreasonable income and illegal income widened the income gap. During rapid economic development, distribution system was also adjusted continually. In the meantime, legal systems related to income management were also promulgated continuously, but dislocation and absence problems still existed. This enabled some people to obtain income by unreasonable and even unlawful means. As mentioned earlier, absence and incompleteness of resource taxes allowed some people to take forcible possession of the income from selling resources. In addition, in recent years, the scale of invisible income is expanded continuously, also widens income gap. When invisible income is considered, the Gini coefficient calculated based on "total family income of urban residents" rises from 0.31–0.34

---

[6]Zhang and Zhao (2015).

[7]Li (2012).

in raw data to 0.45–0.51, the scale of "invisible income" caused by hidden income accounts for about 19–25% of corresponding GDP of China from 2002 to 2009.[8]

Regulation force of redistribution is limited, primary distribution pattern basically determines the disposable income pattern after redistribution. Firstly, tax regulation is an important means of redistribution regulation, but individual income tax in China is manifested as progressive tax amount yet regressive tax rate, tax amount of high income group is high but tax rate is a bit low. Take an example of 2009, if inequity did not exist, individual income tax would decrease Gini coefficient of the pre-tax income of urban residents by 0.018, but actually only decreased by 0.0129.[9] That is to say, such regressivity of individual income tax decreased the regulation efficacy of tax. Secondly, redistribution efficacy could hardly be realized due to the division of social security system. Social security system is an important redistribution means, it narrows the income gap in the form of social solidarity. However, vulnerable groups that should be supported cannot be supported via social security due to urban and rural division, sector division and other problems in the social security system of China, even "reverse regulation" exists. For example, rural migrant workers who work in cities could hardly obtain social security. Even after permitted by the systems, participation rate of rural migrant workers is still very low, mainly because it is difficult for rural migrant workers to meet the requirements for receiving social security due to transfer connection and other problems. Non-contributory social security (such as subsistence allowance) is mainly given to local urban residents, it is difficult for rural migrant workers to obtain such security.

Urbanization was lagged behind industrialization, weakened the capability of industrialization process to narrow income gap. With rapid development of industrialization, a large number of surplus rural labor moved from rural areas to urban areas, their employment changed from agriculture to industry, and their life also changed from rural areas to urban areas, promoted the urbanization process. However, restricted by household registration system, China's urbanization process may be divided into two stages, peasants became rural migrant workers, rural migrant workers became citizens. The essential public services behind household registration system became obstacles in the transition of rural migrant workers to citizens. In other words, although rural migrant workers were employed in cities, yet they could enjoy essential public services still according to rural standard, based on huge difference of essential public services between rural and urban areas in China, this reduced capability of industrialization to narrow the income gap. With continuous development of industry, the scale of rural migrant workers increases continuously, in 2015, the scale of rural migrant workers reached 277.47 million, accounting for 35.8% of total working population.[10] The expanded scale of rural migrant workers further weakened the capability of industrialization to narrow the income gap.

---

[8]Bai (2015).

[9]Xu and Yue (2014).

[10]2015 Statistical Report on National Economy and Social Development, http://www.gov.cn/xinwen/2016-02/29/content_5047274.htm.

To sum up, we may see from the reasons of yawning income gap of residents that, yawning income gap is mainly reflected between urban and rural areas, between regions and between industries, and the share of labor remuneration is a bit low. On this basis, we analyze the macro distribution pattern between urban and rural areas, between regions, between industries, and the change rules of labor remuneration in the distribution of national income as follows.

3 Difference in the Macro Distribution Pattern Between Urban and Rural Areas, Between Regions and Between Industries

Calculation and measurement of income gap to reflect the income distribution status is an important aspect in income distribution research. When too wide income gap exists, it's more important to find out the source of income gap, and indicate the direction to further narrow the income gap. From the perspective of Gini coefficient, income gap is still large in China. Social structure also reflects bottom class accounting for about a half. We analyze the income gap between urban and rural areas, between regions, and between industries in combination with the discussions on the reasons of income distribution gap.

3.1 Analysis of Income Gap Between Urban and Rural Areas

Before reform and opening up, China gave priority to heavy industry development, developed typical urban and rural distribution structure. Rural area provided significant financial support to urban area through scissors difference. After reform and opening up, although reform was firstly implemented in rural areas, yet urban and rural division existed all along. The restriction on labor mobility between urban and rural areas was concentrated reflection of urban and rural division. Therefore, we firstly discuss the income gap between urban and rural areas.

From the decomposition result of Gini coefficient, urban-rural income gap was uppermost contributor to national Gini coefficient. Rural Gini coefficient increased from 0.21 in 1978 to 0.34 in 1997, 0.38 in 2002, while urban Gini coefficient was 0.30, 0.29 and 0.34 respectively, national Gini coefficient in these three years was 0.30, 0.38 and 0.45 respectively, it may be seen that national Gini coefficient was larger than that in urban and rural areas in each period, it means huge income gap between urban and rural areas.[11]

Thereafter, urban-rural income gap has already been main source of income gap. According to Fig. 3, urban-rural income gap fluctuated in the period of 1978–1997. Income ratio between urban and rural areas decreased gradually from 1978 to 1985,

[11]Cai and Wan (2006).

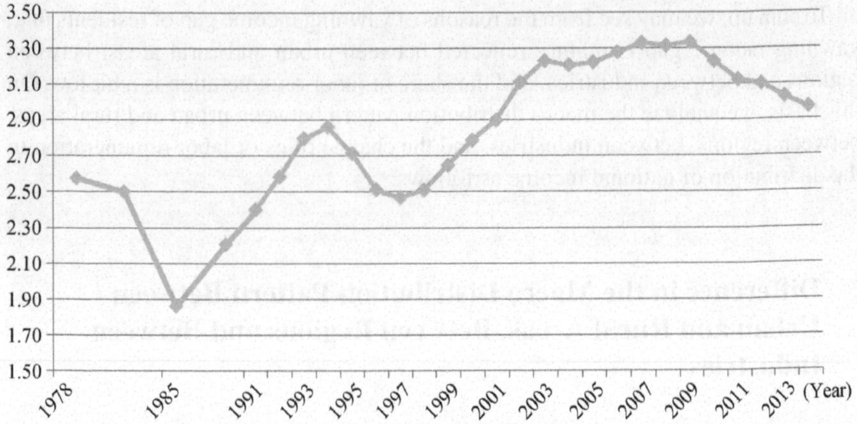

Fig. 3 Resident income gap between urban and rural areas. *Data source* Calculated according to 2015 *China Statistical Yearbook*, per capita disposable income for urban residents, per capita net income for rural residents

dropped from 2.57:1 in 1978 to 1.86:1 in 1985. Because reform and opening up was firstly carried out in rural areas, extensive popularization of household contract responsibility system with remuneration linked to output released rural economic vitality, aroused the enthusiasm of peasants. In addition to the increase in productivity, under the policy "grain rendering to state, sufficient reserve for collective, the rest is own", income level of peasants increased greatly, so urban-rural income gap was narrowed significantly. In 1984, the focus of reform changed from rural area to urban area. With the introduction of market mechanism in urban economic development, urban development speed also increased quickly. Income level of urban residents also increased greatly, growth rate exceeded rural area, yawning trend was developed in the income gap between urban and rural residents. In 1994, income ratio of urban and rural residents reached maximum value 2.86 in this period. Thereafter it decreased, income ratio of urban and rural residents in 1997 was equivalent to that in 1980.

In the period of 1997–2014, income ratio of urban and rural residents firstly rose then dropped. With gradual promotion of the reform in state-owned enterprises, increasing efficiency while reducing the staff, factor distribution tended more to market-dominated. The 15th National Congress of CPC Report put forward to "combine distribution to each according to work with distribution according to productive factors, insist on priority to efficiency with due consideration to fairness, optimize allocation of resources to promote social development". With higher market degree, the income of urban residents increased faster than rural residents; in the period of 1997–2003, urban-rural income gap widened continuously and quickly. Although "Rush of Migrant Workers" broke out in China in 1989, a large number of rural migrant workers went to urban areas for work, obtained wages higher than farming, yet rural migrant workers were deeply discriminated in urban employment, their income was a bit low. Although the income of rural residents increased, yet the growth amplitude was still lower than the income growth of urban resident. In the period of 2003–2009, urban-rural income gap still widened continuously, but the widening speed was far lower than the widening speed in the period of 1997–2003. Income ratio of urban and rural residents rose slowly from 3.23:1 in 2003 to 3.33:1 in 2009. This growth rate was equivalent to the growth rate from 2002 (3.11:1) to 2003. After peak value in 2009, income ratio of urban and rural residents decreased, dropped to 2.97:1 in 2014, basically restored to the level in 2001.

In the same time sections, the changes of urban-rural income gap were basically consistent with the changes of Gini coefficient, turning points of rise and fall were almost the same. It may be seen that, urban-rural income gap constitutes main part of national income gap, urban-rural income gap basically determines the trend of Gini coefficient.

3.2 *Analysis of Income Gap Between Regions*

Hu Line divided China into two regions according to population distribution, about 96% of Chinese population resided in the Southeastern Region which accounted for about 36% of Chinese land area, about 4% of Chinese population resided in the Northwestern Region which accounted for about 64% of Chinese land area. Although this is rougher than the division of eastern middle western and northeast regions, yet it fully shows the differences of natural environment, population distribution in different regions of China. With gradual deepening of reform and opening up and the implementation of two overall strategic thoughts, different regions faced different development opportunities, and marketization degree varied. So regional difference is also a long-term concern for income gap in China (Fig. 4).

Utilizing the data of per capita disposable income of urban residents and per capita net income of rural residents in all provinces, we calculate the coefficient of variation per capita income for urban and rural areas respectively in all provinces from 1991 to 2014 to reflect the changes of income gap between regions. Firstly, income difference in both urban and rural regions experienced the process from widening to narrowing. Income difference between regions narrowed continuously after 2006, compared with urban regions, income difference between rural regions decreased faster. In 2011, income difference between rural regions was already less than the all-time low in 1998 since 1991, and dropped to below 0.35 in 2013. Similarly, income difference between urban regions also decreased since 2006, in 2010, it dropped to the level in 1997, and dropped to below 0.25 in 2013. Next, at decrease stage, the difference decrease speed between rural regions was faster than urban regions. That is to say, convergence of income difference between rural regions was faster than urban regions. Finally, income difference between urban regions was lower than rural regions all along. The income difference between different urban regions was very slight, relatively balanced between different urban regions, coefficient of variation per capita disposable income is 0.25–0.30. In contrast, income difference was very huge between different rural regions, coefficient of variation per capita net income of rural residents was above 0.40 before 2012, and even above 0.45 in some years.

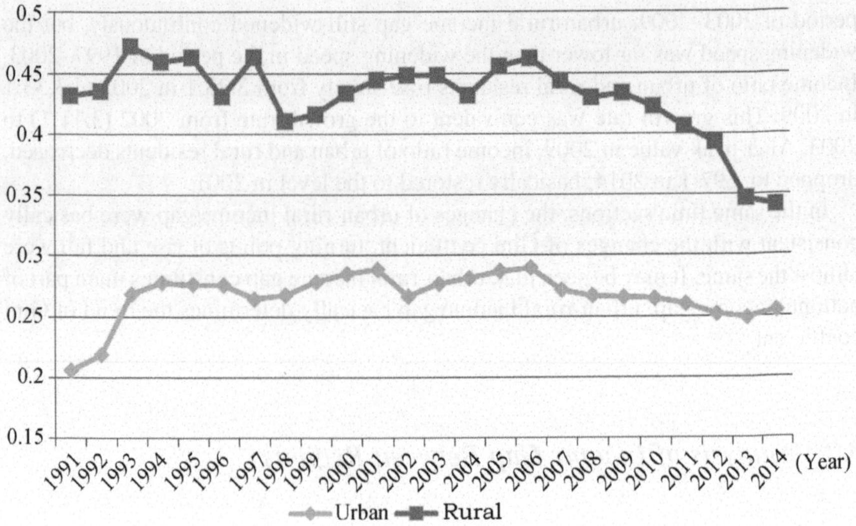

Fig. 4 Change trend of the coefficient of income variation between urban and rural regions. *Data source* Calculated according to *China Statistical Yearbook* in past years, per capita disposable income for urban resident income, per capita net income for rural resident income

Although income gap between rural regions has been narrowed quickly since 2006, yet still far greater than urban regions in 2014.

3.3 *Analysis of Income Gap Between Industries*

With the deepening of reform and opening up, and gradual increase of market degree, income gap between industries has been widened continuously while efficiency is increased. Income gap between industries also becomes a hot spot issue. We calculate coefficient of industry income variation in the period of 1990–2014 according to the data from National Bureau of Statistics of China.[12] Since industry classification criteria were adjusted in 2003, comparability of the data before and after that was not very strong. Industry classification in 2003 was more meticulous than previous classification, this enabled previous income gap within some industries to become income gap between industries. It may be seen from Fig. 5 that, income gap between industries was higher than previous level after industry breakdown.

From overall trend, income gap between industries widened continuously in the period of 1990–2008; after 2008, income gap between industries narrowed, and was kept at 0.33 after 2012.

[12]Here industry average income only refers to the average income of unit employees in specific industry.

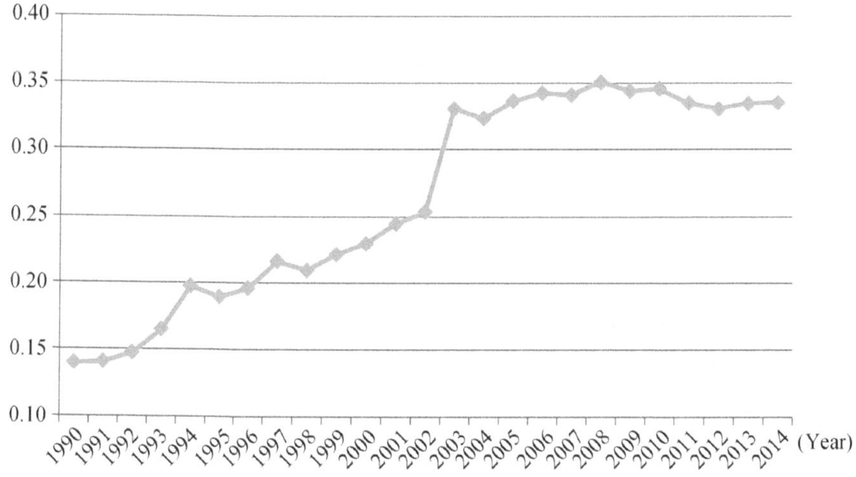

Fig. 5 Change trend of coefficient of income variation between industries. *Data source* Calculated according to *China Statistical Yearbook* in the past years

By stages, income gap between industries rose quickly before 2002. After industry standard was adjusted in 2003, income gap between industries was pulled up sharply, continued small rise from 2003 to 2008. Up to peak value 0.35 in 2008, then sustained slight decrease.

Income gap between monopoly industry and competitive industry has always been concerned. We regard manufacturing industry as competitive industry, regard real estate industry and financial industry as monopoly industry. And compare the income gap between monopoly industry and competitive industry in the period of 1990–2014. Gap between real estate industry and manufacturing industry is analyzed, in the period of 1990–1997, income gap between real estate industry and manufacturing industry increased continuously, thereafter income gap between real estate industry and manufacturing industry dropped continuously, dropped to 1.1 times in 2014. With respect to the income gap between financial industry and manufacturing industry, the gap rose continuously in the period of 1990–2010. Up to peak in 2010, per capita wage in financial industry was 2.27 times of that in manufacturing industry; the gap was narrowed gradually since 2010, dropped to 2.11 in 2014, equivalent to that in 2007 (Fig. 6).

To sum up the change trend of income gap between urban and rural areas, between regions, and between industries, by comparing with overall Gini coefficient, we may find that, income gap between urban and rural areas, between regions, and between industries changed synchronously with Gini coefficient, both decreased around 2009. Income difference between urban and rural areas, between regions, and between industries decreased in 2009, 2006 and 2008 respectively, the gap between urban and rural areas decreased quickly, and the income gap between rural regions also decreased quickly. We can see from the income ratio between urban and rural areas versus the income ratio between monopoly industry and competitive industry that,

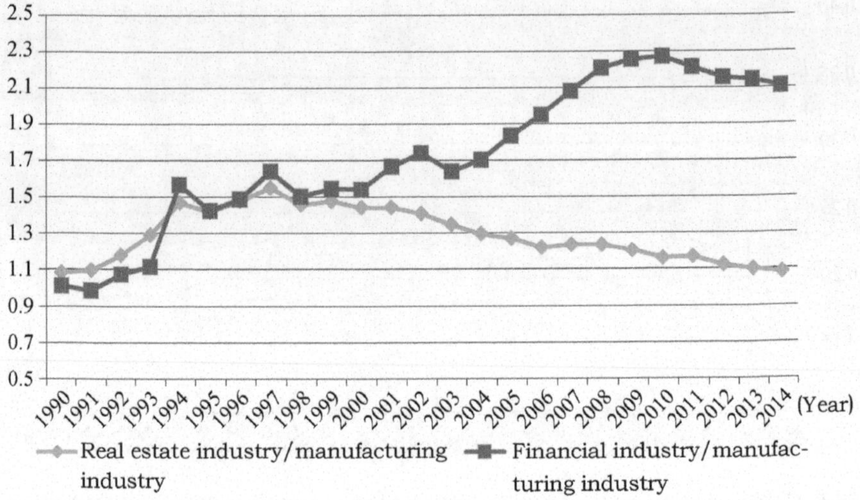

Fig. 6 Chnage trend of income gap in monopoly industry and competitive industry. *Data source* Calculated according to *China Statistical Yearbook* in the past years

the income gap between urban and rural areas was still large, and was the main source of income gap. From the coefficient of income variation in rural, urban areas, the income difference within rural areas was still large. This means that, narrowing the income gap between rural and urban areas, between different rural regions is still an important link in narrowing the income gap.

4 Analysis of the Change Trend of Labor Remuneration in the Distribution of National Income

Based on funds flow statement, we analyze the distribution pattern of three subjects, i.e. government, business, household, and the proportion of labor remuneration. National Bureau of Statistics of China started to prepare funds flow statement from 1992, adjusted China's national economic statistics system in 2005, and adjusted funds flow statement since 2000 at the same time. Therefore, funds flow statement may be divided into two stages, namely, 1992–1999 and 2000–2013 according to different statistics systems. Data in these two time sections are interconnected, but hopping existed between two time sections. In view of this, the analysis on funds flow statement will be divided into two time sections, and prone to trend analysis for the comparison across time sections.

4.1 Changes in the Primary Income Distribution Pattern of Three Subjects

In primary distribution, income of government sector mainly comes from net taxes on production of business sector, a small part comes from household sector; main income of household sector is remuneration for workers, from government sector and business sector respectively, remuneration for workers provided by business sector is dominant.

During rapid economic development of China, interest distribution relationship among governments, businesses and individuals was not changed significantly. This may be seen clearly from the changes in distribution principle of macro pattern since the 14th National Congress of CPC. After "plan and consider the interests of state, collective and individual as a whole" was put forward at the 14th National Congress of CPC, macro distribution pattern was concerned again at the 17th National Congress of CPC. That is to say, in the period of 1992–2007, the distribution principles of three subjects in macro distribution pattern were basically consistent. In nominal terms, at the stages of 1992–1999 and 2000–2013, income of government, business and household sectors was at ascent stage (see Table 1). For the period of 1992–1999, gross income experienced decelerated growth from 1996 to 1998, income of business sector in primary distribution decelerated more quickly, this is probably the interaction result of Asian Financial Crisis and the reform of state-owned enterprises in China. For the period of 2000–2013, the most evident deceleration occurred in 2009, in primary distribution, nominal value of gross income only increased 7.69% over preceding year, annual growth rate of business sector was merely 0.10%, on the contrary, annual growth rate of household sector was higher than total income growth rate, which was very rare. Decelerated growth rate in 2009 was mainly affected by global financial crisis. Due to higher degree of openness in China, and more close link with world economy, business sector received greater impact in this financial crisis.

The proportion of government, business and household sectors in primary distribution of macro distribution pattern is analyzed below (see Table 2). In the period of 1992–1999, proportion of government sector in primary distribution was basically smooth, without significant fluctuation. Only the proportion in 1992 and 1995 was relatively low. The decreased proportion of government sector in 1995 might be affected by tax sharing system reform. Although the proportion of business sector fluctuated to certain degree, yet not significantly, only proportion in 1993 and 1995 was relatively high, up to 20%. Except 1993, for government and business sectors, the decline of one meant the growth of the other, so proportion of household sector was stable at about 66%. In 1993, the proportion of government and business sectors grew simultaneously, so proportion of household sector decreased significantly, from 66.06% down to 62.61%. Although the proportion of household sector increased continuously after that, yet until 1998, it restored to the level in 1992.

From 2000 to 2013, proportion of government sector went all the way up, from 13.13% in 2000 to 15.63% in 2012. Proportion of business sector also increased

Table 1 Income of the sectors in primary distribution

Year	Nominal value (RMB hundred million)				Annual growth rate[a] (%)			
	Gross income in primary distribution	Government	Business	House-hold	Gross income in primary distribution	Government	Business	House-hold
1992	26937	4462	4680	17795				
1993	35260	6098	7087	22075	30.90	36.67	51.43	24.05
1994	48109	8217	8551	31341	36.44	34.75	20.66	41.98
1995	59810	9103	11683	39025	24.32	10.78	36.63	24.52
1996	68143	11660	11854	44629	13.93	28.09	1.46	14.36
1997	78061	13334	13189	51538	14.55	14.36	11.26	15.48
1998	83024	14729	13445	54850	6.36	10.46	1.94	6.43
1999	88479	15171	15755	57553	6.57	3.00	17.18	4.93
2000	98001	12865	19324	65811				
2001	108068	13697	23122	71249	10.27	6.47	19.65	8.26
2002	119096	16600	25694	76802	10.20	21.19	11.12	7.79
2003	134977	18388	30077	86512	13.33	10.77	17.06	12.64
2004	159454	21913	40051	97490	18.13	19.17	33.16	12.69
2005	183617	26074	45026	112517	15.15	18.99	12.42	15.41
2006	215904	31373	53416	131115	17.58	20.32	18.63	16.53
2007	266422	39267	68350	158805	23.40	25.16	27.96	21.12
2008	316030	46549	84086	185395	18.62	18.54	23.02	16.74
2009	340320	49606	84170	206544	7.69	6.57	0.10	11.41
2010	399760	59927	97968	241865	17.47	20.81	16.39	17.10
2011	468562	72067	112213	284283	17.21	20.26	14.54	17.54

(continued)

Table 1 (continued)

Year	Nominal value (RMB hundred million)				Annual growth rate[a] (%)			
	Gross income in primary distribution	Government	Business	House-hold	Gross income in primary distribution	Government	Business	House-hold
2012	518215	80976	117776	319462	10.60	12.36	4.96	12.37
2013	583197	88745	140692	353760	12.54	9.59	19.46	10.74

Note [a]Due to the changes of statistics system in the period of 1992–1999 and the period of 2000–2014, growth rate of 2000 compared to 1999 is not calculated. The same below

Data source The data of 1992–2011 came from Wei Zhong (2015), the data after that were calculated by the author according to the funds flow statement provided in *China Statistical Yearbook*

Table 2 Proportion of government, business, household sectors in primary distribution unit (%)

Year	Government	Business	Household	Total
1992	16.57	17.37	66.06	100
1993	17.29	20.10	62.61	100
1994	17.08	17.77	65.15	100
1995	15.22	19.53	65.25	100
1996	17.11	17.40	65.49	100
1997	17.08	16.90	66.02	100
1998	17.74	16.19	66.06	100
1999	17.15	17.81	65.05	100
2000	13.13	19.72	67.15	100
2001	12.67	21.40	65.93	100
2002	13.94	21.57	64.49	100
2003	13.62	22.28	64.09	100
2004	13.74	25.12	61.14	100
2005	14.20	24.52	61.28	100
2006	14.53	24.74	60.73	100
2007	14.74	25.65	59.61	100
2008	14.73	26.61	58.66	100
2009	14.58	24.73	60.69	100
2010	14.99	24.51	60.50	100
2011	15.38	23.95	60.67	100
2012	15.63	22.73	61.65	100
2013	15.22	24.12	60.66	100

Data source The data of 1992–2011 came from Wei Zhong (2015), the data after that were calculated by the author according to the funds flow statement provided in *China Statistical Yearbook*

continuously in the period of 2000–2008. While the proportion of both government sector and business sector rose together, the proportion of household sector decreased continuously, from 67.15% in 2000 down to 58.66% in 2008. In the period of 2009–2012, the proportion of government sector still rose, but since the proportion of business sector decreased significantly, the proportion of household sector rose correspondingly. Proportion of household sector in 2012 basically restored to the level in 2005, but large gap still existed compared with the proportion in 2000.

The changes of macro distribution pattern were closely linked to the income growth of three subject sectors. We may find the difference of macro distribution pattern in two time sections 1992–1999 and 2000–2013 by linking the growth rate of gross income and income of the sectors in Table 1 with the proportion of the sectors in Table 2. In the period of 1992–1999, income growth of household sector was faster than the growth speed of gross income from 1994 to 1998, only in 1993 and 1999, income growth of household sector was slower than growth rate of gross income.

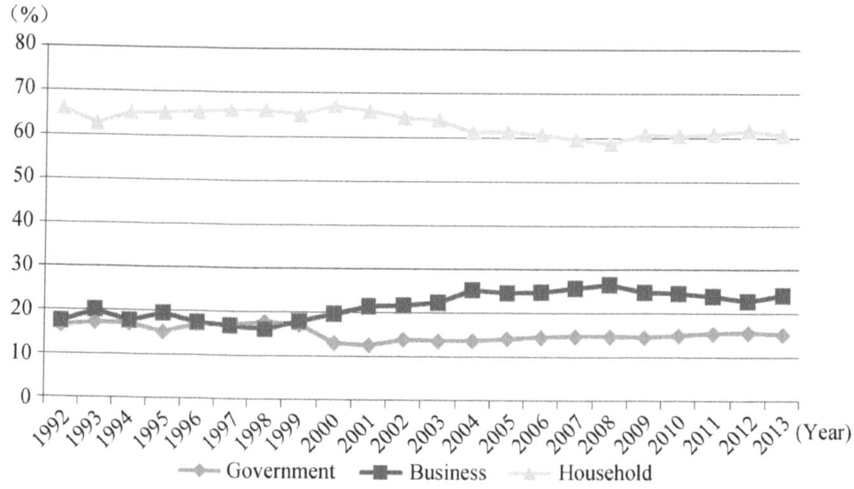

Fig. 7 Proportion trend of government, business, household sectors in primary distribution

This led to continuously increasing proportion of household sector from 1994 to 1998. The relationship between government and business sectors against growth rate of gross income was mostly in reverse state, when growth rate of government sector was higher than gross income, the growth rate of business sector was lower than gross income.

In the period of 2000–2013, growth rate of household sector was higher than the growth rate of gross income only in 2005, 2009, 2011 and 2012. While growth rate of government sector was lower than growth rate of gross income only in 6 years, and the decrease amplitude was very limited every time. Growth rate of business sector was lower than gross income only in 5 years, i.e. 2005, 2009–2012. This means that, income growth rate of household sector rose mainly during the "Twelfth Five-Year Plan" after the 17th National Congress of CPC, the increase in growth rate of household sector came from the decrease in growth rate of business sector. That is to say, measures for adjusting proportion of household sector after the 17th National Congress of CPC aimed to the adjustment between business and household sectors, continuous increasing trend of government sector did not decline (Fig. 7).

4.2 Changes in the Distribution Pattern of Disposable Income of Three Subjects

Disposable income of the sectors may be obtained after adjustment is made on social insurance payment and expenditure, social welfare income and expenditure, society subsidy income and expenditure and other transfer income and expenditure based on primary distribution.

Similar to the trend of primary income distribution, disposable income after redistribution also kept rise basically. In the periods of 1992–1999 and 2000–2013, nominal value of disposable income of all government, business and household sectors were higher than previous year, only disposable income of business sector decreased in 1996, lower than nominal value in 1995. Disposable income of household sector rose continuously, without sudden drop, then rise in government and business sectors. From the perspective of growth rate, growth rate of disposable income was also similar to primary distribution, it decreased from 1996 to 1998 (Table 3).

Redistribution of primary distribution intends to distribute income again, balance the distribution among three subjects, i.e. government, business and household sectors. Based on the difference in statistics systems, we still discuss the redistribution pattern in the periods of 1992–1999 and 2000–2013 respectively. In the period of 1992–1999, proportion of government sector in disposable income firstly decreased then increased from 1992 to 1997, 1995 became turning point, then the proportion in 1998 and 1999 basically remained at the level in 1997. Proportion of business sector in disposable income decreased continuously from 1992 to 1997, although it increased once in 1995. Thereafter, proportion of business sector rose in 1998 and 1999. In the process of government sector and business sector when the decline of one meant the growth of the other, except 1993, proportion of household sector in disposable income basically remained stable.

In the period of 2000–2013, proportion of the sectors in disposable income was quite different from that in the period of 1992–1999. Proportion of government sector in disposable income increased continuously from 2000 to 2007, rose from 14.53% in 2000 up to 19.01% in 2007 by 4.5% points. Decreased slightly in 2008 and 2009, thereafter increased slightly, in 2011, it even exceeded the highest point in 2007, and further increased to 19.54% in 2012. The proportion of business sector in disposable income increased continuously from 2000 to 2004, from 17.49% in 2000 up to 22.51% in 2004, fell slightly in 2005 and 2006, continued to increase in 2007 and 2008, the proportion reached 22.74% in 2008, thereafter the proportion of business sector in disposable income decreased. Different from the uptrend of government sector and business sector, proportion of household sector in disposable income dropped continuously from 2000 to 2008, from 67.54% in 2000 down to 58.28% in 2008 continuously, proportion of household sector changed to uptrend from 2009.

After 2008, the proportion of government, business and household sectors in disposable income changed mainly in business sector and household sector. While the proportion of government sector still kept slight increase, the increasing proportion of household sector came from the decreasing proportion of business sector. This was basically consistent with the change trend of primary distribution (Table 4 and Fig. 8).

We analyze the adjustment direction and strength in redistribution process below. And we subtract the proportion of three subject sectors in primary distribution from their proportion in disposable income to show interest distribution in the redistribution process (see Table 5). Firstly, the impact of redistribution process on income distribution share of the subjects is not significant, basically within 4% points, only

Table 3 Disposable income of the sectors after redistribution

Year	Nominal value (RMB hundred million)				Annual growth rate (%)			
	Disposable gross income	Government	Business	Household	Disposable gross income	Government	Business	Household
1992	27001	5389	3159	18453				
1993	35328	6943	5557	22827	30.84	28.84	75.91	23.70
1994	48224	8927	7005	32292	36.50	28.58	26.06	41.46
1995	59930	9916	9723	40292	24.27	11.08	38.80	24.77
1996	70320	12570	9625	48125	17.34	26.76	−1.01	19.44
1997	78487	14363	10282	53842	11.61	14.26	6.83	11.88
1998	83379	15120	11216	57043	6.23	5.27	9.08	5.95
1999	88888	16089	13067	59733	6.61	6.41	16.50	4.72
2000	98523	14314	17670	66539				
2001	108771	16324	20582	71865	10.40	14.04	16.48	8.00
2002	120170	19506	23241	77423	10.48	19.49	12.92	7.73
2003	136421	21947	27206	87268	13.52	12.51	17.06	12.72
2004	161349	26518	36322	98509	18.27	20.83	33.51	12.88
2005	185572	32574	40089	112910	15.01	22.84	10.37	14.62
2006	218142	39725	46991	131426	17.55	21.95	17.22	16.40
2007	269243	51192	59492	158559	23.43	28.87	26.60	20.65
2008	319027	60544	72557	185926	18.49	18.27	21.96	17.26
2009	342482	62603	72577	207302	7.35	3.40	0.03	11.50
2010	402514	74116	85276	243122	17.53	18.39	17.50	17.28
2011	470145	90203	94170	285773	16.80	21.71	10.43	17.54

(continued)

Table 3 (continued)

Year	Nominal value (RMB hundred million)				Annual growth rate (%)			
	Disposable gross income	Government	Business	Household	Disposable gross income	Government	Business	Household
2012	518432	101301	95731	321399	10.27	12.30	1.66	12.47
2013	582657	110376	115168	357113	12.39	8.96	20.30	11.11

Data source The data of 1992–2011 came from Wei Zhong (2015), the data after that were calculated by the author according to the funds flow statement provided in *China Statistical Yearbook*

Table 4 Proportion of government, business, household sectors in disposable income unit (%)

Year	Government	Business	Household sector	Total
1992	19.96	11.70	68.34	100
1993	19.65	15.73	64.62	100
1994	18.51	14.53	66.96	100
1995	16.55	16.22	67.23	100
1996	17.88	13.69	68.44	100
1997	18.30	13.10	68.60	100
1998	18.13	13.45	68.41	100
1999	18.10	14.70	67.20	100
2000	14.53	17.94	67.54	100
2001	15.01	18.92	66.07	100
2002	16.23	19.34	64.43	100
2003	16.09	19.94	63.97	100
2004	16.43	22.51	61.05	100
2005	17.55	21.60	60.84	100
2006	18.21	21.54	60.25	100
2007	19.01	22.10	58.89	100
2008	18.98	22.74	58.28	100
2009	18.28	21.19	60.53	100
2010	18.41	21.19	60.40	100
2011	19.19	20.03	60.78	100
2012	19.54	18.47	61.99	100
2013	18.94	19.77	61.29	100

Data source The data of 1992–2011 came from Wei Zhong (2015), the data after that were calculated by the author according to the funds flow statement provided in *China Statistical Yearbook*

a few adjustments exceeded 4% points. This means that, the income distribution pattern in China is mainly determined by primary distribution pattern, the impact of redistribution is very limited on the distribution pattern. Next, in the process of redistribution, proportion of business sector in disposable income was lower than its proportion in primary distribution, but benefits of government sector and household sector in the process of distribution varied evidently at two stages. From 1992 to 1999, government obtained more income from redistribution only in 1992 and 1993, expanded its share, but in the period of 1994–1999, only household sector obtained more income from redistribution. That is to say, redistribution process inclined to household sector. However, in the period of 2000–2013, interest distribution in the redistribution process was completely different from this. During this period, not only business sector became injured party in redistribution process, even household sector also became injured party in redistribution process.

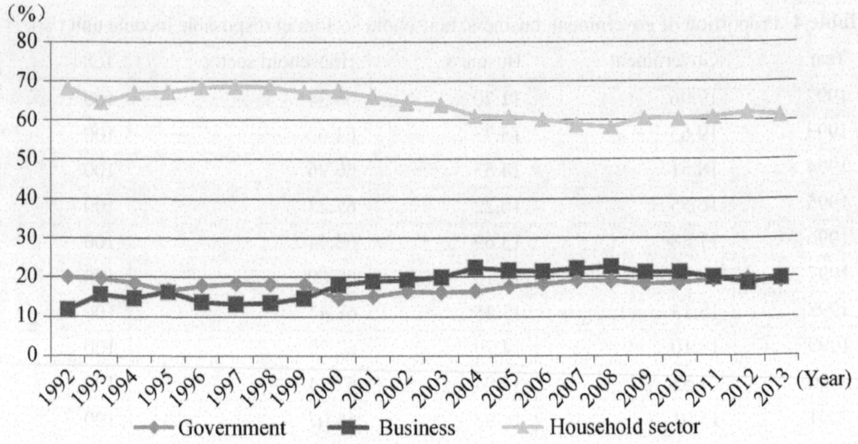

Fig. 8 Trend of the proportion of government, business, hosuehold sectors in disposable income

Table 5 Adjustment direction and strength of redistribution

Year	Government	Business	Household
1992	3.39	−5.67	2.28
1993	2.36	−4.37	2.01
1994	1.43	−3.24	1.81
1995	1.33	−3.31	1.98
1996	0.77	−3.71	2.95
1997	1.22	−3.8	2.58
1998	0.39	−2.74	2.35
1999	0.95	−3.11	2.15
2000	1.40	−1.78	0.39
2001	2.34	−2.48	0.14
2002	2.29	−2.23	−0.06
2003	2.47	−2.34	−0.12
2004	2.69	−2.61	−0.09
2005	3.35	−2.92	−0.44
2006	3.68	−3.2	−0.48
2007	4.27	−3.55	−0.72
2008	4.25	−3.87	−0.38
2009	3.70	−3.54	−0.16
2010	3.42	−3.32	−0.10
2011	3.81	−3.92	0.11
2012	3.91	−4.26	0.34
2013	3.73	−4.36	0.63

Data source The data of 1992–2011 came from Wei Zhong (2015), the data after that were calculated by the author according to the funds flow statement provided in *China Statistical Yearbook*

Until 2011, household sector changed to beneficiary party again. This reflected government sector taking more income in the process of redistribution relying on its dominant position, seized the income of household sector. Even when household sector was also benefited from redistribution process from 2011 to 2013, yet the income obtained by household sector was merely a tiny part of the income obtained by government sector.

4.3 Changes in the Proportion of Labor Remuneration in National Income

Government, business and household sectors include labor remuneration expenditures, which all together constitute labor remuneration income of household sector. Proportion of labor remuneration in GDP, proportion of labor remuneration in the subjects are calculated in this part respectively (see Table 6).

In the period of 1992–1999, proportion of labor remuneration in GDP was about 52%, the proportion of labor remuneration decreased continuously after 2000, and reached the lowest point 47.30% in 2011, yet increased greatly in 2012, restored to the level in 2006, reversed the continued downtrend of labor remuneration. But it is noteworthy that, the trend of proportion of labor remuneration varied among the subjects. With respect to government sector, in the period of 1992–1999, proportion of labor remuneration in added value of government sector was about 75%. After 2000, proportion of labor remuneration in government sector increased significantly. This was opposite to continuous decrease trend of the proportion of labor remuneration in GDP. As it were, the increased proportion of labor remuneration in government sector offset the decreased trend of proportion of labor remuneration in GDP to certain degree. Yet also reflected the income of public servants in government sector relatively higher. In recent years, Craze for Civil Service Examinations is a powerful evidence of higher wages of the public servants. In the period of 1992–1999, proportion of labor remuneration in business sector always fluctuated slightly, basically around 40% as a whole, it rose continuously from 1994 to 1997, and fell back again in 1998 and 1999 to the level in 1994. Quite contrary to the continuous rise of proportion of labor remuneration in government sector, proportion of labor remuneration in the added value of business sector decreased continuously from 2000 to 2008. Dropped from 44.89% in 2000 to 35.58% in 2008, decreased by nearly 10% points, it rose again in 2009, but entered downtrend again thereafter, and increased somewhat in 2013. In two different periods, proportion of labor remuneration in household sector maintained a relatively stable level, without continuous rise or fall. In the period of 1992–1999, except 1998 and 1999, proportion of labor remuneration in household sector basically maintained 39%; in the period of 2000–2012, proportion of labor remuneration in household sector was basically about 36%; yet it fell in 2013, became the lowest point since 2000, merely 33.92%.

Table 6 Proportion of labor remuneration in the sectors and GDP unit (%)

Year	Proportion of labor remuneration in GDP	Government	Business	Household
1992	54.43	62.48	42.06	39.04
1993	51.44	76.00	38.42	38.23
1994	52.27	77.01	40.59	39.08
1995	53.54	75.00	41.35	38.13
1996	52.74	77.98	42.81	38.49
1997	53.35	70.48	43.10	38.81
1998	53.15	73.49	40.93	40.28
1999	53.03	78.70	40.13	40.83
2000	53.03	83.69	44.89	36.63
2001	52.89	82.44	42.99	35.98
2002	53.68	88.39	42.62	35.69
2003	52.58	85.28	41.94	35.86
2004	50.17	88.35	38.21	36.62
2005	50.19	88.18	38.15	36.74
2006	48.76	84.56	36.98	36.81
2007	47.51	83.61	35.84	36.44
2008	47.18	84.93	35.58	36.36
2009	48.75	80.47	36.62	36.05
2010	47.40	85.14	35.85	35.90
2011	47.30	85.23	35.58	36.14
2012	49.49	86.05	38.31	36.51
2013	51.31	87.13	39.82	33.92

Data source The data of 1992–2011 came from Wei Zhong (2015), subsequent data were calculated by the author according to the funds flow statement in *China Statistical Yearbook*. In addition, the proportion data of labor remuneration in government sector in 1992 were calculated by the author according to the 1992 Funds Flow Statement in *China Statistical Yearbook* of 1999

From a perspective of international comparison, proportion of labor remuneration showed uptrend in U.S., Japan and U.K., while the proportion of labor remuneration in China showed an opposite trend.[13] Although the proportion of labor remuneration in GDP rose in 2012 and 2013, yet due to data limitations, we cannot tell continuous rise in the proportion of labor remuneration. In addition, from the perspective of proportion value of labor remuneration, the proportion of labor remuneration in China is kept at low level. When the U.S., Japan, U.K. were at the stage of development similar to current stage of China, proportion of household sector in primary distribution was higher than China. For example, the proportion of household sector in primary distribution of the U.S. was 81.08% in 1929. Although this proportion decreased

[13]Xie et al. (2014).

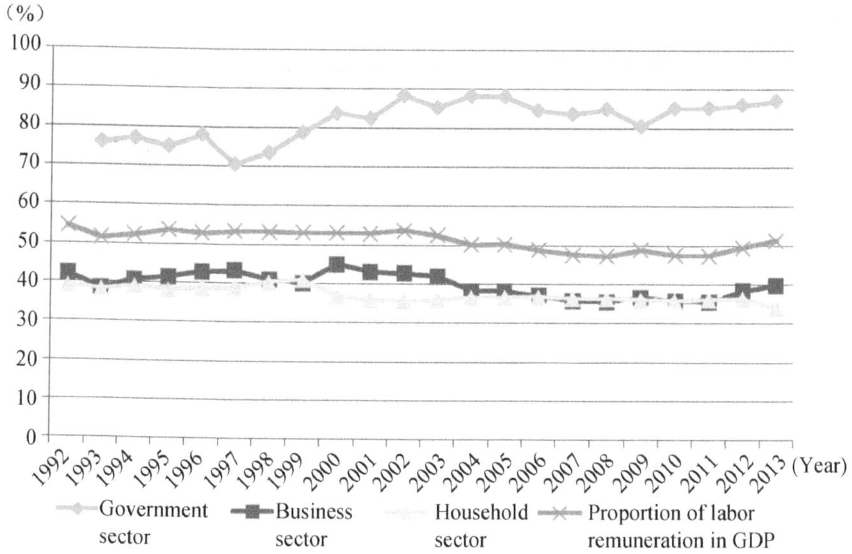

Fig. 9 Change trend of the proportion of labor remuneration in the sectors and GDP

somewhat later, yet still 75.50% till 1965. In the period of 1955–1975, average proportion of household sector in primary distribution was 81.78% in Japan. In contrast, although the proportion of household sector in primary distribution increased since the "Twelfth Five-year Plan" of China, yet the proportion of household sector in primary distribution was not high, the proportion was merely 61.65% in 2012. Labor remuneration is the uppermost source of income of household sector, we may deduce by comparing the proportion of income of household sector that, the proportion of labor remuneration in China's GDP is lower than the level in developed countries (Fig. 9).

References

Bai Chongen, Tang Yanhua, Zhang Qiong, the Estimate of China's Invisible Income Scale–based on Extended Consumer Spending Model and Data Interpretation, *Economic Research Journal*, 6th Issue, 2015.

Cai Fang, Wan Guanghua, Research on the Income Gap and Poverty in China: What We Know, What We should Know?, published in *Income Gap and Poverty in Transition Period of China* by Cai Fang, Wan Guanghua, Social Sciences Academic Press, 2006 Edition.

Li Qiang, Social Stratification, Fairness and Equity in Social Space, *Journal of Renmin University of China*, 1st Issue, 2012.

Lin Yifu, Poverty, Growth and Equity: China's Experience and Challenges, *China National Conditions and Strength*, 8th Issue, 2004.

Lin Yifu, Cai Fang, Li Zhou, *Chinese Miracle: Development Strategy and Economic Reform*, Truth & Wisdom Press, 2010 Edition.

National Bureau of Statistics, the People's Republic of China, *Poverty Monitoring Report in Rural China 2009*, China Statistics Press, 2010 Edition.

Su Hainan, Wang Xueli, Liu Zhaoquan, Liao Chunyang, Some Hot Spot Issues in the Discussion of Minimum Wage System, *China Opening Journal*, 6th Issue, 2006.

Xie Pan, Li Wenpu, Gong Min, Economic Development and Changes in National Income Distribution Pattern: International Comparison, *Finance and Trade Research*, 3rd Issue, 2014.

Xu Jing, Yue Ximing, How Tax Injustice Influences Income Distribution Effect, *Economic Perspectives*, 6th Issue, 2014.

Zhang Chewei, Zhao Wen, Share of Labor Remuneration Issue in China–Calculation and Analysis Based on Employee Economy and Self-Employed Economy, *Social Sciences in China*, 12th Issue, 2015.

Chapter 4
Redistribution of National Income

In macro pattern, income distribution mainly focuses on primary distribution. There is generally a redistribution process after primary distribution. If primary distribution embodies the result of market operations, it is a functional distribution, then redistribution (or secondary distribution) is adjustment of primary distribution made by the government and society by public means or non-economic means. Redistribution of income is a major approach to realize social equality, an important component of socialist market economy. Since the reform and opening up of China, especially since establishment of the framework of socialist market economy system, redistribution of income has been strengthened continuously, and has become a main policy means to uphold social justice. In this chapter, the concept, connotation, necessity and main policy means of income redistribution are firstly analyzed; then the status and problems of income redistribution in China are analyzed in three aspects, namely, tax, public finance, social security.

1 Redistribution of Income and Its Policy Framework

1.1 Redistribution of National Income in Marxian Economics

Redistribution of Income has different meanings in different economic contexts: in traditional Marxist political economics, redistribution refers to the redistribution of national income. In the textbook of traditional Marxist political economics,[1] National income refers to, after the value of consumed means of production is deducted from

[1]At the early stage of socialist construction in Soviet Union, someone thought redistribution of national income only existed in a society of class antagonism, denied redistribution in socialist society. But traditional Marxist political economics textbook admitted redistribution of national income later. See Liu (1957).

C. Pei et al., *The Basic Income Distribution System of China*, China Governance System Research Series, https://doi.org/10.1007/978-981-15-3461-4_4

aggregate social product (C + V + M), the new value created in that year, it is equal to "V + M". In the definition of national income, it only includes the new value created by workers in material production sectors, service sector, government administration, social service and other sectors do not create new value, therefore, transfer from material production sectors to these sectors is also included in the scope of redistribution.

In popular textbooks of Marxist political economics,[2] the reasons of redistribution of national income are summarized as follows: firstly, transfer of income from material production sectors to non-material production sectors. Although non-material production sectors do not produce value, yet necessary for value realization and social development. Secondly, an instrument of the state to control overall balance in national economy. Thirdly, social security fund, for coping with various social risks, and providing social welfare and public services for residents.

Correspondingly, national policy instruments for income redistribution include: firstly, service fee and public finance, redistribution between material production sectors and non-material production sectors is made in the form of service fee paid by the producers in production sectors to non-material production sectors (service sector etc.); redistribution of national income of material production sectors to public sector, administration sector in the form of public finance. Secondly, national economic construction expenditure, mainly manifested as direct investment of government in economic field. This is related to traditional definition of socialist state responsibility. Especially under Soviet-style planned economic socialism, the state of course assumes the responsibility of economic construction, manages the assets of ownership by the whole people on behalf of all people. Thirdly, transfer payment in the form of financial or social security fund, "government transfers income from one person or one organization to another person or another organization, without exchange of corresponding product or labor service".[3] Such transfer payment is generally defined as social risk fund, or "fund for people losing ability to work" in the framework of traditional Marxist political economics.[4]

1.2 *Redistribution of Income in Western Economics*

Analytical framework of western economics for the income distribution and redistribution of income varies greatly from Marxist political economics. Income distribution was defined as distribution according to factors and contribution in western economic framework from the very beginning: newly produced products (and services) should be distributed according to the contributions of labor, land and capital, this is primary distribution. Individual income distribution of residents has

[2]Pang et al. (2007), Song (2008).

[3]Pang et al. (2007, p. 289).

[4]*Critique of the Gotha Programme*, translated by Central Compilation and Translation Bureau of Marx, Engels, Lenin and Stalin Works, People's Publishing House 1965, p. 12.

been developed after the primary distribution. On this basis, government or society transfers the income of some people to some other people by compulsory or non-compulsory means such as tax, public financial expenditure, social security, social welfare, charitable donation.[5]

Major viewpoints of western economics on the theoretical basis of income redistribution policy: firstly, to realize income justice and social equality, under certain social welfare function, redistribution of income could increase total social welfare. Secondly, efficiency viewpoint, equal distribution of income could increase overall social production efficiency. Thirdly, in a democratic voting society, policy orientation of income redistribution is determined by the distribution of votes in different voters and the preference of median voter.[6]

The policy means of income redistribution in western economics is different from that in Marxian economics, major differences: firstly, definition of national income in western economics (Gross Domestic Product or Gross National Product, GDP or GNP) is different from that in Marxist political economics. In western economics, services including government management services belong to newly generated value, no redistribution from material production sectors to service sectors. Next, definition of state responsibility is different in western economics. In traditional western economics (before Keynes), government played the role of "night watchman", did not intervene economic operation actively, so did not make redistribution via economic construction expenditure of the government. After Keynes, although governments of major western countries started to intervene economic operation actively, yet still based on private ownership of means of production, the redistribution made by government via economic intervention was very weak.

Both western economics and Marxist political economics agree redistribution of income via tax, public finance and transfer payment of social security programs. After the framework of socialist market economy system was established in China, income redistribution was strengthened policy in this aspect, and became main policy means to realize common prosperity, share economic goals.

1.3 Changes of Income Redistribution Policy in China

In the planned economic period, income redistribution policy in China adhered to the pattern in the planned economy period of Soviet Union, transfer payment-dominated individual income redistribution was very rare, redistribution of income was concentrated in national economic construction and redistribution from material production sectors to non-material production sectors. Even after reform and opening up, until the beginning of the 1990s, there was no evident redistribution policy in which individual income redistribution was dominant. This was related to relatively equal personal income, inconspicuous income gap under planned economic conditions, but

[5]Eatwell et al. (1996, pp. 116–118).

[6]Meltzer and Richard (1981, pp. 89, 914–927).

more important, redistribution means of modern market economy such as tax, public finance and social security have been embedded in primary distribution and macro distribution pattern under planned economic conditions, not an independent policy domain. For example, there was no tax type of individual income tax in planned economy era of China until the beginning of the 1980s, nor independent social security fund.

Establishment of the socialist market economy system, the tax system, modern public finance system and social security system adaptive to modern market economy, provided conditions for the implementation of modern income redistribution policy; on the other hand, the deteriorated income distribution status of residents since the reform and opening up also required government to strengthen the redistribution of income. Although redistribution of income was not mentioned clearly in the Decision on the Establishment of Socialist Market Economy System at the 14th National Congress of CPC, the Third Plenary Session of the Fourteenth Central Committee of the CPC and in the 15th National Congress of CPC Report, yet relevant redistribution policy had been defined in several aspects: firstly, tax policy was required to adjust income gap, "establish the system of the declaration of individual incomes for tax payment gradually, strengthen the collection and management of individual income tax according to law, levy estate and gift tax in due time. Avoid growing income disparity due to extremely high income of a few people via distribution policy and tax regulation",[7] "regulate over high income, improve individual income tax system, levy estate tax and other new tax types".[8] Secondly, establish social security system that combines social pooling and individual accounts, "establish multi-level social security system, ... Social security system should include social insurance, social relief, social welfare, veteran benefit and placement, social mutual aid, personal savings accumulation security".[9] These two aspects have actually covered main redistribution policies.

CPC put forward the concept of redistribution clearly in the 16th National Congress of CPC Report, required efficiency in primary distribution, "In redistribution, we should pay more attention to fairness and strengthen the function of the government in regulating income distribution to narrow the gap if it is too wide".[10] In the 17th National Congress of CPC Report, "Primary distribution and redistribution should deal with the relationship between efficiency and fairness, more attention should be paid to fairness in redistribution".[11] The expressions of redistribution of income were more complete and well organized in the 18th Party Congress Report and the Third Plenary Session of the Eighteenth Central Committee of the CPC,

---

[7]Decision of the CCCPC on Some Major Issues Concerning Decision on the Establishment of Socialist Market Economy System, the Third Plenary Session of the Fourteenth Central Committee of the CPC, 1993.

[8]The 15th Naitonal Congress of CPC Report, 1997.

[9]Decision of the CCCPC on Some Major Issues Concerning Decision on the Establishment of Socialist Market Economy System, the Third Plenary Session of the Fourteenth Central Committee of the CPC, 1993.

[10]The 16th National Congress of CPC Report, 2002.

[11]The 17th National Congress of CPC Report, 2007.

basic framework of income redistribution policy under modern socialist market economy was put forward: "we should take speedy steps to improve the mechanism of redistribution regulating income distribution mainly through taxation, social security, and transfer payments",[12] "improve the mechanism of redistribution regulating income distribution mainly through taxation, social security, and transfer payments, strengthen tax regulation. We should establish a mechanism for equitable sharing of proceeds from public resource transfers. We should improve tax reduction or exemption system for charitable donation, support active role of charity for helping the poor".[13]

Based on the analysis above, and income redistribution policy framework promulgated at the Third Plenary Session of the Eighteenth Central Committee of the CPC, the income redistribution policy of China in recent years, policy effect and existing problems are analyzed here in the following aspects: firstly, income redistribution effect of tax; secondly, supply of public services and public goods; thirdly, reform of social security system; fourthly, poverty alleviation policy. Of course, redistribution of income should also include voluntary social transfer payments, such as charitable donations, yet such payments are not analyzed here, because our concern is the income redistribution policy related to government.

2 Taxation and Redistribution of Income

Government is the subject of redistribution of income in modern market economy. Main policy means of government for redistribution of income is public finance, including taxation and public spending. Income redistribution effect of taxation, and the influence of current Chinese taxation structure on income distribution are discussed in this section.

2.1 Taxation and Redistribution of Income

Taxation is one of the major functions of modern government, main source of finance for government running. With respect to economic running, main functions of taxation: firstly, balancing macroeconomic operation as main means of fiscal policy; secondly, allocation of resources via supply of infrastructure and public goods, public services; thirdly, role of redistribution, government realizes income transfer via different taxation structures and tax rates.[14]

---

[12]The 18th National Congress of CPC Report, 2012.

[13]The Central Committee of the Communist Party of China the Decision on Major Issues Concerning Comprehensively Deepening Reforms, 2013.

[14]Musgrave (1959).

Different taxation structures have different redistribution effect, generally speaking, income redistribution effect of direct tax in which income tax, property tax are dominant is the strongest, progressive rate is mostly implemented to achieve more obvious redistribution effect; income redistribution effect of indirect tax in which business tax, commodity tax, value-added tax are dominant is relative weak. Although taxation could realize equality objective of income redistribution, yet since taxation distorts market structure, it inevitably brings about efficiency loss. Research on the theory of optimal tax systems in western economics thinks that, a "neutral tax" may be designed to realize income transfer payments without distorting market structure and production structure. But theoretical assumptions are too rigorous to realize the so-called "neutral tax", for example, completely free market economy is required, while this is impossible in reality.[15] A large number of empirical researches also show that, it's impossible for government to raise the required income without any cost in the real world, and such cost is mainly loss of economic efficiency when taxation interferes resource allocation.[16] Balance of "equality-efficiency" has to be faced between different taxation structures. Empirical researches also show that, the substitution of indirect tax for direct tax will often deteriorate income distribution status, but will increase economic efficiency, the substitution of direct tax for indirect tax will narrow income distribution gap, but will decrease economic efficiency.[17]

For use of taxation as policy means of income redistribution, in addition to considering the above-mentioned distortion of resource allocation and balance between "equity and efficiency", the collection cost and management cost of different tax types should also be considered. Although direct tax including income tax, property tax has stronger effect of income redistribution, yet collection of direct tax imposes higher requirements for government management capacity and collection capacity. For example, the collection of individual income tax and property tax not only requires government to fully grasp the income and property information of residents, have complete personal income records of residents, but also requires government to collect a large number of incomes in kind, design different deduction proportion for households of different dependency burden. With respect to different taxation structures in all countries, proportion of direct tax is high in developed countries, proportion of indirect tax is high in developing countries. Proportion of direct tax in total tax revenue is 30% in developed countries, 20% in middle income countries, and only 17% in low-income countries.[18]

---

[15]Rothbard (2006, p. 108).

[16]Chen (2003).

[17]Yang (2012).

[18]IMF (Fiscal Policy 2014).

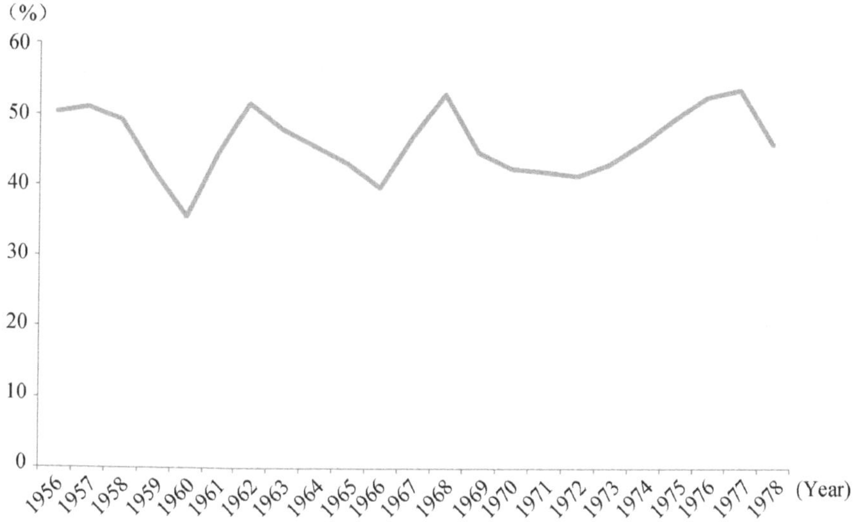

Fig. 1 Proportion of tax revenue in government revenue (1956–1978). *Data source* Compilation of statistics in 60 years of the PRC

2.2 Evolution and Main Features of China's Taxation System

In the period from founding of the PRC in 1949 to basic completion of socialist transformation in 1956, China basically realized public ownership of means of production in cities, and established planned economic system characterized by administrative management preliminarily. Enterprise became a "production workshop" of the government, implemented unified state control over income and expenditure in financial system, lost the role as subject of taxation. "No-tax theory" also appeared in theoretical circle, thought no need of taxation for the distribution relationship in public ownership after socialist system was established.[19] Therefore, government revenue of China from 1956 to 1978 mainly came from profit paid by state-owned enterprises and collectively owned enterprises, there were only a few tax types, including industrial and commercial tax, industrial and commercial income tax. In the period of 1956–1978, proportion of annual tax revenue in total government revenue was roughly below 50%, minimum only 35.6% (1960), proportion of grand total tax revenue in government revenue of these years was merely 45.9% (see Fig. 1). Taxation basically lost its regulation function of economic operation, also lost its function of income redistribution.

After the reform and opening up in 1978 till 1993, with the reform of state-owned enterprises and appearance of diversified economic sectors, especially a great number of foreign-funded enterprises and employees of foreign-funded enterprises, tax system adaptive to commodity economy was established gradually in China. Firstly,

[19]Jia and Zhao (2008, p. 34).

Table 1 Proportion of main tax types in total tax revenue in the past years of China (1999–2014) unit (%)

Year	Main turnover tax	Wherein				Income tax	Wherein	
		Value-added tax	Business tax	Consumption tax	Tariff		Individual	Business
1999	64.9	36.3	15.6	7.7	5.3	11.5	3.9	7.6
2000	63.8	36.2	14.9	6.8	6.0	13.2	5.2	7.9
2001	60.1	35.0	13.5	6.1	5.5	23.7	6.5	17.2
2002	58.9	35.0	13.9	5.9	4.0	24.4	6.9	17.5
2003	60.9	36.2	14.2	5.9	4.6	21.7	7.1	14.6
2004	62.7	37.3	14.8	6.2	4.3	23.6	7.2	16.4
2005	61.6	37.5	14.7	5.7	3.7	25.8	7.3	18.6
2006	60.2	36.7	14.7	5.4	3.3	27.3	7.1	20.2
2007	56.3	33.9	14.4	4.8	3.1	26.2	7.0	19.2
2008	55.3	33.2	14.1	4.7	3.3	27.5	6.9	20.6
2009	56.7	31.0	15.1	8.0	2.5	26.0	6.6	19.4
2010	55.1	28.8	15.2	8.3	2.8	24.2	6.6	17.5
2011	52.9	27.0	15.2	7.7	2.9	25.4	6.7	18.7
2012	52.5	26.3	15.7	7.8	2.8	25.3	5.8	19.5
2013	51.5	26.1	15.6	7.4	2.4	26.2	5.9	20.3
2014	50.7	25.9	14.9	7.5	2.4	26.9	6.2	20.7

Note Data of six main tax types are shown in the table; excluding other tax types
Data source China Statistical Yearbook in the past years

"substitution of tax payment for profit delivery" reform of state-owned enterprises, the profit paid by state enterprises at that time was changed to corporate income tax; secondly, foreign-related tax system for foreign-funded enterprises and employees of foreign enterprises, income tax of foreign-funded enterprises and joint venture, as well as individual income tax were set up.[20] Tax started to be main source of Chinese government revenue. Proportion of tax in government revenue increased rapidly from 49.3% in 1980 to 97.8% in 1993. China established the reform goal of socialist market economy system at the 14th National Congress of CPC and the Third Plenary Session of the Fourteenth Central Committee of the CPC. On this basis, China established multiple tax types, multi-level levied complex tax system with bi-subject of turnover tax and income tax in the tax sharing system reform started from 1994.[21]

China's tax system has main features as follows: firstly, although equal emphasis was placed on bi-subject of the tax system, i.e. turnover tax and income tax, yet indirect tax, especially value-added tax in turnover tax, was dominant in the structure of tax revenue. From 1999 to 2014, although the proportion of indirect tax revenue including value-added tax, business tax, consumption tax and tariff in total tax revenue decreased, yet still above 50% (see Table 1). Of which value-added tax was the

[20]Deng (2009).

[21]Deng (2009).

unique main source of tax revenue. Only the revenue of value-added tax accounted for 20–30% of total tax revenue. Although the proportion of value-added tax revenue decreased in recent years, yet still accounted for above ¼ of total tax revenue.

Secondly, proportion of direct tax was low, in which income tax and property tax were dominant. Income tax in China mainly include individual income tax and corporate income tax. These two income tax types accounted for less than 30% of total tax revenue, in which corporate income tax was dominant. Individual income tax which has the most obvious income redistribution effect has always been kept at 5–7% in recent years, little has changed. The rise in proportion of income tax was mainly the rise of corporate income tax in recent years (see Table 1).

Thirdly, too low proportion of property tax, some tax types with obvious income redistribution effect, such as estate tax, have not been levied yet. At present, property tax in China includes five items: land use tax in cities and towns, land value-added tax, house property tax, deed tax, vehicle and vessel tax. Although the proportion of property tax revenue in tax revenue rose in recent years, from 5.8% in 2007 to 10.3% in 2014, yet, mainly from rapid rise of land value-added tax from less than 1% in 2007 to 3.3% in 2014 due to unreasonable tax structure (see Fig. 2). Deed tax is the second largest tax type in property tax, its proportion was 3.4% (2014). These two items accounted for most of the property tax.

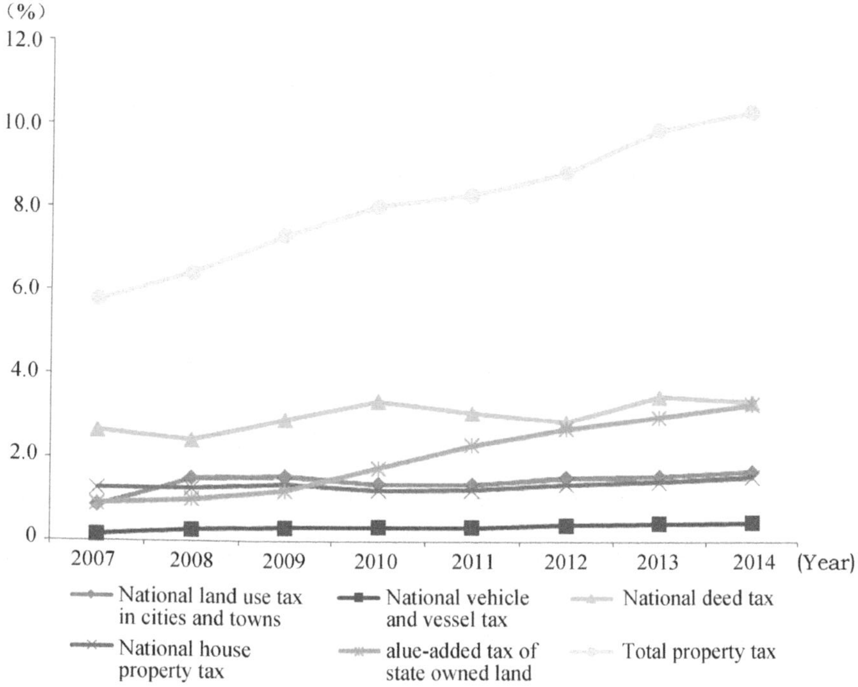

Fig. 2 Proportion of property tax revenue in national tax revenue of China (2007–2014). *Data source China Statistical Yearbook* in the past years

2.3 *The Income Redistribution Effect of Tax in China*

As a main policy instrument of income redistribution, tax has very strong effect on narrowing income gap theoretically, especially the strongly progressive income tax. It may be seen from empirical findings on income redistribution of the tax system in China, the tax system in China has very weak income redistribution effect as a whole, and some tax types have evident reverse redistribution effect.

Progressive income tax is generally believed to be the tax type with the most obvious income redistribution effect, but income tax in China has very weak income redistribution effect,[22] some researches even pointed out that individual income tax in China had no effect to improve income distribution status.[23] In fact, limited income redistribution effect of individual income tax also exists in some other developing countries.[24] Primary reason is backward market, backward government supervision and tax collection capacity in developing countries.[25] In addition, huge invisible income and gray income in China also weakened the income redistribution function of individual income tax obviously, and enabled tax burden of general wage earners income higher than the tax burden of property and other incomes.[26]

Income redistribution effect of indirect tax is not as good as direct tax. Nominal taxpayer of indirect tax is not always actual taxpayer, final tax incidence depends on elasticity of demand for commodity. under turnover tax system in which value-added tax is dominant, low income earners have low elasticity of demand for consumer goods, thus assume more final tax, while high income earners have more choices of consumption, and high overall elasticity of demand, so they assume less final tax. This allows the tax system of China in which indirect tax is dominant further deteriorates income distribution status.[27]

Income redistribution effect of other tax types, such as resource tax, consumption tax and property tax, is also unnoticeable, some of them even deteriorate the income redistribution status.[28] Especially in aspect of property tax, in China, the degree of inequality in distribution of property is far higher than the degree of inequality in distribution of income, this has become an important issue in China's distribution pattern. In the past dozen years, wealth gap wi rapidly in China, in the period of 2002–2010, Gini coefficient of property distribution among Chinese residents rose from 0.45 to 0.71 in rural areas, and rose from 0.45 to 0.66 in urban areas, national

---

[22] Yang (2014), Wang (2008), Wang and Li (2009), Guo (2015), Yue and Xu (2012), Cheng and Wu (2012).

[23] Cheng and Wu (2012); Yang Canming, Alert Against Reverse Regulation of Tax on Personal Income Distribution, *Chinese Social Sciences Today*, July 1, 2010, B3 edition.

[24] Yang (2012).

[25] Bird, M. & Zolt, E. M., Redistribution via Taxation: the Limited Role of Personal Income Tax in Developing Countries, *UCLA Law Review*, Vol. 52, pp. 1627–1696.

[26] Sun and Wang (2013).

[27] Liu and Nie (2004).

[28] Li and Geng (2005), Zhang (2006).

Gini coefficient of property distribution rose from 0.54 to 0.73.[29] Wherein, unequal distribution of property caused by inflation of real estate price played a major role. However, not only proportion of property tax is low in China, and although some important tax types, such as real estate tax, estate tax, gift tax, have been discussed for a very long time, yet are still not introduced.

2.4 *Tax Policy for Redistribution of Income*

In the planned economic period, on the one hand, there was little space for taxation to function in China, low tax revenue and few tax types led to insignificant position of taxation in the entire planned economic operation, on the other hand, in planned economy, all economic activities, including personal income were planned and controlled strictly by administration sector, so there was no policy requirement for taxation to regulate distribution of income. Taxation was put forward as income redistribution policy means at the Third Plenary Session of the Fourteenth Central Committee of the CPC, "we should avoid growing income disparity due to extremely high income of a few people via distribution policy and tax regulation", and should "establish the system of the declaration of individual incomes for tax payment gradually, strengthen the collection and management of individual income tax according to law, levy estate and gift tax in due time".[30]

Taxation was put forward as an important means in the ensuing policy statements of CPC Central Committee concerning distribution of income. The Third Plenary Session of the Eighteenth Central Committee of the CPC further required to "devote greater efforts to tax regulation".[31] In the Outline of the "Thirteenth Five-year Plan", tax regulation policy for distribution of income was further explained specifically and clearly, firstly, "quicken the setup of individual income tax system that combines comprehensive and classified forms", secondly, "include some top grade consumer goods and high consumption behaviors in the collection scope of consumption tax", thirdly, "improve tax policy that encourages contribution to the society and poverty alleviation".[32] However, as mentioned above, it may be seen from empirical research on income redistribution effect of taxation in China that, the role of taxation for regulating redistribution of income has not been fully played. Because of unreasonable design of tax system, for example, some important tax types with evident income redistribution effect have no been introduced, proportion of turnover tax is too high, and because of low tax collection capacity and management level. In

---

[29]Li (2015).

[30]Decision of the CCCPC on Some Major Issues Concerning Decision on the Establishment of Socialist Market Economy System, 1993.

[31]Decision of the CCCPC on Some Major Issues Concerning Comprehensively Deepening the Reform, 2013.

[32]Outline of the Thirteenth Five-Year Plan for National Economy and Social Development of the People's Republic of China, 2016.

addition, tax does not only regulates redistribution of income, but also acts as fiscal policy and works for government financing. These functions should be considered comprehensively.

Under great background of new normality of economic development in China, as major policy for redistribution of income, tax should also be adjusted in the following aspects: firstly, adjust taxation structure, reduce turnover tax rate, especially reduce value-added tax rate for necessities of life, reduce turnover tax burden of income bracket. Secondly, reform property tax system, increase the tax on property held, decrease the tax on property transfer, especially levy real estate tax as soon as possible in cities with excessive expansion of real estate. Introduce estate and gift tax and other new property tax types as soon as possible. Thirdly, strengthen tax collection and management, increase tax collection capacity, especially improve information statistics of resident income and property, devote greater efforts to taxation of invisible income and gray income. Low capacity of collection and management is the main reason of dominant indirect tax in developing countries, but indirect tax not only has poor income redistribution effect, but also has market distortion effect. One of the major tax problems in China is collection and management capacity problem. The Third Plenary Session of the Eighteenth Central Committee of the CPC required to improve modern national governance capacity, important of which was government monitoring and supervision capacity for economic operation. In aspect of tax collection and management, information system should be firstly set up and consummated for economic activities of residents, government and enterprises, so as to fully grasp fund flow information, lay a foundation for effective supervision and collection.

3 Redistribution of Income Through Public Spending

3.1 Income Redistribution Effect of Public Spending

Income redistribution effect of fiscal policy includes two aspects, firstly, "receive", i.e. progressive taxation structure, high income earners pay more tax, low income earners pay less tax, so as to adjust income distribution; secondly, "pay", government makes transfer payment to low income group through public spending, so as to improve income distribution status. The income redistribution effect of tax is analyzed in the previous section, the income redistribution effect of public spending and transfer payment will be analyzed in this section. Fiscal public spending with income redistribution effect includes the following categories: firstly, transfer payment in the form of cash mainly refers to various social assistance programs, poverty alleviation programs and disaster relief expenditures supported by government finance.[33] Such

[33]Such program belongs to social assistance in the generalized social security system, it is different from social insurance program in social security: social insurance program is payment type social security, payment obligations should be equivalent to benefit, no benefit if there is no payment; fund of social assistance program comes from financial payment, does not require obligations equivalent

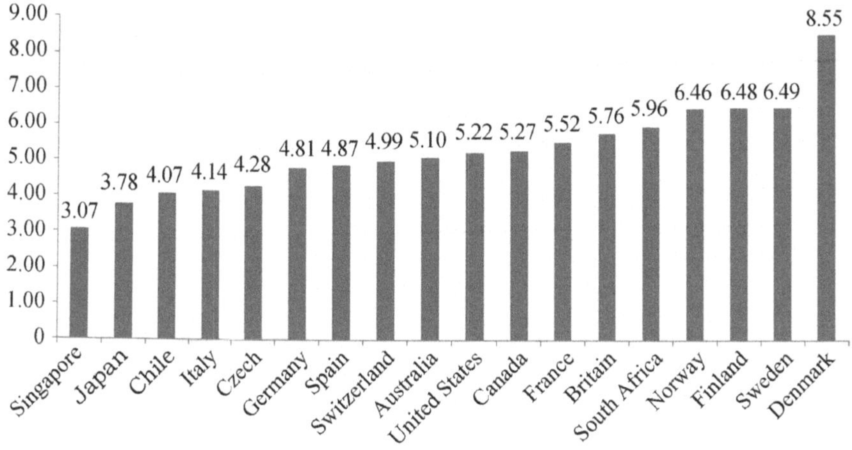

Fig. 3 Proportion of government educational expenditures in GDP of some countries (%). *Data source* http://data.Uis.Unesco.Org/?Queryid=181

public spending plays the role of "social security net", provides assistance for low income group and poverty group. Secondly, supply of public goods and public services. Supply of various public goods and public services for the society has become an important function of modern government. Including spending for public education, spending for health care and spending for employment security. Although public spending for education, medical care and employment does not exert direct influence on income, yet it influences income distribution status indirectly in two aspects: firstly, provision of public services reduces cash expenditure of residents for these services directly; for low-income families, the income substitution effect brought by these services through public channel is higher than high-income families theoretically. Next, these services are actually investments in human capital, increase income capacity of residents, is a primary approach to cut off intergenerational transmission of poverty on a long view. Public spending for such goods and services also becomes main fiscal spending items of some countries. For example, government educational expenditures, government educational expenditures in Northern Europe and other welfare states account for over 6% of GDP (see Fig. 3).

Income redistribution effect of public spending is stronger than tax, and has smaller market distortion effect.[34] Research reveals that, in OECD countries, contribution of average social transfer payment (public spending for public service and social assistance) to income distribution gap (Gini coefficient) is 75%, while that of

to rights, its principle is Need principle, it's available as long as the helpee meets certain conditions. Income redistribution effect of social insurance program is analyzed in the next section of this chapter.

[34]Prasad (2008).

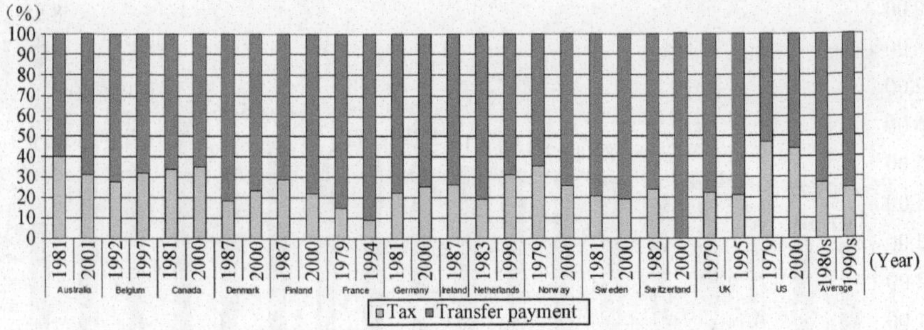

Fig. 4 Contribution of tax and social transfer payment to narrow income gap in OECD countries. *Data source* Mahler, V. A., Jesuit, D. K., Fiscal redistribution in the developed countries: new insights from the Luxembourg income study, *Socio-Economic Review*, vol. 4, no. 3, pp. 483–511

tax is only 25%; and the contribution of tax to narrowing income gap decreased from 27% in the 1980s to 24% at the end of the 1990s[35] (see Fig. 4).

3.2 *Public Spending, Transfer Payment and Supply of Public Goods in China*

Fiscal public spending, transfer payment and supply of public goods are also main policy means of income redistribution in China. In the 17th National Congress of CPC Report, social policies related to public service provision, social security and transfer payment were discussed under the topic "Social Development with the Focus on Improving People's Livelihood" unifiedly for the first time; this framework was further determined at the 18th National Congress of CPC, the Third Plenary Session and the Fifth Plenary Session of the Eighteenth Central Committee of the CPC, the connotation of construction of people's livelihood and relevant social policies were extended and deepened. At the 18th National Congress of CPC, these construction objectives of people's livelihood were deemed as "the most direct and most realistic issues of interests concerned by the people", and described specifically in six aspects: firstly, make efforts to provide education satisfactory to people; secondly, promote employment of higher quality; thirdly, do everything to increase resident income; fourthly, promote social security construction in both urban and rural areas; fifthly, increase health level of the people; the sixth, strengthen and make innovations in social administration.

In recent years, fiscal public spending increased very rapidly in these important people's livelihood fields related to vital interests of residents. China's fiscal expenditures in education, social security, employment and health care from 2007 to 2014 are shown in Table 2. In aspect of education spending, fiscal education spending was

[35] Mahler, V. A., Jesuit, D. K., Fiscal Redistribution in the Developed Countries: New Insights from the Luxembourg Income Studyw, *Socio-Economic Review*, Vol. 4, No. 3, pp. 483–511.

Table 2 China's fiscal expenditures in education, health care, social security and employment (2007–2014) unit (%)

	Proportion in GDP				Proportion in total fiscal expenditure			
	Education spending	Social security and employment expenditure	Health care expenditure	Education + social security + health expenditure	Education spending	Social security and employment expenditure	Health care expenditure	Education + social security + health expenditure
2007	2.6	2.0	0.7	5.4	14.3	10.9	4.0	29.2
2008	2.8	2.1	0.9	5.8	14.4	10.9	4.4	29.7
2009	3.0	2.2	1.1	6.3	13.7	10.0	5.2	28.9
2010	3.0	2.2	1.2	6.4	14.0	10.2	5.3	29.5
2011	3.4	2.3	1.3	7.0	15.1	10.2	5.9	31.2
2012	3.9	2.3	1.3	7.6	16.9	10.0	5.8	32.6
2013	3.7	2.4	1.4	7.5	15.7	10.3	5.9	31.9
2014	3.6	2.5	1.6	7.6	15.2	10.5	6.7	32.4

Note All expenditures in the table are fiscal expenditures; fiscal expenditure in social security includes the fiscal subsidy for social security fund, supplementary national social security fund expenditure, expenditure for retired persons in administrative public institutions, social assistance expenditure etc., excluding expenditure of social security fund

Data source China Statistical Yearbook in the past years

2.3 trillion Yuan in 2014, accounting for 3.6% of Gross Domestic Product in that year, accounting for 15.2% of total fiscal expenditure in that year; fiscal health care expenditure was 1 trillion Yuan, accounting for 1.6% of GDP in that year, accounting for accounting for 6.7% of total fiscal expenditure in that year; fiscal expenditure in social security and employment was 1.6 trillion Yuan, accounting for 2.5% of GDP in that year, accounting for 10.5% of total fiscal expenditure. Proportion of these three expenditures in GDP of that year was 7.6%, accounting for 32.4% of total fiscal expenditure in that year, i.e. nearly 1/3 of total fiscal expenditure in that year was spent in education, health care and social security. And this proportion rose continuously. Proportion of these three expenditures in total fiscal expenditure was 29.2% in 2007, rose to 32.4% in 2014. Of which health care expenditure increased faster, its proportion rose from 4.0% of total fiscal expenditure in that year to 6.7%, increased by 2.7 percentage points.

Another important aspect of fiscal public spending is direct fiscal transfer payment, which involves two aspects, firstly, social assistance for low income group, including minimum living standard security system for urban and rural residents and rural five guarantees system, as well as medical assistance system for urban and rural residents; secondly, poverty alleviation/reduction expenditure for poverty-stricken areas. Fiscal social assistance belongs to non-contributory assistance policy in social security system. Different from social insurance, social assistance adheres to "Need" principle, i.e. no matter paid or not, assistance may be obtained as long as income is lower than certain standard (or other conditions).

Average standard and expenditure level of minimum living security of Chinese urban and rural residents have been enhanced greatly in recent years. Urban minimum living security standard and average expenditure level of minimum living security increased from 182.4 Yuan/person per month, 102.7 Yuan/person per month in 2007 to 451.1 Yuan/person per month and 316.6 Yuan/person per month in 2015; rural minimum living security standard and average expenditure level of minimum living security increased from 70.0 Yuan/person per month, 38.8 Yuan/person per month in 2007 to 264.8 Yuan/person per month and 147.2 Yuan/person per month in 2015 (see Fig. 5).[36] Other social assistance programs, including rural extremely poor people relief and support, traditional relief, medical assistance and temporary assistance have also been set up comprehensively. In 2014, social service fee made by fiscal payment to civil affairs department was over 440 billion Yuan, accounting for 2.90% of total fiscal expenditure in that year, of which social assistance was main part, about half of the social service fee in that year. In social assistance expenditure, urban and rural minimum living standard security accounted for a large proportion, their sum was 138.92 billion Yuan, next was medical assistance, up to 33.24 billion Yuan (see Table 3).

---

[36]Data in 2015 originate from Ministry of Civil Affairs, *The People's Republic of China 2015 Statistical Report on Social Service Development.*

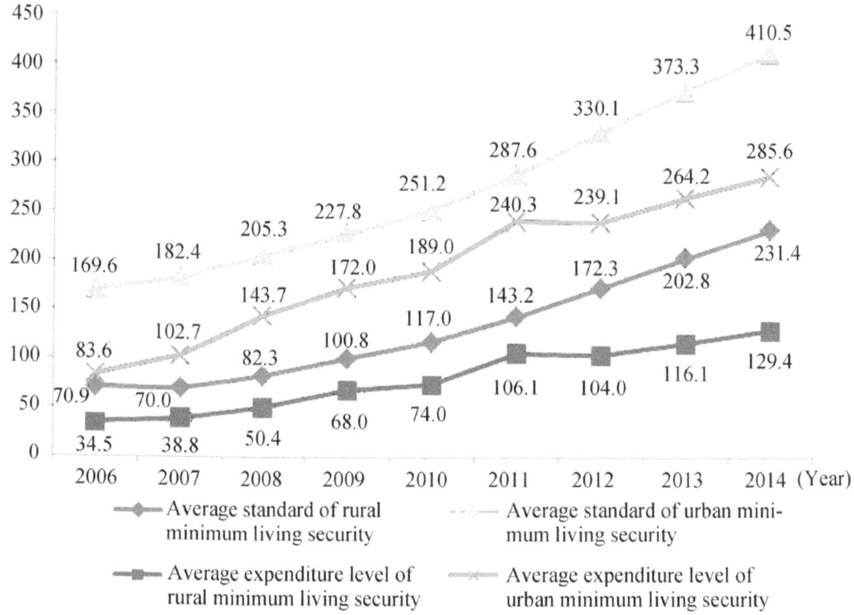

Fig. 5 Average standard of minimum living security and average expenditure level of minimum living security in rural and urban China (in RMB/person • month). *Data source China Civil Affairs' Statistical Yearbook 2015*

Table 3 Expenditure on civil administration undertakings and expenditure on social assistance (2014)

Item	Amount (RMB hundred million)	Proportion in total fiscal expenditure of that year (%)
Social service fee	4404.1	2.90
Social assistance	2197.5	1.45
Urban minimum living security	518.9	0.34
Rural minimum living security	870.3	0.57
Rural five guarantees	189.8	0.13
Medical assistance	332.4	0.22
Temporary assistance	57.6	0.04
Other	228.5	0.15

Note Social service fee refers to the fiscal allocation to people's livelihood department, includes pension cost, retirement settlement cost, social welfare cost, social assistance, natural disaster relief cost, local retiree cost, other civil administration costs, of which social assistance cost is main part, accounting for nearly half of all social service expenditures

Data source China Civil Affairs' Statistical Yearbook 2015

3.3 Income Redistribution Effect of Public Spending

Theoretically speaking, fiscal public spending has positive income redistribution effect. Increasing fiscal public spending is helpful to narrow income gap, this also becomes mainstream view of policy analysis, in various policy suggestions, increasing public spending and transfer payment becomes one of the main policy suggestions. However, whether public spending generates positive income redistribution effect in reality also relies on a series of systems and realistic conditions, relies on management level of policy implementation. This also leads to quite different income redistribution effect of the same public spending policy in different countries: the redistribution effect of public spending is significant in developed countries, while income redistribution effect of public spending in developing countries is relative weak, even reverse redistribution effect exists.[37]

Fiscal public spending of China for people's livelihood undertaking is no lower than the countries and regions at the same stage of development in aspect of total amount, growth rate is also very fast, this plays certain role for alleviating poverty, narrowing income gap. Especially social assistance program and poverty alleviation program play positive role in narrowing income gap. But as a whole, income redistribution effect is not evident, even reverse redistribution effect exists, i.e. the interests obtained by the rich from public spending exceed the poor. This is more obvious in aspect of public service, such as public education expenditure, government health care expenditure.[38] In aspect of public service, although original intention of government is to provide public services free of charge or at low price for low income group.

However, on the one hand, due to imbalanced distribution of public service resources, for example, large-scale high grade hospitals and institutions of higher education are mainly distributed in major cities, on the other hand, cost to obtain these services is unaffordable to low income group. So a large number of medical and educational resources supported by public finance are mainly obtained by high income group.[39] For example, in the student groups receiving higher education, the proportion of students from high income class and cities is far higher than the proportion of students from low income group and countryside. Government investment in higher education has been obtained mainly by high income group and "dominant group".[40] This violates the original intention of public spending to narrow income gap, make transfer payment to the poor. Reverse income redistribution effect also exists in medical and health services paid by the government, degree of inequity in rural area is more serious than urban area, such inequity has not been improved evidently with social and economic development.[41] Of course, education and medical

[37] Lindert et al. (2006).

[38] Wang (2010), Ran et al. (2009), Wang (2007), Liu (2007).

[39] Guo et al. (2006).

[40] Jiang (2002).

[41] Wu et al. (2011).

treatment also assume functions in other aspects, for example, increase human capital accumulation. Yet income redistribution effect of public spending is also worthy of attention.

4 Social Insurance System and Redistribution of Income

4.1 Social Insurance and Its Redistribution Effect

The generalized social security (social security) includes three parts: firstly, social insurance based on mutual aid, mutual relief among social members. Social insurance adheres to general principles of insurance industry, reciprocity principle of rights and obligations, yet different from commercial insurance, social insurance is mandatory, all eligible members of society must participate. Secondly, social assistance program funded by government financial allocation, its feature is no need of payment by the members who receive assistance, nor other contributions, based on "Need principle", i.e. as long as members of society meet certain conditions, and "Need", they may achieve assistance. For example, the urban and rural minimum living standard security systems, medical assistance system analyzed above. Social assistance is a "safety net" of modern society, could ensure groups got stuck in low income for whatever reason to obtain the most fundamental material assistance. Thirdly, social welfare program. The nature of social welfare program is different from social insurance and social assistance, the goal of social welfare is not to deal with risk, nor rescue the weak, but to provide welfare treatment for certain group in the members of society, for example, family policy in some countries, provides physical goods, services or cash for multiple-child family, women who stay at home to care for young children. In recent years, the concept of international social security has been expanded, some human capital investment type public services are also included in the concept of social security. The concept of "social protection" substitutes the concept of social security increasingly.[42]

Social assistance program has been analyzed in fiscal public spending above, so income redistribution effect of social insurance program is focused in this section. Social insurance is a product of modern industrial society. Social medical insurance established by German Bismarck government in 1893 was the first program of social insurance. Thereafter main industrial countries established social insurance systems gradually, including medical insurance, pension insurance, work-related injury insurance, unemployment insurance and maternity insurance.

Main functions of social insurance, firstly, risk diversification, risk is diversified via mutual assistance, mutual relief among members of society. For example, medical insurance deals with disease risk of the insured, pension insurance deals with old-age risk of the insured. Social insurance diversifies risks among different members of

[42]Norton et al. (2001).

society, so as to enhance capability of the members of society to deal with impact of risks. Secondly, income redistribution function. Since a main feature of social insurance is mandatory, i.e. eligible members of society, regardless of their income, occupation, age, gender etc., must participate in social insurance. This mandatory nature evades adverse selection in commercial insurance program: those members of good conditions and low risks evade participation. On the other hand, contribution principle of social insurance is "pay-by-capacity", at uniform rate, high income earners pay more, low income earners pay less; yet benefit is given according to "Need" principle: those under higher impact of risk may gain more. For example, in medical insurance, high income earners pay more, but when reimbursement is needed in case of illness, the basis is not high or low payment and high or low income, but uniform reimbursement proportion, the more spent, the more reimbursement will be given. Mandatory contribution irrelevant to benefit is the main reason of income redistribution function of social insurance. The third function of social insurance is compulsory saving, this function exists in social insurance program of funded scheme, it is very weak or does not exist in insurance program of complete pay-as-you-go system.

4.2 The Social Insurance System in China

The social insurance system in China has been established gradually after reform and opening up, especially after reform of socialist market economy system was determined at the 14th National Congress of CPC. Urban and rural division feature of social security system in the planned economic period of China: social insurance program only existed in urban areas; only security programs provided by collective economic organizations were available in rural areas, for example, rural five guarantees, cooperative medical care. China established labor insurance system for urban enterprise employees in the 1950s, enterprises paid certain insurance premium to form labor insurance of the whole society, employees may obtain assistance in case of diseases, old-age risks. However, with the establishment of planned economic system, state-owned enterprises and collectively owned enterprises became attachments to administration sector, lost independent operating status and function. under such conditions, it was necessary for social insurance to exist. After reform and opening up, with the reform of urban industrial enterprises, enterprises were burdened with heavy social responsibilities in the planned economic period, some enterprises were at a disadvantage in market competition due to a large number of old employees and heavy social burden. Therefore, in the 1980s, at the beginning of reform and opening up, unified social insurance system was explored in many regions.[43] Such exploration continued till the mid 1990s. At the 14th National Congress of CPC, target model of China's reform and opening up was determined to be socialist market economy system, which required reform of state-owned enterprises, and establishment of modern

[43]Zhao (1987).

enterprise system. This inevitably required to strip off social functions originally assumed by the enterprises, so the enterprises may become true market subject.

Under such conditions, construction principle of China's social security system was determined as "social pooling plus individual account" at the Third Plenary Session of the Fourteenth Central Committee of the CPC, basic pension, basic medical insurance systems would be established for enterprise employees. China's basic pension and basic medical systems for urban enterprise employees was established in accordance with the Decision of the State Council on the Establishment of Unified Basic Pension Insurance System for Enterprise Employees in 1997, as well as the Decision of the State Council on the Establishment of Basic Medical Insurance System for Urban Employees in 1998. Work-related injury insurance, unemployment insurance, maternity insurance were also established gradually in this period.

In rural area, with the collapse of people's commune system, social security function of collective economic organization for rural residents was also weakened gradually. Except five guarantees supporting system, there was no complete and unified social insurance program in rural area before 2002. In 2002, the Chinese government decided to establish new rural cooperative medical system all over China, covered all rural areas in China rapidly. In 2010, new rural cooperative medical system was determined as social insurance program in *Social Security Act*. In 2007, basic medical insurance for urban residents was established for unemployed group in urban areas. In 2016, the State Council determined to consolidate the new rural cooperative for rural residents with medical insurance for urban residents, and establish unified medical insurance program for urban and rural residents. In aspect of pension insurance for rural residents, the Chinese government determined to carry out new rural pension insurance program in rural areas in 2009, and consolidated it with the pension insurance program for urban residents in 2014, established pension insurance system for urban and rural residents.

From the perspective of current social insurance coverage in China, full coverage of system (each group is covered by at least one social insurance program) and actual full coverage (see Fig. 6, Table 4M) have been basically realized, this is an amazing achievement in the history of social insurance in the world.

4.3 Characteristics and Income Redistribution Effect of the Social Insurance System in China

The social insurance system in China originated in the planned economic period, still had some characteristics of the planned economy era, main institutional characteristic that influenced the fairness of social insurance system was "fragmented" social insurance system in China: different social insurance programs were established for different groups; and regional segmentation existed in the same social insurance program. With respect to these two segmentations, the former is "institutional segmentation", the latter is "regional segmentation". Institutional segmentation

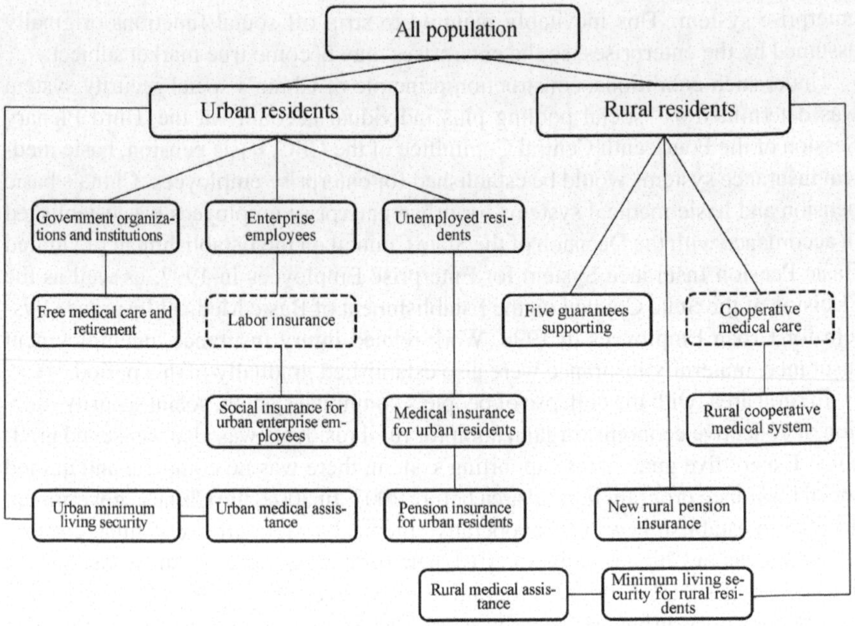

Fig. 6 Social security programs in China

and regional segmentation broke the social insurance program in China into "fragments". In the planned economic period, when population movement and employment did not change frequently, such "fragmented" social insurance program had its own rationality; however, with the establishment of socialist market economy system, massive domestic migration became normal state, and employment changed more frequently, fairness of the "fragmented" social insurance system decreased, and income redistribution effect was affected greatly.

Firstly, institutional segmentation of social insurance program. The social insurance program in China was designed for different groups: firstly urban and rural segmentation, different social insurance programs were designed for rural residents and urban residents. Next, segmentation existed inside the urban and rural areas respectively. Different social insurance programs were designed for urban employees and unemployed urban residents respectively. While different social insurance programs also existed among urban employees: different social insurance programs were established for enterprise employees and employees of government organizations and institutions respectively. Treatment difference between these different social insurance programs was evident, and they could not be transferred to each other. In 2012, average pension of the pension insurance for urban employees was above 20,000 Yuan per year, while average pension for urban and rural residents was only less than 900 Yuan per year; per capita financing of basic medical insurance for urban employees was up to 2288.8 Yuan/year, per capita financing of basic medical insurance for urban residents was only 322.9 Yuan/year, per capita financing of

Table 4 Coverage rate of social insurance programs for different groups in China unit (%)

		2006	2007	2008	2009	2010	2011	2012
Social security system for government organizations and institutions		100.00	100.00	100.00	100.00	100.00	100.00	100.00
Basic social insurance for urban enterprise employees	Pension	49.15	50.80	53.71	55.37	58.29	63.29	65.51
	Medical	29.69	34.95	39.05	42.27	44.74	46.24	47.12
	Unemployment	28.15	28.36	29.84	29.65	30.30	31.56	32.90
	Work-related injuries	24.58	30.32	34.78	37.10	39.41	42.27	44.51
	Maternity	9.74	14.00	18.64	23.38	26.90	30.21	33.53
Pension insurance for urban and rural residents								56.78
Medical insurance for urban residents			29.96	55.56	76.10	78.88	85.62	99.12
Rural cooperative medical system		80.70	86.20	91.50	94.20	96.00	97.50	98.26
Social security system for government organizations and institutions		100.00	100.00	100.00	100.00	100.00	100.00	100.00
Participation of rural migrant workers in social insurance for urban employees	Pension	10.80	13.40	17.20	18.20	21.40	26.10	27.81
	Medical	18.00	22.70	30.40	29.80	29.90	29.30	30.58
	Unemployment	17.90	28.80	35.20	38.40	41.10	43.00	43.95
	Work-related injuries	–	8.30	11.00	11.30	13.00	15.10	16.54

Note 1. Coverage rate of basic pension and medical insurance for urban enterprise employees refers to the coverage rate of on-the-job workers and staff, excluding number of retirees participating in social insurance for urban employees; the number of retirees participating in social insurance for urban employees is included in pension and medical insurance for residents. 2. The former pension insurance for urban residents and new rural pension insurance have been consolidated into pension insurance for urban and rural residents. 3. Denominator of social insurance for urban enterprise employees is urban employees not in government organizations and institutions; numerator is number of on-the-job workers and staff participating in social insurance for urban employees. 4. Denominator of pension insurance for urban and rural residents is number of urban unemployed residents plus rural residents, numerator is number of persons covered by pension insurance for urban and rural residents plus number of retired residents covered by social insurance for urban employees. 5. Number of rural migrant workers covered by social insurance for urban employees has been included in the number of persons covered by basic social insurance for urban enterprise employees
Data source China Statistical Yearbook, *China Labor Statistical Yearbook*, *China Population and Employment Statistics Yearbook* of relevant years

rural cooperative medical system was only 308.5 Yuan/year (see Table 5). Among urban employees, monthly pension of the employees of government organizations and institutions was above 2500 Yuan, but monthly pension of enterprise employees was only above 1500, monthly difference was more than 1000 Yuan (see Table 6).

Table 5 Urban–rural and institutional gaps in social security level of China (2012)

Social insurance program		Amount	Unit
Basic pension insurance for urban employees	Average pension	20900.4	Yuan/year
Pension insurance for urban and rural residents	Average pension	879.5	Yuan/year
Basic medical insurance for urban employees	Per capita financing	2288.8	Yuan/year
Basic medical insurance for urban residents	Per capita financing	322.9	Yuan/year
Rural cooperative medical system	Per capita financing	308.5	Yuan/year

Note In August 2012, pension insurance for urban residents was consolidated with new rural pension insurance for statistics; data originate from 2012 *Statistical Bulletin of Human Resource and Social Security Undertakings*. Average pension of pension insurance was equal to fund expenditure in that year divided by number of retirees; per capita financing of medical insurance and cooperative medical care was equal to the fund income in that year divided by number of insured at the end of that year

Data source China Civil Affairs' Statistical Yearbook, China Labor Statistical Yearbook

Table 6 Pension gap after retirement under different urban employment status in China (2010)

		Retirement pension/pension given by social security		Gross monthly income	
Employment status before retirement	Number of observations (persons)	Average value (Yuan/month)	Gini coefficient (%)	Average value (Yuan/month)	Gini coefficient (%)
A Informal employment	2325	260.62	61.65	376.54	65.45
B Government organizations and institutions	2007	2508.19	29.04	2632.37	30.40
C Enterprise employees	5605	1528.15	20.83	1600.51	22.42
D Government agencies plus enterprises	123	2847.91	26.14	2903.97	26.07
B + C + D	7735	1803.43	27.03	1888.97	28.35
Total	10060	1446.86	39.72	1539.43	40.54

Data source Social security research group of the institute of economics, Chinese academy of social sciences: transition path of multi-track social security pension system, *Economic Research Journal*, 12th issue, 2013

Such inequality in social security benefits was "Reverse" income distribution, i.e. low income group (urban unemployed group, rural residents) got lower benefits, while high income group got higher benefits.

Next, social insurance pooling faced low regional level, and serious regional segmentation. Pooling region of social insurance program in China was basically pooling at county level, the pooling level was low, and transfer and renewal between different pooling regions was difficult. Nowadays, the goal of pension insurance for enterprise employees is to realize national pooling, however, except a few provinces, pooling at provincial level has not been fully realized yet. While in those provinces where pooling at provincial level has been realized, only adjustment fund system has been realized at provincial level, rather than pooling in the full sense of the word; the goal of medical insurance for enterprise employees is to realize pooling at district and city level, but only pooling at county/district level has been realized in most regions; with respect to pension insurance and medical insurance for residents, although urban-rural pooling has been realized, yet registration and participation are still carried out according to registered permanent residence, so regional segmentation still exists. Due to huge difference in economic and social development level between regions, income distribution consequence brought by such regional segmentation is huge regional segmentation of social insurance benefits, and its trend is still "reverse" income distribution: social security benefits in high income region are higher than social security benefits in low income region. Take an example of the pension of urban enterprise employees, although all of them participate in pension insurance for urban enterprise employees, yet regional disparity of benefits is very significant: pension in the highest region is 2.15 times of that in the lowest region, pension in the second highest region is 1.78 times of that in the second lowest region (see Table 7). Among other provinces and regions except Tibet Autonomous Region, generally pension level in eastern coastal region is high, and pension level in midwest undeveloped region is low.

Table 7 Annual average pension of urban enterprise employees and regional gap in minimum living security between urban, rural areas (2012)

Region	Average pension of enterprise employees (Yuan/year)	Urban minimum living security (Yuan/person, month)		Rural minimum living security (Yuan/person, month)	
		Average standard	Subsidy level	Average standard	Subsidy level
Minimum	7573	251	189	115	81
Second lowest	7996	253	192	115	82
Second highest	14212	520	435	427	229
The highest	16251	570	463	430	318
Gini coefficient (%)	10.27	12.05	13.92	22.56	18.02
The highest/lowest	2.15	2.27	2.45	3.75	3.96
Second highest/second lowest	1.78	2.06	2.27	3.72	2.79

Data source China Civil Affairs' Statistical Yearbook 2012, China Labor Statistical Yearbook 2012

Income redistribution effect of social insurance. As mentioned earlier, social insurance has income redistribution function, is one of the main policy means of government to achieve income redistribution objective. This was defined in the 18th Party Congress Report, in which the objectives and principles of China's social insurance reform are "full coverage, basic security, multi-level, sustainable", and "enhance fairness, adapt to mobility, guarantee sustainability".

But since institutional segmentation and regional segmentation still exist in social insurance system, positive income redistribution effect of social insurance exists as a whole, yet not evident, even "reverse" income redistribution effect appears. Take an example of the pension insurance for urban enterprise employees, reverse income redistribution existed ever since national unified pension insurance for urban enterprise employees was established in 1997; after the reform proposal in 2005, such reverse income transfer effect was improved. However, under the reform proposal in 2005, obvious reverse income transfer trend still existed in population above 40 years old.[44] Intragenerational redistribution effect and intergenerational redistribution effect of China's pension insurance system analyzed using actuarial method also show that, intragenerational redistribution effect of pension insurance system is relative weak, and might cause severe intergenerational inequality.[45] Research on income redistribution effect of pension insurance for urban and rural residents also reveals that, positive income redistribution effect of pension insurance for urban and rural residents is limited, and reverse income redistribution effect still exists on some vulnerable groups.[46] Although researches show positive income redistribution effect in aspect of medical insurance, yet this effect only exists in the same pooling area of the same medical insurance system.[47] Most researches still find that, regulating effect of medical insurance on income distribution is weaker.[48]

As a whole, China's social insurance system does not play its due role in regulating income distribution. Mainly because institutional design of different social insurance programs is determined according to groups. under planned economic conditions, residents needed to attach themselves to a unit, social security was mainly provided by units. Such unitized social security itself contained inequality result, as long as income capacity of units was different, social security benefits were different; while different units differed greatly in geographic location, functions in the planned economy and bargaining power with government, so social security benefits of different groups were different. And because of correlation with the units they belonged to, those units with good income capacity not only had high income, but also high security benefits. This is institutional source of reverse redistribution.

It was put forward at the 17th National Congress of CPC, 18th National Congress of CPC to establish unified social insurance system, adaptive to mobility, definite requirements for the reform of social insurance system were put forward at the Third

[44]He (2007).

[45]Peng and Shen (2007).

[46]Wang and Xue (2012).

[47]Jin and Yu (2016).

[48]Jin (2005), Zhao and Ma (2012).

Plenary Session and the Fifth Plenary Session of the Eighteenth Central Committee of the CPC for the above mentioned. It was proposed in the Outline of the "Thirteenth Five-year Plan" to "implement full coverage program to realize full coverage of statutory personnel by and large", "establish more convenient social insurance transfer and renewal mechanism". In recent years, institutional integration, increasing pooling level of social insurance intended to reduce institutional segmentation and regional segmentation of social insurance, so it may play the role of income redistribution better.

5 Suggestions for Improving Income Redistribution Policy

Income redistribution is main policy means of modern market economy to regulate the inequality of income distribution. China has established socialist market economy system, also requires to fully utilize income redistribution policy means to realize common prosperity, share development results. This has been embodied in income distribution policy of CCP expressly. Establishing perfect income redistribution policy system is also realistic requirement of sharing economy concept. It may be seen from the analysis above that, China's income redistribution policy, including tax, government spending and social security system, has been improved obviously in recent years, for example, taxation adaptive to socialist market economy system, perfect public spending and public service system as well as social security system covering all people. under the policy framework of develop people's livelihood undertaking vigorously, government at all levels increased expenditure in various public services. This is a great achievement. However, from the viewpoint of income redistribution, these policy means did not play the role of income redistribution well, some programs even brought about reverse income redistribution. Main reasons are as follows.

Firstly, the development stage of China is primary stage of socialism, China is still a developing country, and its development is extremely unbalanced. Therefore, China's income redistribution policy instruments, including taxation, public spending and social security, have multiple objectives in the development framework. In these multiple objectives, efficiency objective and equality objective are most important of all. Specific form of efficiency objective is economic growth rate. For example, tax policy, in addition to redistribution of income, it should also motivate regional economic growth; public spending should also finance some large-scale economic construction projects; social security system should also safeguard social stability. This is different from single objective of income redistribution policy in western countries. Of course, central policy objectives also vary, the principle "giving priority to efficiency with due consideration to fairness" has been evolved gradually to the principle "efficiency and fairness should be considered in both primary distribution and redistribution, and more attention to should be paid to fairness in redistribution".[49]

---

[49]The 18th National Congress of CPC Report, 2012.

Secondly, institutional legacies of the planned economy still exist, the most important one is division of various public spending programs and social security programs according to different groups, and higher income group could obtain more public services. Take an example of urban and rural division, household registration system is an instrument to control population movement for successful implementation of planned economy. However, household registration system still exists tenaciously up until now, and tends to be solidified in some regions. Although a large floating population work and live in urban areas, yet due to segmentation of household registration system, they cannot enjoy various public services fairly in employment place. Social security program is still divided according to the registered permanent residence. Such actual "identity system" restricts the effect of income redistribution policy severely.

Thirdly, huge regional gap and subsequent sustainability risk have to be considered in the implementation of various income redistribution policies. To maximize the effect of income redistribution policy, unified policies should be applicable all over China; however, due to huge regional development gap, tremendous risk of fund sustainability exists to increase public spending in backward regions to the same as developed regions, and even higher than the developed regions, although very evident income redistribution effect may be achieved. Take an example of rural social pension insurance, good benefits may be obtained in the eastern region due to developed economy and high subsidy given by the government. However, basic pension in central and western regions mainly comes from central fiscal transfer payment, if it is increased to the same as that in the eastern region, the central government finance will inevitably be under tremendous pressure.

Fourthly, insufficient governing capacity and management level for implementation of income redistribution policy. Good income redistribution effect of taxation, public spending and social security programs require good governing capacity and management level, especially economic behavior information of residents should be fully grasped. However, China is still backward in this aspect, low management level, insufficient governing capacity are among the major obstacles that restrict the implementation of income redistribution policy in China. After some very good policies were promulgated, no good "feedback" was obtained from ordinary residents, the so-called "good intentions don't work", primary reason was insufficient management capability.

With respect to the above-mentioned reason, according to the development reality of the primary stage of socialism in China, and the objective of completing the building of a moderately prosperous society in all respects in 2020, income redistribution policy should be improved in the following aspects.

Firstly, cancel urban and rural division pattern in steps, realize integrated development in both urban and rural areas. X this is also an important content in the "Thirteenth Five-year Plan". Restriction of registered permanent residence should be released gradually in some large and medium-sized cities to promote citizenization of rural migrant workers. Urbanization of two hundred million people should be quickened in the coming decade according to central deployment. This also means gradual disappearing of urban-rural dual structure, it's an important step to realize public service equalization.

Secondly, adapt to the reality of normalized mass population movements, frequent employment transition, break up institutional segmentation and regional segmentation of social security system gradually, establish unified national social insurance system based on national identity. Unified basic national social insurance system provides equal, basic social security for all nationals; diversified security requirements may be met by different supplementary insurance on the basis of national social insurance.

Thirdly, break up the segmentation of sector interests, integrate public spending, increase fairness of public spending. Now, public services related to people's livelihood are managed and implemented by different sectors, so sector interests are solidified, this aggravates institutional segmentation, and is unfavorable to give play to the efficiency of public spending. Public spending in China mainly adopts government production mode, i.e. government provides directly; it is various public institutions at all levels affiliated with government sector that provide public services. These public institutions and competent administration sector lead to low efficiency, insufficient fairness, dense "administrative" color due to no distinction of government organs or institutions, no separation of management and implementation. For this, "de-administration" reform of public institutions was proposed at the Third Plenary Session of the Eighteenth Central Committee of the CPC, public services should be provided to the whole society in procurement mode as long as the services may be purchased.

Fourthly, improve governing capacity and management level. Fine management is required to implement income redistribution policy well. For example, taxation, insufficient supervisory capacity and collection capacity might bring about reverse income redistribution effect. Governing capacity and management level should also be improved for public services, social security etc. Low governing capacity should be changed gradually according to national governance capacity improvement requirements mentioned at the Third Plenary Session of the Eighteenth Central Committee of the CPC.

References

Bird, M. and Zolt, E.M., Redistribution via Taxation: the Limited Role of Personal Income Tax in Developing Countries, *UCLA Law Review*, Vol. 52, pp. 1627–1696.

Chen Qingsong: Enlightenment of Western Theory of Optimal Taxation on the Design of Tax System in China, *Journal of Finance and Economics*, 1st Issue, 2003.

Cheng Ying, Wu Jian, Research on the Orientation of Three Functions of Individual Income Tax in China at This Stage—Empirical Analysis Based on 2000-2010 Provincial Panel Data, *Collected Essays on Finance and Economics*, 5th Issue, 2012.

Critique of the Gotha Programme, translated by Central Compilation and Translation Bureau of Marx, Engels, Lenin and Stalin Works, People's Publishing House, 1965 Edition.

Deng Ziji, the Achievements and Prospects of Tax System Reform in the 60 Years of The PRC, *Taxation Research*, 10th Issue, 2009.
Guo Xiaoli, Research for the Effect of Individual Income Tax on Regulating Income Redistribution of Urban Residents, *Research on Financial and Economic Issues*, 6th Issue, 2015.
Guo Zhenyou, Chen Ying, Zhang Yuhui, Benefit Incidence Analysis of Government Health Subsidy, *Soft Science of Health*, 2nd Issue, 2006.
He Lixin, Income Distribution Effect of the Reform in Urban Pension Insurance System in China, *Economic Research Journal*, 3rd Issue, 2007.
IMF, Fiscal Policy and Income Inequality, *IMF Policy Paper*, 2014, Washington, D. C., http://www.imf.org/external/pp/ppindex.aspx.
Jia Kang, Zhao Quanhou, *30 Years of China's Economy Reform: the Volume of Revenue Tax*, Chongqing University Press, 2008 Edition.
Jiang Hong, Ma Guoxian, Zhao Haili, Distribution and Genesis of the Benefit Incidence of Public Higher Education, *Journal of Finance and Economics*, 3rd Issue, 2002.
Jin Caihong, Research on Income Redistribution Regulation Mechanism of Chinese Medical Security System, *Reform of the Economic System*, 6th Issue, 2005.
Jin Shuanghua, Yu Jie, Empirical Research for the Impact of Medical Insurance System on Different Income Brackets—Analysis Based on Urban Residents in Liaoning Province, *Research on Economics and Management*, 2nd Issue, 2016.
Li Shaorong, Geng Ying, Tax Structure, Economic Growth and Income Distribution in China, *Economic Research Journal*, 5th Issue, 2005.
Li Shi, Property Distribution Gap and Redistribution Policy Options in China, *Reform of the Economic System*, 1st Issue, 2015.
Lindert, K, Skoufias, E., and Shapiro, J., Redistributing Income to the Poor and the Rich: Public Transfers in Latin America and the Caribbean, *SP Discussion Paper* No. 0605, the World Bank, 2006.
Liu Gugang, Some Issues Concerning the Primary Distribution and Redistribution of National Income—Overview of the Soviet Union Discussions in 1957, *Economic Research Journal*, 3rd Issue, 1958.
Liu Qiongzhi, Incidence of Public Spending: are Chinese Government Public Services Delivered to Poor Population? *Management World*, 4th Issue, 2007.
Liu Yi, Nie Haifeng, Impact Analysis of Indirect Tax Burden on Income Distribution, *Economic Research Journal*, 5th Issue, 2004.
Mahler, V. A., Jesuit, D. K., Fiscal Redistribution in the Developed Countries: New Insights from the Luxembourg Income Study, *Socio-Economic Review*, Vol. 4, No. 3, pp. 483–511.
Meltzer, A. H. And S. F. Richard, A Rational Theory of the Size of Government, *Journal of Political Economy*, 1981, 89, 914–927.
Musgrave, R. A., 1959, *The Theory of Public Finance*, New York: McGraw-Hill.
Norton, A., Conway, T., and Foster, M., Social Protection Concepts and Approaches: Implications for Policy and Practice in International Development, London: Overseas Development Institute, *Working Paper 143*, 2001.
Pang Jinju et al as editors in chief, *Political Economy* (3rd Edition), Higher Education Press, 2007 Edition.
Peng Haoran, Shen Shuguang, Comparative Study on Income Redistribution Effect of the Pension Insurance System before and after the Reform in China, *Statistical Research*, 2nd Issue, 2007.
Prasad, Naren, Policies for Redistribution: the Use of Taxes and Social Transfers, *Discussion Paper*, 2008, International Institute for Labor Studies.
Prepared by John Eatwell, Murray Milgate, Peter Newman, *The New Palgrave Dictionary of Economics*, Chinese version, Volume 4, Economic Science Press, 1996 Edition.
Ran Guanghe, Pan Hui, Research on Income Distribution Effect of Government Public Spending–Testing Based on VAR Model, *Journal of Chongqing University* (Social Science Edition), Volume 15, 2nd Issue, 2009.

Rothbard, M. N., *Power and Market: Government and the Economy* (Fourth Edition), Alabama: Ludwig von Mises Institute, 2006.

Song Tao as editor in chief, *Political Economy Tutorial* (Eighth Edition), China Renmin University Press, 2008 Edition.

Sun Jing, Wang Yali, Research on the Redistribution Effect of Tax on the Income of Urban and Rural Residents in China, *Journal of Zhongnan University of Economics and Law*, 3rd Issue, 2013.

Wang Cuiqin, Xue Huiyuan, Research on the Income Redistribution Effect of New Type Rural Social Pension Insurance, China Population, *Resources and Environment*, 8th Issue, 2012.

Wang Li, Measurement of the Fairness Effect of Fiscal Expenditure, *Finance Forum*, 7th Issue, 2007.

Wang Shaoguo, Li Wei, Empirical Analysis of the Role of Redistribution Mechanism in Regulating Income Gap between Urban Residents, *Economic Review*, 3rd Issue, 2009.

Wang Shijie, Correlational Research on Public Financial Expenditure and Inequality of Income Distribution in China, *Shandong Economy*, 5th Issue, 2010.

Wang Zhigang, Progressivity Analysis of China's Tax System, *Taxation Research*, 9th Issue, 2008.

Wu Ning, Jiang Qicheng, Wang Congcong, Wan Quan, Zhao Yuxin, Benefit Incidence Analysis of Government Subsidies for Medical Institutions in A Western Province, *Chinese Health Economics*, Volume 30, 5th Issue, 2011.

Yang Ju, New Advances in the Research on Income Distribution Effect of Foreign Tax Structure, *Shanghai Journal of Economics*, 2nd Issue, 2012.

Yang Yuping, Analysis on the Income Redistribution Effect of Individual Income Tax in China–the Perspective Based on Income Composition, *Journal of Shenzhen University* (Humanities & Social Sciences), 2nd Issue, 2014.

Yue Ximing, Xu Jing, Resident Income Distribution Effect of Individual Income Tax in China, *Economic Perspectives*, 6th Issue, 2012.

Zhang Bin, Tax System and Redistribution of Income, *Taxation Research*, 8th Issue, 2006.

Zhao Bin, Ma Xiaomao, Research on "Reverse Transfer" of Social Medical Insurance in China, *Chinese Health Economics*, 2nd Issue, 2012.

Zhao Jie, Discussion on Rebuilding the Distribution Relationship between State and Enterprises after Separation of Two Rights, *Public Finance Research*, 10th Issue, 1987.

Chapter 5
New Concepts, New Ideas of Shared Development

Five development concepts, i.e. innovative, coordinated, green, open, and shared, were put forward in the Recommendations for the 13th Five-Year Plan for Economic and Social Development at the Fifth Plenary Session of the Eighteenth Central Committee of the CPC, "sharing is an essential requirement of socialism with Chinese characteristics, we must insist on the development for people, development based on people and development results shared by people, make more effective institutional arrangement, so all the people could have more sense of gain in the joint development and sharing, enhance development motivation, enhance unity among people, make steady progress towards common prosperity". Shared development is an important concept of economic development after China's economy entered new normality, will guide the direction of economic development in China. Meanwhile, income distribution is an important component of shared development concept, closely linked to resident income growth. In view of this, we analyze the new concepts of primary distribution, redistribution under the concept of sharing, and discuss the impact of social and economic transformation on income distribution.

1 New Concept of Shared Development

Near-term goal of shared development is to build a moderately prosperous society in all respects by 2020, yet shared development is consistent with the ultimate goal of socialism "achieve common prosperity". Shared development not only includes several levels, but also has historical origins, we will firstly define "what is shared development", then explain the necessity to promote shared development at this stage of China.

C. Pei et al., *The Basic Income Distribution System of China*, China Governance System Research Series, https://doi.org/10.1007/978-981-15-3461-4_5

1.1 Staged Goals of Economic Development

The essence of socialism is to release and develop the productive forces, eliminate exploitation and polarization, finally achieve common prosperity. To shake off poverty, increase people's living standard, at the early stage of reform and opening up, Deng Xiaoping put forward new development concept at the Third Plenary Session of the Eleventh Central Committee of the CPC, which was the preliminary explanation of common prosperity. In the Southern Tour Talks in 1992, Deng Xiaoping gave a comprehensive explanation of common prosperity "where conditions permit, some areas may develop faster than others; those that develop faster can help promote the progress of those that lag behind, until all become prosperous". It may be seen that, common prosperity may be achieved only when conditions permit at the primary stage of socialism when the development level of productive forces is relatively backward. Where conditions are limited, only areas where conditions permit may be developed first. Final common prosperity is established on the basis of development, rather than equalitarianism under the conditions of backward development.

Common prosperity is the ultimate goal of socialist development, this goal will not be achieved overnight. So several staged goals have been set up in China's economic development process. "Three-Step" strategy was put forward expressly in the 13th Party Congress Report, setting up corresponding development goals for each stage of economic development. "Step 1 is to double Gross National Product, solve the problem of food and clothing for people from 1981 to 1990; Step 2 is to double Gross National Product again, let people live a fairly comfortable life from 1991 to the end of the 20th century; in Step 3, the average per-capita GNP will reach the standard of moderately developed countries, people live a better life, and basically achieve modernization in the mid 21st century." "live a fairly comfortable life" became main goal after the 13th Party Congress. With rapid economic development in China, China's GDP per capita exceeded 900 USD in 2000, thus China became a lower middle developing country according to the standard of World Bank. Development results were summarized and new development goals were put forward in the CPC Central Committee Recommendations for the 10th Five-Year Plan for Economic and Social Development passed at the Fifth Plenary Session of the Fifteenth Central Committee of the CPC, "we have attained the objectives of the first two steps of the three-step strategy for China's modernization drive, all-round economic and social development, and by and large, the people have become well-off, now we begin to implement the third step of strategic deployment. This is a new milestone in the history of the development of the Chinese nation".

Although China became a lower middle income country in 2000, Seven-Year Priority Poverty Alleviation Program was basically completed, on the whole, the people have reached a well-off standard of living, yet the rate of subsistence poverty in rural China is still up to 3.4%. To calculate according to the subsistence poverty line, poor population in rural China was still up to 32.09 million in 2000. Poor population scale in China will increase if calculated according to low income line or poverty line of the World Bank.[1] The well-off standard of living reached in 2000 was low standard, incomplete, unbalanced well-off, "the goal of building a moderately prosperous society in all respects" was thus put forward on this basis. Economic development and narrowing gap is primary goal of building a moderately prosperous society in all respects, "efforts will be made to quadruple the GDP of the year 2000 by 2020, and China's overall national strength and international competitiveness will increase markedly. We will in the main achieve industrialization and establish a full-fledged socialist market economy and a more open and viable economic system. The proportion of urban population will go up considerably and the trend of widening differences between industry and agriculture, between urban and rural areas and between regions will be reversed step by step. We will have a fairly sound social security system. There will be a higher rate of employment. People will have more family property and lead a more prosperous life". Two Centenary Goals were further defined in combination with the goal of building a moderately prosperous society in all respects after the 18th National Congress of CPC, "complete the building of a moderately prosperous society in all respects when the Communist Party of China celebrates its centenary and turn China into a modern socialist country that is prosperous, strong, democratic, culturally advanced and harmonious when the People's Republic of China marks its centennial".

1.2 The Concept of Shared Development

To complete the building of a moderately prosperous society in all respects and to finally achieve common prosperity are goals of socialist development. With respect to the development strategy at two stages of common prosperity, at the first stage, some people and some areas getting rich first might bring about growing income disparity, but socialist system should be able to avoid growing income disparity. Overall situation should be considered at the early stage of economic development, and development should be dominant. With rapid economic development in China, its economic aggregate becomes the second in the world, according to the standard of World Bank, China became an upper middle income country in 2011, per capita GDP increased to about 7,800 USD in 2015. More capable in aspect of narrowing the income gap, and this is consistent with the assumptions of Deng Xiaoping in the Southern Tour Talks, i.e. "We should study when to raise this question and how to settle it. I can imagine that the right time might be the end of this century, when our people are living a fairly comfortable life". That is to say, the problem of growing income disparity should be solved when up to a well-off standard of living. The problems of growing income disparity and growing income gap should still be solved

[1]Data originate from Poverty Monitoring Report in Rural China. According to the level in current period, subsistence poverty line in 2000 was 630 Yuan/person per year; low income poverty line proposed in 2002 was 869 Yuan/person •year; low standard poverty line of the World Bank is 1.25 dollars/person per day.

in two ways according to the methodology of dialectical materialism. Although the level of economic development increases in China, yet it's still a middle income country, still at the primary stage of socialism, top priority is still to maintain stable economic growth, and promote economic development. under the dual goals of both guaranteeing development, and narrowing the income gap, the concept of shared development emerge as the times require. On this basis, shared development is surely the sharing not to damage the development efficiency of market economy. In the principles of development relying on people and development results shared by people, shared development focuses more on the equality of opportunity, guaranteeing basic livelihood of the people and narrowing income gap.

Firstly, in view of the equality of opportunity, starting point equity and process justice should be realized. Supply of essential public services should be increased to ensure equal access to basic public services, so as to realize starting point equity. Shared development requires development relying on people, not only to rely on quantity of people, but also rely on quality of people with continuous economic transformation in China, especially the quality of labor force. From the perspective of economics, it means the increase of educational attainment of labor force to achieve higher human capital. Equal access to education is an important aspect of shared development, school-age children and adolescents could access to the same basic public educational resources, especially children of low-income families, so they will not lose at the starting line. While sharing economic development results, this could promote human capital accumulation, enhance development motivation. In addition, equal access to education embodies the thought of teaching how to fish better, could avoid transferring poverty to next generation to a great degree.

Employment guarantees labor force to get more income, and is one of the core objectives of macroeconomic development. Equitable access to jobs and equal pay for equal work rare mainly embodied on process justice. It's more favorable for labor migration to establish unified labor market, break up urban and rural division, regional and industry segmentation, eliminate or weaken identity, gender discrimination. Breaking up institutional barriers to promote labor migration is an important embodiment of shared development, through labor migration, workers may get more employment opportunities, helpful for their job matching, this could also mitigate structural unemployment.

Next, from the perspective of guaranteeing basic livelihood of the people, poverty should be eliminated, fair and sustainable social security system should be established. Both the International Labor Organization and United Nations regard prevention and reduction of poverty as the primary function of social security. The first of United Nations Millennium Development Goals is to eradicate extreme poverty and hunger. Poor population is vulnerable group in the society, supporting poor population to get rid of poverty is something inherent in shared development.

Social security system embodies social solidarity, the rich help the poor, the healthy help the sick, young help the old, safe people help those affected by disasters, and so on. Social security system under solidarity thought supports relatively disadvantaged groups, promotes social stability. This shows that social security system is an important embodiment of members of the society sharing economic development.

However, it is noteworthy that, social security system should not impair marketization, so basic guarantee and sustainability are more emphasized in the concept of shared development. Although social security system embodies social solidarity, yet government expenditure is still required in some cases. Too high social security level will inevitably bring huge burden to government finance, sustainability cannot be guaranteed. In the meantime, too high social security level might break the rules of market development. For example, too high unemployment compensation will decrease the employment possibility of unemployed workers, thus decrease labor participation rate of the whole society, unfavorable to economic development. Bottom line requirements and survival guarantee comprise the starting point of a perfect social security system.

Finally, from the perspective of narrowing income gap, regulation of redistribution and normalization of income system should be strengthened. The ultimate goal of shared development is common prosperity, now narrowing income gap becomes the staged goal of shared development. China should quicken the establishment of comprehensive and classified individual income tax system. Progressive individual income tax should be used to regulate the income of high income group, estate tax and gift tax should be used to reduce intergenerational wealth transfer, improve intergenerational starting point equity. In addition, while legal income is protected, invisible income should be normalized to inhibit corruption, and illegal income should be banned. Normalizing income distribution order enables personal income to be more transparent, so that market may play a dominant role in income distribution.

1.3 Necessity of Shared Development

Large basic education supply gap increases unemployment risk by influencing human capital accumulation of labor force. Dual structure between urban and rural areas in China, is not only embodied in economy, but also embodied in essential public services, huge difference exists in the supply of basic public education between urban and rural areas. Although urbanization rate calculated according to resident population exceeds 50%, yet nearly half of the population still live in rural areas. It is difficult for the children of rural migrant workers to get basic education in urban areas, most of them still receive education in rural areas, this further highlights the difference in basic education supply between urban and rural areas. With the economic development in China entering new stage, surplus rural labor decreases continuously, demographic dividend disappears gradually, economic development will change from labor intensive to capital intensive and technology intensive little by little. The transformation process puts forward higher requirements for human capital of labor force, it is difficult for labor force with low educational background to get employment opportunity under capital intensive and technology intensive conditions, they will more easily get stuck in unemployment and even unable to be employed, poverty is more likely to follow.

Large basic education supply gap hinders economic development by influencing the stock of human capital of economically active population. China's economy enters a new phase of development, in order to keep sustainable and stable development, technological advance has to be more relied on in case demographic dividend disappears gradually and return on capital decreases. Improving human capital is an important source of technological advance. Education quality of the children from rural families is generally low due to large basic education supply gap, relatively high education cost of senior high school hinders children from rural families from studying in senior high school. Urban low-income families also face relatively high education cost of senior high school. Therefore, the difference in education supply hinders the accumulation of human capital, unfavorable to economic development.

Large education supply gap hinders the expansion of middle-income group via labor productivity structure. With the increase of labor marketization degree, market plays a leading role in the allocation and remuneration of labor resources. In case of market allocation, labor remuneration is closely linked to marginal productivity of labor. The key to the expansion of middle-income group is that, workers with moderate marginal productivity become dominant among all workers. Education is an important factor that influences marginal productivity of labor. In other words, expansion of middle-income group relies on workers with high education degrees becoming dominant in economically active population. However, large education supply gap becomes a bottleneck of rural families and low-income families for investment in education, thus will inevitably hinder scale expansion of workers with high education degrees. This will fundamentally hinder the expansion of middle-income group.

Eliminating poverty in rural areas is the most difficult challenge to building a moderately prosperous society. With rapid economic development in China, poor population decreases greatly, yet overall elimination of poverty still faces great difficulties. Existing poverty line is 2300 Yuan set down in 2011 (constant price in 2010). Along with economic development and implementation of poverty alleviation policies, the scale of rural poor population decreased from 165.67 million in 2010 to 70.17 million in 2014, incidence of rural poverty also decreased greatly from 17.2% to 7.2% accordingly, decreased by 10% points.[2] The scale of 70.17 million poor population is still huge, it's an arduous task to help them get rid of poverty completely.

Urban poverty should also arouse attention. Compared with rural areas, although the scale of urban poor population is small, yet the absolute quantity is a large number. There are approximately 18 million urban population living on minimum living security, over 9 million registered urban unemployed persons. Even if there is any overlap between them, yet about 18 million urban population living on minimum living security is really a large number, and big challenges have to be confronted to provide training and employment opportunities for over 9 million urban registered unemployed persons.

---

[2] *China Yearbook of Household Survey 2015.*

Although China's social security system has achieved full coverage, yet many problems still exist in the social security from planned economy. The most prominent is that, fragmentation reduces fairness of social security; overprotection, historical debt and aging reduces sustainability of social security. Fragmentation is reflected in three aspects, namely, institutional segmentation, regional segmentation and sectoral segmentation. Institutional segmentation is reflected in significant difference of benefits between different groups, poor fairness between groups. Regional segmentation is reflected in difficult connection and transfer, inconvenient, unfavorable to labor migration, it hinders the unification of labor market. While sectoral segmentation causes poor information sharing and poor social solidarity, reduces overall function of social security, so social security is only limited within certain scope and under certain conditions. Fragmentation allows the groups having the right to speak to compare unrealistically with each other to get the social security of higher gains step by step, at the same time, it aggravates the tension between different groups, adverse to social stability.

Overprotection, historical debt and aging reduce the sustainability of social security. Institutional fragmentation overprotects some people, forms a high plateau of welfare, thus attacks unrealistic comparison of other groups. Overprotection increases payment burden of social security. The reform of state-owned enterprises and institutional updating require supplementary payment for social security of those "middlemen" who started to work before the system was established and retired after the system was established, government finance should assume this burden according to the settings at that time, the limited local financial resources led to "empty account operation" of individual accounts, with the retirement of this part of labor force, it is imperative to make up empty accounts, this exerts huge pressure on the payment of social security. On the other hand, the aggravated aging of population increases old age dependency ratio, less and less on-job population make payment, expenditure for social security increases, its sustainability decreases.

Large income gap generates adverse impact on economic growth by influencing total consumption. From the viewpoint of effective demand, consumption, investment and export form the troika to promote economic growth. China's economic development is export-oriented, investment and export become two engines of China's economic growth, by comparison, pull effect of consumption is relative weak. Small consumption scale, poor economic pull effect are closely linked to large income gap. According to Keynesian theory of consumption, marginal propensity to consume (and then average propensity to consume) decreases with the increase of income. That is to say, low income earners spend a higher proportion of income for consumption, while high income earners spend a lower proportion of income for consumption. China has pyramid-shaped income structure and inverted T-shaped social structure, both indicate large scale of low income group. Low income group has relatively high propensity to consume, but low income leads to low total consumption. Large income gap centralizes income to high income earners, propensity of society to consume will fall, total consumption of the society becomes insufficient, adverse to fuel economic growth. In case of sluggish growth of overseas market demand, the expanding of domestic demand becomes particularly important, narrowing income gap on this basis becomes an important content of shared development. This does not only intend to achieve common prosperity, but also enable economic development to rely more on the consumption of people.

Narrowing income gap is favorable to promote human capital accumulation, and break up vicious cycle of poverty. The findings show that, education has intergenerational immobility, parents with relatively high educational level correspond to children with relatively high educational level. Because parents with relatively high educational level could obtain higher income, then invest more in children's education. The researches in China also show that, when household income decreases, education spending will decrease significantly. Large income gap will inevitably reduce the investment of low-income families in education, their children will still have low educational level, thus obtain low income in labor market, and get stuck in the vicious cycle of poverty. Although access to public education has become much more equitable, may offset the influence of a bit low investment in education by some low-income families, yet the importance of family investment in education should not be neglected.

Narrowing income gap is helpful to reduce credit constraints of the residents. Credit constraints make steady consumption in life cycle impossible. Similarly, low-income families face credit constraints in the process of entrepreneurship, it is difficult for them to obtain sufficient funds because of too wide income gap. And low-income families face credit constraints even for the investment in education of their children. Nationwide enterprise-starting requires entrepreneurs to obtain sufficient funds, especially medium and low income earners. Large income gap reduces the credit capacity of residents, unfavorable to the development of nationwide enterprise-starting.

China is in a critical period to build a moderately prosperous society in all respects, and should keep continuous and stable economic growth. More supply of essential public services could realize equal access to basic public services, eliminate poverty, achieve fair and sustainable social security, narrow income gap, offer more benefits of economic development results to people, enhance social stability and cohesion, and provide new power for further economic development.

2 New Ideas of Primary Distribution Under the Shared Development Concept

The Chinese characteristics at the primary stage of socialism require development to be the precondition of shared development, promote enhance result sharing on the basis of development. Just as that mentioned at the Fifth Plenary Session of the Eighteenth Central Committee of the CPC, we must ensure that development is for the people, by the people and with the people sharing in its fruits. Primary distribution is the direct embodiment of development results, so we firstly analyze the impact of policies concerning minimum wage system, increasing productivity, narrowing regional gap and narrowing urban-rural gap on primary distribution under the shared development concept.

2.1 The Impact of Minimum Wage System on the Increase in Labor Remuneration

As mentioned in the 17th National Congress of CPC Report "Vigorous efforts will be made to raise the income of low-income groups, gradually increase poverty-alleviation aid and the minimum wage, and set up a mechanism of regular pay increases for enterprise employees and a mechanism for guaranteeing payment of their salaries". After the 18th National Congress of CPC, it was mentioned in the Opinions on the Deepening of Income Distribution System Reform that "minimum wage standard should be adjusted timely according to economic development, commodity price variation and other factors, minimum wage standard in most regions should reach forty percent and above of the average wage of local urban employees by 2015." In addition, International Labor Organization has paid special attention to the determination of minimum wage standard ever since its establishment in 1919. Driven by International Labor Office, minimum wage system has been recognized by international community as a legal system of state to intervene distribution, guarantee basic rights of workers.

Minimum wage refers to the wage higher than labor market clearing level specified by systems, it aims to guarantee basic rights of workers, ensure their wage levels. However, minimum wage system has been controversial since its establishment. With respect to the impact of minimum wage, the focus of discussion is the impact of minimum wage on employment. From the viewpoint of labor economics, when minimum wage is higher than market clearing level, it will inevitably lead to the increase of supply and decrease of demand, the gap between supply and demand becomes the unemployed group. Of course, because the elasticity of supply curve is different from the elasticity of demand curve in different labor markets, the scale of unemployment brought by minimum wage is also different. For example, when demand curve remains unchanged, the larger the elasticity of supply curve is, the larger the scale of unemployment brought by minimum wage becomes. Therefore, the impact of the same minimum wage standard on unemployment might vary greatly in different labor markets. In addition, the impact of minimum wage on employment is related to minimum wage standard. If the difference between minimum wage and market clearing level is small, the scale of unemployment is also small. On the contrary, large difference leads to large scale of unemployment.

From the perspective of international empirical findings, the impact of minimum wage on employment also varies greatly. Bell's comparative study of Columbia and Mexico reveals that, if minimum wage is implemented effectively, it will generate adverse impact on employment.[3] Neumark analyzed 6 OECD countries in the

[3]Bell (1997), pp. S102–S135.

period of 1975–1997 and found that, increase of minimum wage will reduce youth employment, and negative effect of minimum wage on employment leads to different results in different countries.[4] Abowde et al. studied the relationship between increase of minimum wage and employment in France and the United States and found that, increase of minimum wage will lead to decrease of employment.[5] Card and Krueger found from research on fast food industry in the United States that, the implementation of minimum wage does not decrease employment.[6] Fields and Kanbur found that, the effect varies under different conditions, depending on the set level of minimum wage relative to poverty line, elasticity of labor demand, income sharing mechanism and nature of poverty and other factors.[7]

While minimum wage system was introduced in China from 1993, academic world discussed a lot on whether it should be introduced and the impact of introduction. Focus at the first stage was whether minimum wage system should be introduced. Some scholars thought minimum wage system inappropriate for China at this stage. Firstly, from the perspective of employment, minimum wage system hinders low income group from finding jobs, contrary to the original intention of safeguarding the interests of low income earners[8]; about 65% of rural labor force in China is still willing to accept work below minimum wage standard, minimum wage is unenforceable in such circumstances.[9] Next, from the perspective of enterprise cost, minimum wage is a kind of price regulation, decreases the competitiveness of Chinese enterprises.[10] At the same time, some other scholars think it necessary to implement minimum wage system,[11] under "non-collective bargaining" labor relations in China, government sets minimum wage to provide basic guarantee for the negotiation between workers and enterprises, so as to ensure the interests of workers without prejudice.[12] Focus at the second stage was discussion on the impact of minimum wage system. Target group of minimum wage is low income earners in labor market, mainly blue-collar employees. Rural migrant workers in cities become the target group of many researches on the impact of minimum wage system. From the perspective of employment, increase of minimum wage standard will promote the employment of rural migrant workers.[13] From the perspective of wage, minimum wage plays a significant role in the wage growth of rural migrant workers.[14] From the perspective of

---

[4]Neumark (1999).

[5]Abowd et al. (2009).

[6]Card (1993).

[7]Fields (2005).

[8]Zhang (2000).

[9]Ping (2005).

[10]Zhang (2000), Xue (2004).

[11]Fu (1995), Yang Shuxia, A Brief Discussion on Minimum Wage Security System in China, *Journal of Henan University*, 5th Issue, 1996.

[12]Qiao (2006).

[13]Luo (2007).

[14]Sun (2011).

narrowing income gap, the increase of minimum wage standard narrows the income difference within rural migrant worker group significantly.[15]

According to the implementation effect of minimum wage system in China, minimum wage system plays an active role in the employment and income of rural migrant workers, and narrowing income gap. However, minimum wage system in China also faces coverage problem. Quite a few people are not covered by minimum wage system even in developed countries with mature labor market. Although China's labor market has been developed substantially, yet still immature. The groups covered by minimum wage system are workers who provide normal work in legal working hours or in the work time under the labor contract signed according to law. It is relatively easy to supervise the enterprises that sign labor contracts according to law, but it's difficult to supervise enterprises that do not sign contracts. The Regulations for Labor Supervision promulgated by the State Council in 2004 and the Labor Contract Law promulgated in 2008 intensified the supervision on implementation of minimum wage system. However, since rural migrant workers are mostly self-employed informally, minimum wage coverage of migrant worker group is still lower than urban local labor force. The coverage of monthly minimum wage is not significantly different between external labor force and urban local labor force. The coverage of hourly minimum wage in migrant worker group is far lower than urban local labor force. With respect to each age group, the coverage of both monthly minimum wage and hourly minimum wage in external labor force is lower than urban local labor force.[16] In view of this, the coverage of minimum wage in rural migrant workers needs to be further increased, especially the coverage of hourly minimum wage.

2.2 *The Impact of Increase in Labor Productivity and Human Capital on the Increase in Labor Remuneration*

Labor remuneration is the concentrated reflection of labor income, remuneration of workers depends on marginal productivity of workers according to the factor allocation and price determination principles. Just as Marshall said "the distribution of national income to labor, capital and land is in proportion to people's need for their services. But such need is not total need, but marginal need".[17] While other conditions are unchanged, marginal productivity is mainly determined by characteristics of workers themselves. Mincer put forward the Mincer equation, in which education is an important factor that influences labor income.[18] The findings show that, labor income will increase with the increase of years of education. The significant

[15] Ye (2013).

[16] Du (2008).

[17] Marshall (1981).

[18] Mincer (1974).

existence of rate of return to education reveals that education increases labor productivity, workers with higher educational level also have higher labor productivity, so the return is enhanced in labor market. However, another parallel viewpoint thinks that, education only embodies "sheepskin" effect,[19] and education only plays a role of signal, persons with higher labor productivity are identified via education system, they show their competence in work after they have obtained degree diploma. Persons with stronger competence have lower learning costs, could obtain higher educational background more easily. In order to reject the part in education related to competence, scholars have researched the rate of return to education in case competence is considered or competence is rejected,[20] the research reveals that, higher educational level still means higher income, education could increase labor productivity. Both of the above theoretical and empirical results embody the impact of human capital on increasing the remuneration for workers.

On the other hand, with respect to sources of economic growth, capital, labor, technological advance are main sources of potential economic growth. Increase in labor productivity and human capital will be helpful to increase economic growth potential. Solow said, economic growth originates from increase in labor productivity and technical progress when population is unchanged, increase in human capital is one of the important source of technological advance.[21] Salai Martin listed a series of factors closely related to economic growth through a great number of empirical research, educational level is one of the important items.[22] Educational level is converted into labor force of higher skills and higher labor productivity, promotes economy to a higher level. When growth theory turns to endogenous growth model, human capital especially externality of education, becomes the source of increasing returns to scale, and an important power to promote economic growth. Schurz thinks the most important investment to be investment in human capital in a long run.[23] From the perspective of macro distribution pattern, labor remuneration is a part of economic aggregate, only keeping continuous and stable economic development, and "making the pie bigger" continuously could prepare better material basis to increase labor remuneration.

The empirical research results using China's data show that, increase in human capital will increase labor remuneration, and human capital will contribute more to economic growth. From a microscopic view, education has a significant impact on remuneration for workers. According to the survey data in 2004, for every increase of 1 year education, personal income will increase 4.34%; meanwhile, rate of return to education also presents an up trend with the increase of income level, rate of return to education of the highest 95% income earners exceeds twice of that of the lowest 5% income earners.[24] From a macro view, the breakdown of China's GDP growth factors

[19] Spence (1973).

[20] Angrist (1991), pp. 979–1014; Ashenfelter (1994), pp. 1157–1173.

[21] Solow (1957).

[22] Sala-I-Martin (1997).

[23] Theodore (2001).

[24] Zhang (2006).

shows that, human capital plays an important role in China's economic growth. In the period of 1978–2008, among the factors such as capital stock, labor force, stock of human capital measured by years of education and total factor productivity, contribution rate of human capital is 11.7%; considering that different educational level corresponds to different productivity, the contribution rate of human capital further increases to 38%.[25]

It's also noteworthy that, while determining labor income, human capital also determines the distribution structure of labor income. Workers with lower human capital have lower income level, the higher the human capital is, the higher the income level becomes. Therefore, with respect to labor group, structure of human capital will influence the distribution structure of labor income to a great degree. The sixth population census data show that, average years of education of population over age 16 are 8.91 years in China, and are 10.84 years, 9.21 years, 7.57 years respectively for populations in cities, towns and villages. With respect to social structure, most bottom workers are peasants. With respect to socio-economic index, 96.7% of all rural workers are below Score 40.[26] Low level of human capital, especially in towns and villages, hinders low income group from entering middle-income group due to limited human capital. Increase in human capital is helpful to upgrade human capital structure of labor group, expand medium and high human capital groups gradually, enable them to become core force of labor group. This will lay foundation to expand middle-income group fundamentally.

In the meantime, with the disappearance of demographic dividend, China has entered a new phase of development. This phase is more in line with "constant population" assumption in Solow growth model, in this case, source of economic growth is the continuously improved human capital. In view of this, human capital is not only micro-level labor income increase, the foundation to improve income distribution structure, but also the core power to promote sustained economic growth.

2.3 The Role of Development Policies for Narrowing Regional Disparity

In 2000, China crossed over low-income countries, and entered middle income countries, the people have reached a well-off standard of living as a whole. Although on the whole, the people have reached a well-off standard of living, yet development level is still relatively low, disparity between eastern and western regions is still very large. With respect to the difference between eastern and western regions, China decided to implement Western Development Strategy one year before reaching a well-off standard of living as a whole, i.e. in 1999. The scope of Western Development includes 12 provinces, cities, autonomous regions, namely, Yunnan,

[25] Whalley and Xiliang (2010).

[26] In the calculation of socio-economic index of total working population, score 90 is the highest score, score 40 is middle lower level. Li (2005).

Sichuan, Guizhou, Shaanxi, Gansu, Ningxia, Xinjiang, Qinghai, Tibet, Chongqing, Inner Mongolia and Guangxi. According to resource endowment conditions, there are rich mineral resources in the western region, which may provide a large number of mineral resources for the eastern region. Before the Western Development, the industrialization development process in the western region relies more on resource advantage, relies on transport of resources to the eastern region. However, from international experience, rich resources will not always lead to economic development and well-off residents. Dutch disease and "resource curse" are general terms of such problems. Dutch disease refers to the adverse effects on manufacturing, domestic price increase and home currency appreciation after discovery of natural resources. "resource curse" is broader, generally refers to the paradox that per capita income of a country or region does not increase with the development of resources, or refers to the paradox that income growth of a country or region with abundant resources is slower than a country or region with poor resources.

In addition to simple reliance on resource development that leads to Dutch disease and "resource curse", primary products are often dominant in resource export. under core-periphery hypothesis, technological advance of developed countries does not improve the trade conditions of developing countries, but deteriorates the conditions. Labor income gap between core countries that mainly produce industrial products and periphery countries that mainly produce primary products will be larger and larger. Although this is comparison between countries with different trade conditions and resource endowment, yet because of large regional disparity in China, huge difference in resource endowment exists between different regions. Therefore, if the western region always takes selling resources as its development core, it will become a periphery region very easily, the gap between it and developed eastern region will continue to become larger.

In order to avoid Dutch disease, "resource curse" and gap widening under core-periphery hypothesis, appropriate preferential policy and support should be provided to promote sustainable development of central and western regions. For economic development conditions, capital, labor and technical progress are important sources. For underdeveloped countries or regions, physical capital accumulation and human capital accumulation will become important pillars to promote economic development. In this way, preferential policy and support should be provided towards physical capital accumulation and human capital accumulation. The implementation of Western Development has increased annual average economic growth rate of the western region by about 1.5% points since 2000, promoted China's regional economy to converge from divergence; these are realized mainly by vast investment in physical capital especially infrastructure, while educational development, technological progress and soft environment have not been improved notably in the Western Development.[27] But some researches reveal that, the Western Development has not promoted rapid growth of GDP and GDP per capita in the western region effectively. Both central government and local government overfocus on the investment in fixed assets and development of resource energy, yet neglect institutional reform and soft

[27] Liu (2009).

environmental construction, leading to extrusion of human capital, lagged industrial restructuring, so the effect of Western Development policy has not been achieved effectively.[28] This means that, the role of Western Development policy in promoting western economic development is limited, the prominent reason lies in only focusing on investment and accumulation of physical capital, yet neglecting the investment and accumulation of human capital.

According to the above analysis on the increase in human capital versus economic growth, in case demographic dividend disappears gradually, population basically keeps certain scale and even decreases, increase in human capital will become a source of economic growth. In view of this, support for western and other backward regions should be embodied more in human capital to promote rapid development in the western region and provide power for stable and continuous economic development in China. In addition, yield period of investment in fixed assets, especially investment in infrastructure, is relatively long, could provide basis for follow-up economic development. In the near term, the return on investment in infrastructure or its promoting effect on economic growth is limited, but investment in infrastructure is a prerequisite for economic development. For example, in the Western Development process of the United States, the construction of traffic line became the development power of American West.[29]

After Western Development Strategy was implemented in 1999, "Northeast Area Revitalization Plan" and "Rise of Central China" strategies were implemented in 2003 and 2006 successively, provided policy support for the development of northeast and central regions. From the perspective of economic theory, promoting development of backward regions mainly means promoting local physical capital accumulation and human capital accumulation. Although the level of economic development in the northeast and central regions is higher than that in the western region, yet large gap with developed eastern region also exists. Under this common law, both investment in physical capital and investment in human capital should be considered for policy support in the northeast and central regions.

Promoting the development of backward regions to realize regional balanced development is a specific embodiment of common prosperity. After some regions become rich, they may support the development of backward regions to realize common prosperity step by step. This is a core content in the concept of common prosperity. The concept of shared development is established on the basis of common prosperity, it enables economic development results to be more shared, so as to promote further economic development by sharing more economic results. With respect to specific regional balanced development policies, preferential policies may provide more supports and opportunities for western, northeast and central regions, promote development of these regions. Since the 18th Party Congress, changes in microenvironment have been resorted to narrow regional income gap, give full play to the role of market. For example, promote employment equity, increase vocational

[28] Liu (2015).

[29] Gu (2002).

skills, encourage social capital investment, improve equal access to basic public services.

2.4 *The Role of Industrial Development Policies in Narrowing the Difference Between Urban and Rural Areas*

Agrarian reform is closely linked to economic growth. As economies grow, the portion of agriculture in gross output will decrease if calculated according to per capita growth rate. Because, according to Engel's law, with the increase of people's real income, the proportion of their income spent on food will become smaller and smaller. This means that, with continuous economic growth, the increase in demand for agricultural products will decrease relatively. If the growth rate of agricultural supply is faster than the growth rate of demand, then "When the grain is cheap, the farmers suffer" is bound to happen. From the perspective of GDP structure, with economic development, the proportion of agriculture will decrease continuously. It may be seen from Fig. 1 that, in rapid economic development process of Japan, the proportion of agriculture in GDP decreased quickly and continuously, down to 2.12% in 1990. Japan was already a developed country in 1990, in combination with the situations in USA and UK, the proportion of agriculture in GDP was below 2% in all these countries, and even tended to decrease gradually, although very slowly. In

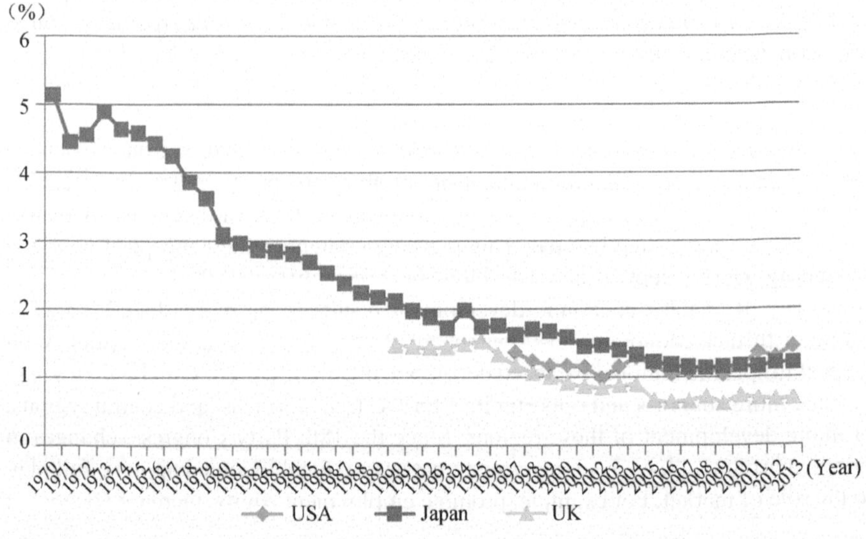

Fig. 1 Change trend of the proportion of agriculture in developed countries. *Data source World Development Indicators 2016*

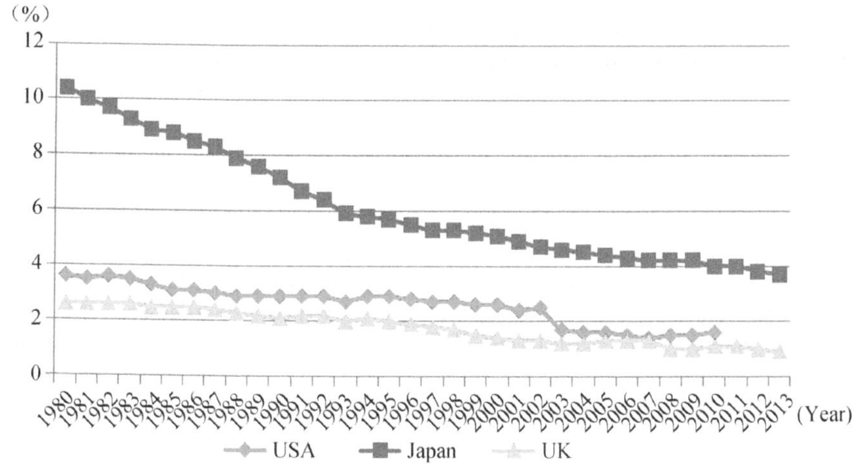

Fig. 2 Change trend of the proportion of agricultural working population in developed countries. *Data source World Development Indicators 2016*

2013, the proportion of agriculture in GDP was 1.45, 0.69 and 1.21% in USA, UK and Japan respectively. While the proportion of added value of agriculture decreased, the proportion of agricultural labor force also decreased continually (see Fig. 2).

This shows that while growing increase of domestic demand for agricultural products may be met, both the proportion of agriculture in GDP and the proportion of agricultural working population in total working population decrease, this requires agricultural labor productivity to increase greatly. In other words, along with economic development, the development of mechanization improves agricultural labor productivity continuously, so that a large number of agricultural labor force may turn to industrial production. In this process, thanks to continuous increase in the productivity of agricultural labor force, the income of peasants also increases continuously. At the same time, the labor force transferred from agriculture meets the demand of industrial development for labor force. According to labor migration model, before reaching Lewis Turning Point, labor productivity of surplus rural labor is 0 or close to 0, labor force migrates from countryside to cities continuously; after reaching Lewis Turning Point, the labor productivity of rural labor force increases, if industrial sectors still need to attract labor force from agriculture, they have to increase wages. The continuous migration of agricultural labor force increases agricultural labor productivity, thus increases the income of peasants.

According to the above-mentioned economic development rules as well as international experience, the key to narrow urban-rural income gap is to increase agricultural labor productivity in the process of economic development. Four major factors influence the increase in agricultural labor productivity: firstly, whether surplus labor force may be migrated; secondly, whether agricultural modernization level may be increased; thirdly, whether land may be transferred; fourthly, whether human capital may be improved.

Firstly, the role of surplus labor migration in narrowing urban-rural income gap. Barriers that restrict rural labor migration were weakened gradually in rapid economic development process of China. Notification Concerning the Rural Works in 1984 was published on the People's Daily in 1984, alleviated the restriction on flow of peasants to towns. Blind flow of population was controlled in the period of 1989–1991, flow of rural labor force was encouraged after 1992, Regulations for the Custody and Repatriation of Urban Vagrants and Beggars was abolished in 2003, then a series of policies were promulgated for access of rural migrant workers to essential public services, including social security, accompanying children education, employment training etc. The scale of rural migrant workers expands continuously, although urban-rural income gap is still large, yet migration of rural labor force narrows the urban-rural income gap.[30]

Next, the role of land transfer and agricultural modernization in narrowing income gap. Household contract responsibility system with remuneration linked to output distributes land to peasant households according to the scale of family members, peasant households possess use right, such use right has been kept for a long period by means of systems and policies. This increases enthusiasm of peasants greatly, and further increases agricultural labor productivity. However, land area per household is not large, especially in regions of large population with relatively little land, this becomes huge obstacle of mechanized, modern agricultural development. In addition, with a large number of peasants working in cities, transfer of idle land also becomes an urgent rural problem to be solved. Regulations for land transfer were specified in the Notification of the General Office of CCCPC, General Office of the State Council concerning Further Stabilization and Improvement of Rural Land Contract Relations in 1997, and the content of land transfer was specified in the *Law of the People's Republic of China on Land Contract in Rural Areas* promulgated in 2003. According to research findings, increase in the quantity of land leased and sublet by peasant households will increase per capita net income of peasant households notably.[31]

Finally, the role of increase in human capital in narrowing income gap. According to the analysis of human capital versus labor remuneration in this section, increase in human capital could increase labor productivity, then further increase remuneration. China's urban-biased policies and restrictions of household registration system lead to huge gap between urban and rural areas in aspect of access to public education. According to the sixth population census data of China in 2010,[32] average years of education of population over 16 years old are 8.91 years, and are 10.84 years, 9.21 years, 7.57 years for population of cities, towns and villages respectively. This means that, educational level in villages and towns is far lower than cities, considering the difference in education quality, the education gap between urban and rural areas

---

[30]Cai (2009).

[31]Wang Chunchao, Rural Land Transfer, Labor Resource Allocation and Peasant Income Growth: Empirical Research Based on Rural Household Survey in 17 Provinces of China, *Journal of Agrotechnical*, 1st Issue, 2011.

[32]Calculated according to the sixth population census data at the website of National Bureau of Statistics of China. http://www.Stats.gov.cn/tjsj/pcsj/rkpc/6rp/indexch.Htm.

will be larger. From the perspective of enrollment rate, the difference in enrollment rate of school-age children between villages, towns and cities is not significant at the stages of primary school and junior high school, but huge difference exists in the enrollment rate of senior high school. In 2012, the enrollment rate of ordinary senior high school in cities was 75%, total enrollment rate in villages and towns was merely 34%.[33]

With respect to China's policies for promoting agricultural development, the above-mentioned policies already implemented have achieved positive effect. Based on the objective law of agricultural development slower than industrial development, migration of agricultural population should be encouraged, so they may enter industries and share economic development results. The key to increase agricultural labor productivity lies in mechanization and modernization. Land transfer should be promoted and agriculture organization form should be changed to increase the land area operated by peasant households, so as to provide basis for mechanization and modernization. In the Opinions of the Central Committee of the Communist Party of China, the State Council concerning Quickening the Development of Modern Agriculture and Further Increasing the Vitality of Rural Development promulgated in 2012, with respect to agricultural labor migration, we should promote citizenization of agricultural transfer population orderly to enhance stability of rural migrant workers in cities, and promote agricultural population transfer; with respect to land and modernization development, we should stabilize rural land contract relations, increase intensive operation level of peasant households, support the development of peasants' cooperative organization, mechanization and modernization need infrastructure as an aid, construction and investment of rural infrastructure also becomes an important content; in aspect of improving human capital, we should vigorously develop rural social undertakings, improve long-acting mechanism for the construction and reconstruction of rural secondary and primary schools. Increasing agricultural labor productivity becomes an important content, undoubtedly, this is helpful to increase income of peasants in primary distribution, thus narrow the urban-rural income gap.

[33]Data originate from *China Population and Employment Statistics Yearbook 2013*, right-age population is calculated according to age-specific data. Since entrance age is not unified in different regions, right-age population calculated directly according to national age-specific population is not precise, but will not influence the judgment of large enrollment rate gap between urban and rural areas. Since the State Council promulgated Decision Concerning Basic Education Reform and Development in 2001 to cancel rural middle and primary schools with fewer students and poor school conditions gradully, incorporate them into town/township center schools, so enrollment rate is calculated using the sum data of villages and towns.

3 New Ideas of Redistribution Under the Concept of Sharing

The concept of shared development is an essential requirement of socialism with Chinese characteristics. Chinese economic aggregate has been ranked as the second in the world, but many problems still exist in sharing development results, for example, too wide income gap, a large number of absolute poverty population, unbalanced regional development. If these problems are not solved, it's difficult to realize great rejuvenation of the Chinese nation, nor build a moderately prosperous society in all respects.[34] Such problems are generated in China's rapid economic development process, some problems, such as unbalanced regional development, too wide gap of personal income, are inevitable, and belong to the problems at specific development stages. The concept of shared development put forward by central government is also based on such background, new development concept should be explored in the precondition of adhering to Marxism. On the way to realize shared development, "making more effective institutional arrangement" was put forward at the Fifth Plenary Session of the Eighteenth Central Committee of the CPC.[35] This requirement has very strong practical guiding significance: realize shared development mainly by means of institutional improvement and institutional arrangement. Institutional framework and institutional arrangement of income redistribution is of great importance in the institutional arrangement to realize shared development.[36]

To realize inclusive shared development through income redistribution reform and improvement of relevant systems, in addition to share development results on concept, fairness of development process, sustainability of sharing mode and means should also be considered and analyzed.[37] We should fully absorb frontier concepts, tried and true methods of international community in the redistribution of income to realize fair, sustainable, unified shared development.

3.1 Social Protection and Social Investment in Human Capital

As one of the main income redistribution policies, social security is a main institutional arrangement to realize shared development. Definite policy measures were proposed for the reform and improvement of social security system at the 18th National Congress of CPC, the Third Plenary Session and the Fifth Plenary Session of the Eighteenth Central Committee of the CPC. These policies also fully absorb international frontier concept in the development of social security system.

---

[34]Jiang (2016).

[35]Recommendations for the 13th Five-Year Plan for Economic and Social Development, 2015.

[36]Zhao (2016).

[37]She (2016).

Traditionally, social security exists as a "social security net", it intends to provide assistance for losers in market competition. Since the 1980s, social protection concept has superseded traditional social security concept gradually. Social protection is generally defined as a series of Public Actions taken by the state and society to cope with vulnerability, risk and deprivation; in a given social and political framework, such vulnerability, risk and deprivation are deemed socially unacceptable. The main purpose of providing corresponding protection for members of society to eliminate vulnerability, control risk, and eliminate various forms of deprivation by means of public policies is to improve social fairness and safety, promote social mobility and inclusiveness, and maintain social stability.[38] Compared with traditional social security, social protection has the following characteristics[39]:

Firstly, concern the needs of vulnerable groups based on full consideration of realistic conditions of protected group, provide specific protection according to their real needs. At the same time, the focus of social security program changes from post-event assistance to pre-event intervention, from passive guarantee to active guarantee.

Secondly, attach importance to affordability and sustainability. In the concept and policy framework of social protection, the protection provided by government should be paid by public budget, the affordability of family and society should also be considered. Even receiving protection provided by society, some vulnerable groups are unable to obtain or use such protection. Sustainability includes both political sustainability and financial sustainability.

Thirdly, improve risk response ability of individuals, families and communities, prevent welfare dependency. Social protection, protection for vulnerable populations, intends to improve their own risk response ability, rather than only passive provision of income compensation. In social security system with welfarism, the most common problem is welfare dependency and welfare rigidity of members of the society. In the concept of social protection, support provided by social protection for members of society is mainly improving their risk response ability. Such support also provides human capital base for sustained economic growth.

Fourthly, social protection emphasizes flexibility of protection content, could adapt to quickly changing economic and social environment, meet changing needs of members of society in different life cycle. Members of society face different risk types at different stages of life cycle, and need different protections. Social protection emphasizes adaptation to such changes, for example, provide more specific protection for children, people in working age group yet unable to obtain sufficient income and the aged. Focus of modern social security system reform is to cope with social risk, seek balance point between economic security and economic growth. The concept of social protection finds a connection point between them, this connection point is investment in human capital based on ability enhancement. One of the main ways to enhance risk response ability of members of society is investment in human capital, while investment in human capital is main source of modern economic growth.

---

[38] Norton (2001).

[39] Ge (2014), Gong (2011).

The concept of social protection may be extended to income redistribution policy, it requires more emphasis on investment in human capital in institutional design of social security, so as to enhance individual ability to cope with social risks, combine individual development with social development, regard social redistribution policy as a new type of investment in human capital. This is also the keynote of current international community to promote developmental social policy[40]: pay special attention to human capital accumulation and whether labor force enters labor market successfully; concern the contribution of social policy to economic development, emphasize unified and harmonious economic and social development; social redistribution policy is also social investment, a mean to enhance national competitiveness; emphasize more on "upstream intervention" of social risk, attach importance to front-end intervention strategy.

3.2 *New Ideas of Targeted Poverty Alleviation and Accurate Redistribution*

"Targeted poverty alleviation" was firstly mentioned by Xi Jinping in Nov. 2013, when he visited the west of Hunan and gave important instructions "practical and realistic, adaptive to local conditions, classified guidance, targeted poverty alleviation". In Mar. 2014, Xi Jinping emphasized, when he participated in the NPC and CPPCC delegation review, on the implementation of targeted poverty alleviation, aiming at poverty alleviation object for key policy implementation, he further explained the concept of targeted poverty alleviation. The background of targeted poverty alleviation is that main feature of previous poverty alleviation is regional aiming, no identification of peasant households.[41] From the mid 1980s, main poverty alleviation object in China was poor counties determined by state and provinces, from 2001, poverty alleviation object was changed to 150,000 poor villages, 14 contiguous poor areas were determined in 2011.[42] However, with overall economic development, especially the growing inequality of income distribution, poverty alleviation based on regional development led to deviation from the goal and decreased poverty alleviation effect. Growing income inequality means that poor population on the bottom of income distribution become increasingly difficult to enjoy the advantages of economic growth, i.e. poverty reduction effect of economic growth decreases. It becomes more and more important to implement more specific poverty alleviation policy for direct support of poor population in case poverty reduction effect of economic growth decreases.[43] The idea of targeted poverty alleviation was proposed on this background.

---

[40] Zhang (2007).

[41] Park (2002).

[42] The Central Committee of the Communist Party of China, the State Council: Outline for Development-oriented Poverty Reduction for China's Rural Areas (2011–2020), 2011.

[43] Wang (2015).

The thinking of targeted poverty alleviation is not only an innovation to solve poverty problems in China, but also puts forward a new idea and method for supply of public service, the implementation of transfer payment and other redistribution policies. Redistribution effect of many policy means of income redistribution is not evident in China, a very important reason is insufficient "aiming" mechanism of the policies. The effect of public spending and transfer payment may be enhanced only when population are aimed "accurately". To proceed from the idea of targeted poverty alleviation, the improvement of income redistribution policy needs "accurate identification, accurate support, accurate management and accurate evaluation".

Establish accurate identification mechanism. Accurate identification is the precondition and basis of accurate income redistribution policy, accurate identification emphasizes identification of the residents who need assistance and support through democratic, scientific and transparent procedures, especially identification of the residents who need support the most. Accurate support is critical, special needs of the object to be supported should be fully understood, so as to provide specific support for different persons, households and for different reasons. Accurate management, information of all supported households and persons may be managed by modern, informatization means, dynamic adjustment may be made according to timely index analysis. Accurate evaluation may be achieved by timely, dynamic monitoring of policy implementation process and effect.[44]

3.3 *Promote the Development of Human Capital Investment Type Service Industry*

Education, medical care and other social services are traditionally thought as public services, most countries regard such services as important components of government's public spending, and also main policy means of income redistribution. These public services are regarded as important content of people's livelihood undertaking or social undertaking in China's policy framework. However, with transformation of economic development in China, increase in resident income level and subsequent change in demand structure, innovation should be made in the supply mode of such services. With the support of modern social protection concept and income redistribution concept, social services including education, medical care, culture are also main modes of investment in human capital. This also reflects the transition from adequate food and clothing type moderately prosperous society to a well-off moderately prosperous society.

According to empirical laws of economic development, with the increase of economic development level and resident income level, after "food, clothing, housing" demands are met, social demand structure also changes, mainly turns to "housing,

[44]Ge (2015).

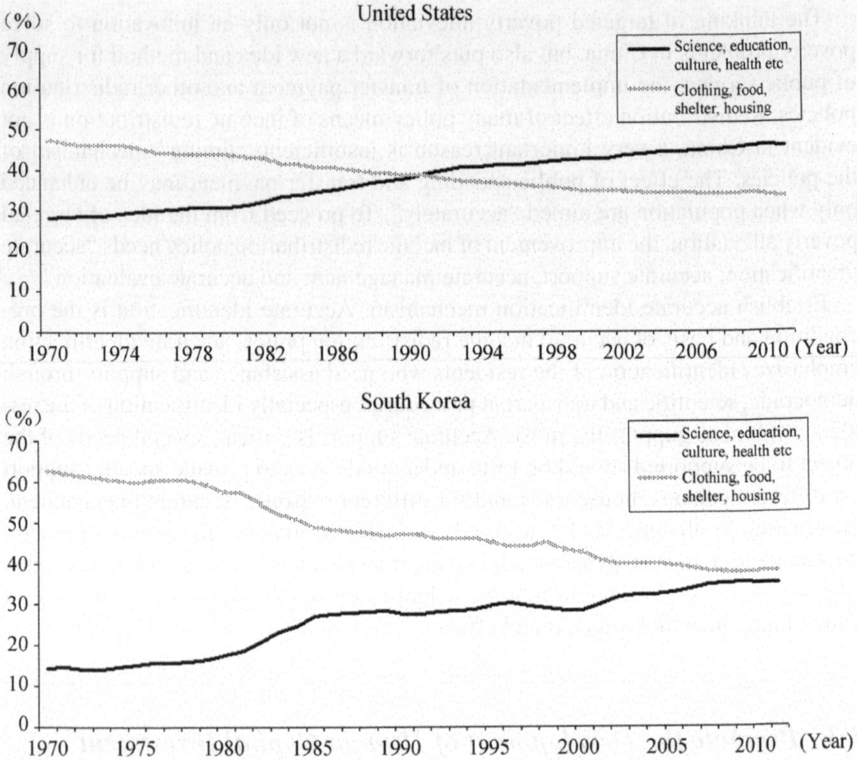

Fig. 3 Proportion of the demand for science, education, culture, health in aggregate demand in the United States and South Korea. *Data source* China's economic growth frontier research group: New factor supply theory, system and policy options for the breakthrough of economic slowdown, *Economic Research Journal*, 11th Issue, 2015

transportation, learning" and other "soft demands",[45] demands for education, medical care, culture, health increase rapidly. These service industries are also human capital investment type service industries, have very strong income redistribution effect. According to international experience, with the increase of economic development level, proportion of demand for "science, education, culture, health" and other human capital investment type service industries also increases quickly in aggregate demand. Demand of the United States as a developed capitalist country for science, education, culture, health and other social services exceeded the demand for food, clothing, housing, transport in ordinary daily life at the beginning of the 1990s, and this trend still rises continuously; such trend also appears in South Korea, with economic growth, demand for science, education, culture, health grows rapidly (see Fig. 3). The change of demand structure relates to the change of industry structure: tertiary industry becomes a leading industry, the industries in the tertiary

[45]Wang (2010).

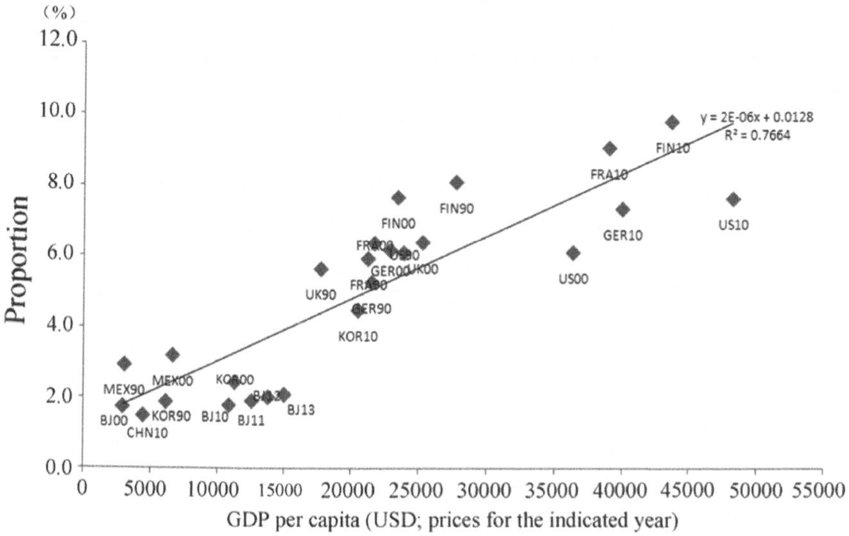

Fig. 4 Proportion of health industry output value in GDP of some countries and regions. *Data source* the data of other countries originate from OECD STAN database for structural analysis, and world bank database. The data of Beijing come from *Beijing Statistical Yearbooks*, the data of Beijing in 2013 come from *2013 Statistical Bulletin of National Economy* in Beijing City

industry related to investment in human capital, such as education, health service, became main industries. Figure 4 shows the proportion of health service industry output value in GDP at different development stages of some countries and regions, after GDP per capita exceeds 20,000 USD, output value of health service industry increases rapidly, the output value of health service industry in some countries approaches 10% of GDP.

Chinese economic aggregate exceeded Japan and became the second largest economy in 2010. As far as the level of economic development is concerned, in aspect of GDP per capita, China exceeded 7600 USD in 2015, became an upper middle income country. Some cities and provinces, for example, Beijing, Shanghai and Jiangsu, also exceed the high income line determined by the United Nations, become developed economic entities (see Fig. 5). This also means that China will enter a demand structure transition period, the demand for investment in human capital such as science, education, culture, health will increase greatly. While these social services are provided directly by government in traditional system. Unique public institutions in China are the subjects to provide these social services. However, from the viewpoint of operating effect, the system of public institutions not only has low efficiency, cannot meet changing demand of residents, its fairness is also very poor. As analyzed above, the income redistribution effect of China's public services is inconspicuous, even reverse income distribution effect exists, which is closely related to such administrative supply system. Therefore, innovation of human capital investment type social service provision system is an inevitable requirement of innovative

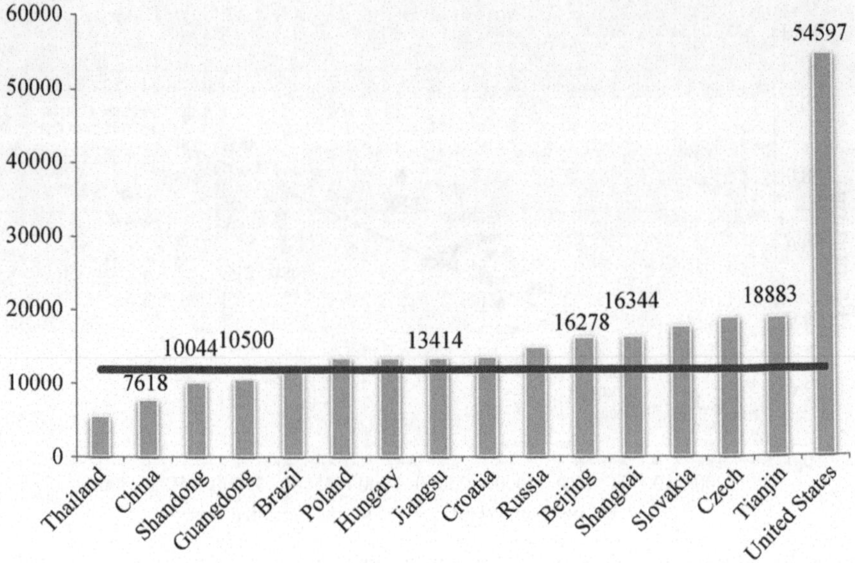

Fig. 5 GDP Per Capita of China and some of its provinces versus other countries and regions (2015). *Data source China statistical yearbook. Note* in USD (prices for the indicated year); transverse line in the figure is the high income line determined by the United Nations (11906 USD)

redistribution policy in the new circumstances. The "de-administration" requirement raised at the Third Plenary Session of the Eighteenth Central Committee of the CPC for public institution reform also has this meaning.

3.4 Develop Public Welfare Organization Vigorously

Not only government sectors, but extensive public welfare organizations also assume the income redistribution function under modern market economic conditions. Since the industrial revolution, although government has become the main implementer of public service, transfer payment and other forms of income redistribution, yet non-government, non-market public welfare organizations have a long history no matter in Western society or in traditional China, and they assume main social security function in traditional society.[46] Due to single stakeholder in the planned economic period of China, a large number of nongovernmental public welfare organizations died or became a part of government agencies, or became quasi-administrative department. After the establishment of socialist market economy, a major social change is the diversification of stakeholders. A middle social class is required between government and individuals to coordinate the relationship between different stakeholders, and

[46]Qin (2004).

assume a large number of social public welfare functions inconvenient for government to assume. These functions include income redistribution function, for example, mass social service provision, nongovernmental charitable donation, mutual assistance and mutual relief in the society.

At this stage, Chinese social organizations may be divided into three categories according to the nature of organization, business content and operation mechanism: firstly, social group, which comprises of citizens or enterprises and institutions voluntarily, carries out activities according to the Articles of Association, including industry association, academic association, professional association and joint association. Secondly, foundation, which is non-profit organization, utilizes donated property for public welfare undertakings, including public-raising foundation and non-public-raising foundation. China Disabled People Union, Soong Ching Ling Foundation belong to social organizations in this category. Thirdly, private non-enterprise unit, which consists of enterprises and institutions, social groups and other social forces as well as individual citizens, that utilize non-state-owned assets to hold, engage in social service activities, may be divided into ten major categories, namely, education, health, science and technology, culture, labor, civil administration, sports, intermediary service and legal services.

Since the reform and opening up, China's social organizations have been developed rapidly, and distributed widely in all walks of life. By the end of 2014, number of registered social organizations in China was up to 606,000, increased 10.8% over preceding year. Of which, 310,000 social groups, including industrial and commercial social service, scientific and technological research, education, health, cultural groups, increased 7.2% over preceding year; 292,000 private non-enterprise units, increased 14.7% over preceding year; 4,117 foundations, increase over preceding year 16.0%.[47] This objectively shows that, social organizations have started to participate in social governance extensively, and become a core force to construct harmonious society.

In 2006, the concept "social organization" was firstly put forward at the Sixth Plenary Session of the Sixteenth Central Committee of the Communist Party of China, and "Improve social organizations, enhance social service function. Encourage social forces to establish private non-enterprise units in education, science and technology, culture, health, sports, social welfare and other fields. Let industry associations, institutes, chamber of commerce and other social groups play their social roles to serve for economic and social development. Develop and normalize various foundations, promote the development of public welfare undertakings" was also proposed. In 2007, to improve and develop social organizations was explicitly included in overall work of social construction and management, constructing harmonious society at the Seventeenth National Congress of the Communist Party of China. In 2013, the following was further recommended at the Third Plenary Session of the Eighteenth Central Committee of the Communist Party of China, "public services that may be

---

[47] Ministry of Civil Affairs, the People's Republic of China, *2014 Statistical Report on Social Service Development*, http://www.Mca.Gov.Cn/article/zwgk/mzyw/201506/20150600832371.Shtml.

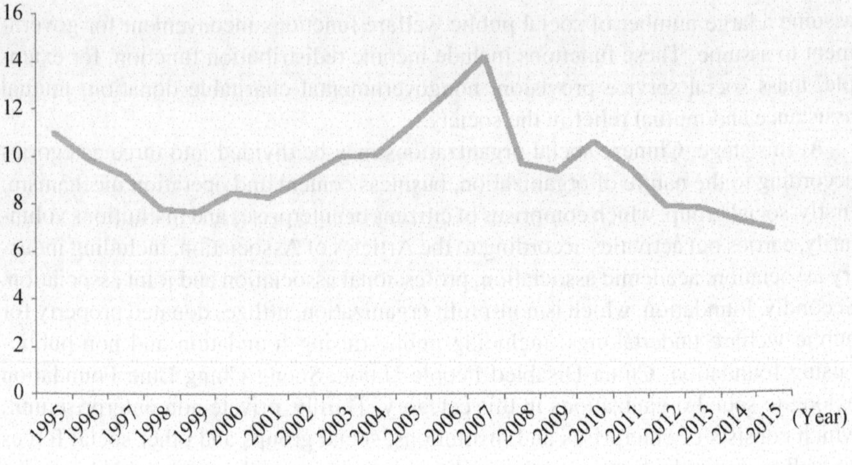

Fig. 6 Actual growth rate changes of China's GDP in the past 20 years. *Data source China Statistical Yearbook* in relevant years

provided and matters that may be solved by social organizations properly should be performed by social organizations".

However, with respect to the development level of social organizations, compared with developed countries, China's social organizations are still at primary development stage. The fundamental cause is that, social service industries, such as education, medical care, scientific research, culture, industry association, are main development fields of social organizations. While public institutions are dominant in these fields of China so far. These public institutions are state-owned administrative organizations, with low operation efficiency, lack of fairness. This promotes government to rethink the positioning of itself and social organizations while changing its functions, reform public institution system, release creativity of talents in the system, let social organizations play a more active role in social governance.

4 Economic Transformation and New Challenges of Income Distribution Policy

Economic development in China has entered a new normal, "L" shape growth path of medium, low speed growth will last for a long period.[48] From the perspective of economic growth rate, this decrease process started from 2008 and 2009. Then after 2010, this process became more evident (see Fig. 6). Entering medium speed and low speed growth period after a high speed economic growth stage is an empirical

[48]Asking for General Trend at the Very Beginning—Talks of Authoritative Source on Current China's Economy, *People's Daily*, May 9, 2016.

law of economic development. This means that "catch-up" growth at early stage is no longer sustainable.

By imitating and learning the experience of developed countries, we should transform the development strategy that utilizes our abundant labor resources, natural resources and land resources to realize high speed economic growth, change the development mode characterized by extended, extensive growth, reconstruct the development motivation in which heavy duty industrialization is dominant. under such conditions, China's income distribution policy faces new adjustment, should be changed fundamentally.

4.1 New Challenges in Economic Transformation Period

1. The impact of new technology development represented by information technology and mobile technology on industrial organizations and employment pattern
   Modern information technology and mobile technology have become frontier of current technology development, the new economy represented by "Internet +" has become new sources of economic growth. "Internet +" reduces information cost and transaction cost significantly, changes the industry organizational structure and employment pattern in traditional industrialization era. In the industrialization period represented by factory system, "employer + employee" is a dominant employment form. Employment without employer is called "informal employment".[49] But since the new economy represented by "Internet +" reduces information cost and transaction cost significantly, so industrial organization mode of factory system is affected greatly. In reality, the business model represented by Taobao and Tmall, travel model represented by Didi and Uber, take-out model represented by Baidu and Meituan impact existing industry organizational structure greatly, so the proportion of free, flexible employment in total employment rises continuously. According to the special research on network entrepreneurship and employment statistics and social security issues carried out jointly by China Association of Employment Promotion and Alibaba Group, if calculate according to average employment per household of network entrepreneurs, overall scale of network entrepreneurship and employment in China approaches 10 million persons. According to statistics, in urban employment groups, self-employed individuals accounted for 16.1% of total urban working population by the end of 2013 (see Table 1).
2. Rapid urbanization and normalization of mass population movements
   Since the 1980s, population movement has become one of the main economic and social features of China, the scale of floating population increased from several million in the 1980s to 220 million in 2010.[50] Among whom, the scale of

[49] Hussmanns (2005).

[50] Zheng (2013).

Table 1 Rural migrant workers and urban self-employed individuals in urban employees

Year	Urban employees (ten thousand persons)	Urban self-employed individuals (ten thousand persons)	Rural migrant workers quantity (ten thousand persons)	Proportion in urban employees (%)	
				Urban self-employed individuals	Rural migrant workers
2004	27293	2521	–	–	–
2005	28389	2778	–	–	–
2006	29630	3012	13181	10.2	44.5
2007	30953	3310	13800	10.7	44.6
2008	32103	3609	14041	11.2	43.7
2009	33322	4245	14533	12.7	43.6
2010	34687	4467	15335	12.9	44.2
2011	35914	5227	15863	14.6	44.2
2012	37102	5643	16336	15.2	44.0
2013	38240	6142	16610	16.1	43.4
2014	39310	–	16821	–	42.8

Note Rural migrant workers refer to the rural migrant workers employed outside hometown
Data source Statistical Bulletin of Human Resource and Social Security Undertaking Development over the years, *China Labor Statistical Yearbook* over the years

rural-urban floating population (rural migrant workers) is the largest. By the end of 2014, number of rural migrant workers in China was 274 million, of whom number of rural migrant workers (flow out of hometown) was up to 168 million, accounting for 42.8% of urban employees. With the changes in China's population structure and industry structure, although absolute number of rural migrant workers increases, yet their proportion in urban employees shows downtrend in recent years (see Table 1). Nevertheless, rural-urban floating population will still constitute main force of mass population movements considering huge rural population base in China and continual urbanization process in the future. Meanwhile, number of urban-urban floating population increases continuously, and their proportion in floating population rises continuously. "the sixth national population census" data in 2010 showed that, the scale of urban-urban floating population was up to 47 million, accounting for 21% of total floating population (the proportion of rural-urban floating population was 63%).[51] On this background, the State Council Report on the Work of the Government in 2014 proposed to solve existing "three one-hundred-million populations" problems in next period, promote permanent residency of about one-hundred-million agricultural transfer population in urban areas, reconstruct urban shanty towns and villages in the city where about one-hundred-million population live, guide nearby urbanization of about one-hundred-million in central and western regions.

[51] Ma (2014).

3. Rapid demographic changes and aging of population
   Huge demographic changes also accompany the economic slowdown in China. The family planning policy implemented in China since the 1980s has changed the demographics of China in very short time, aging increases rapidly. With respect to degree of aging, in 2000, population aged 65 and above accounted for 7.09% of total population, China has entered an aging society. According to predictions, aging of population will develop rapidly in China in the decades to come, aging population of 60 years old and above will account for 19.5% of total population in 2025, and nearly 30% in 2050. With respect to aging speed in China, aging rate will rise 19.8 % points from 2000 to 2050, higher than the aging speed in USA, UK, and also higher than Japan. With rapid increase of aging population, working-age population decreases continuously in China. The proportion of 15–59 years old working-age population in total population of China will decrease from 65% in 2000 to in 53.8% 2050 (Table 2).

4.2 *The Impact of Economic Transformation on Income Distribution and Policy Adjustment*

On the great background of economic transformation, new technologies, new industrial organizations, employment patterns, population movements and demographic changes generate profound impact on China's income distribution status, relevant policies should also advance with times, theory of distribution should be developed continuously for socialist political economics with Chinese characteristics based on adherence to the basic position and methods of Marxism.

Firstly, new technologies and new industrial organization modes require in-depth analysis and research on distribution according to work and distribution according to productive factors, labor theory of value should be further analyzed in the new circumstances. Historical background of labor theory of value put forward by Marx was the establishment and generation period of modern industry when capital and labor were separated, large factories were dominant. Privatization of capital leads to exploitation of labor, this is one of the basic viewpoints of Marx. However, with the development of modern science and technology, especially the development of modern information technology and mobile technology, new industrial organization mode and employment pattern appear, the relationship between capital and labor also changes. Particularly in China where public ownership of the means of production has been dominant, capital contribution, labor value, return of other factors are combined together, the barriers between distribution according to work and distribution according to productive factors need to be broken up, both are socialist methods for sharing economy.

Table 2 Demographic changes and predictions in china and other countries (unit:%)

	1950	1975	2000	2025	2050	Changes (percentage points)
USA						
0–14 years old	27	25.2	21.7	18.5	18.5	10.8
15–59 years old	60.5	60	62.1	56.6	54.6	
60 years old and above	12.5	14.8	16.1	24.8	26.9	
Japan						
0–14 years old	35.4	24.3	14.7	12.1	12.5	19.1
15–59 years old	56.9	64	62.1	52.8	45.2	
60 years old and above	7.7	11.7	23.2	35.1	42.3	
China						
0–14 years old	33.5	39.5	24.8	18.4	16.3	19.8
15–59 years old	59	53.6	65	62.1	53.8	
60 years old and above	7.5	6.9	10.1	19.5	29.9	
South Korea						
0–14 years old	41.7	37.7	20.8	16	16.5	22.2
15–59 years old	52.9	56.4	68.2	59.9	50.4	
60 years old and above	5.4	5.8	11	24.1	33.2	
UK						
0–14 years old	22.3	23.3	19	15.2	15	13.4
15–59 years old	62.1	57	60.4	55.4	51.1	
60 years old and above	15.5	19.6	20.6	29.4	34	

Note 1. "Changes" refer to the changes in the proportion of 60 years old and above population from 2000 to 2050, equal to the proportion of 60 years old and above population in 2050 subtracting the proportion of 60 years old and above population in 2000, it represents aging speed in these 50 years, the larger this value is, the quicker the aging speed becomes in these 50 years. 2. The numbers in 2025 and 2050 are predicted valued of the United Nations

Data source World population ageing: 1950–2050, Department of Economic and Social Affairs Population Division, United Nations, New York: 2001

Secondly, combine equity and sustainability of income distribution, combine equity and efficiency. The relationship between efficiency and equity is one of the topics of traditional economics. It is generally believed that, emphasizing equity in income distribution will decrease efficiency, especially redistribution policy, which will decrease incentives for production, thus reduce efficiency. But as mentioned earlier, modern income distribution policy concept, firstly, takes investment in human capital as a means of intervention at early stage, so as to realize equitable development in the preconditions of improving human capital accumulation; secondly, combine industry development and social service provision, realize effective supply and equitable supply of various social services through industry development. Currently, China faces economic transformation, aging of population and demographic transition, it is of great importance to keep sustainability of income distribution policy.

Thirdly, innovate new social security system, explore the establishment of unified social security system based on residential identity. Mass population movements and frequent change of employment have become main features in current transition period. With respect to current coverage of social security, main issue lies in floating population, especially rural migrant workers. Rural migrant workers are employed and work in cities, yet they could not be covered by urban social security system.

Now, the problems related to two groups hinder the full coverage of social security, the first group is rural migrant workers. According to their registered permanent residence, they should participate in social insurance of rural residents, which includes new rural cooperative and pension insurance for urban and rural residents; yet according to employment relationship, they should participate in social insurance for urban employees. Currently, the proportion of rural migrant workers participating in social insurance for urban employees is less than 20% (see Table 3). According to the provisions for insured workers, they belong to uninsured statutory personnel; but according to social insurance provisions for rural residents, they have already been insured. The second group is urban workers without definite employment relationship. According to the provisions, they should participate in social insurance for employees; however, since employment relationship is indefinite, they may also participate in social insurance for residents. This results in some groups who should participate in social insurance for employees participating in social insurance for residents instead.

Starting from the concept of shared development, China's social security system should establish unified, portable, mobile national social insurance system covering all residents on the basis of social security for residents. This basic national social insurance provide unified, basic social security for residents; at the same time, this system may also serve as a platform, on which various supplementary guarantee items may be established to meet multi-level needs of different groups, so as to realize unified equity and sustainability.

Table 3 Number of rural migrant workers and their participation in basic pension insurance for urban employees

Year	2008	2009	2010	2011	2012	2013	2014
Total number of rural migrant workers (ten thousand persons)	22542	22978	24223	25278	26261	26894	27395
Number of outgoing rural migrant workers (ten thousand persons)	14041	14533	15335	15863	16336	16610	16821
Number of insured rural migrant workers (ten thousand persons)	2416	2647	3284	4140	4543	4895	5472
Number of persons who pay social insurance for urban employees (ten thousand persons)	16588	17743	19402	21565	22981	24177	25531
Number of retirees under social insurance for urban employees (ten thousand persons)	5304	5807	6305	6826	7446	8041	8593
Coverage rate of rural migrant workers under social insurance for urban employees 1 (%)	10.7	11.5	13.6	16.4	17.3	18.2	20.0
Coverage rate of rural migrant workers under social insurance for urban employees 2 (%)	17.2	18.2	21.4	26.1	27.8	29.5	32.5
Proportion of rural migrant workers in all persons who make payment (%)	14.6	14.9	16.9	19.2	19.8	20.2	21.4
Total dependency ratio of social insurance for urban employees	3.13	3.06	3.08	3.16	3.09	3.01	2.97
Dependency ratio of urban employees	2.67	2.60	2.56	2.55	2.48	2.40	2.33

Note 1. Outgoing rural migrant workers refer to those rural migrant workers who work outside their hometown. 2. Coverage rate 1 refers to the coverage rate of all rural migrant workers, coverage rate 2 refers to the coverage rate of outgoing rural migrant workers. 3. Proportion of rural migrant workers in all persons who make payment refers to the proportion of rural migrant workers in on-job payment personnel under social insurance for urban employees. 4. Dependency ratio refers to the ratio of pension system payment personnel to persons who receive pension, i.e. how many on-job payment personnel support a pensioner. Dependency ratio in the table refers to the ratio of all payment personnel participating in social insurance for urban employees to pensioners; dependency ratio of urban employees refers to the ratio of payment personnel after deducting rural migrant workers to all benefit receivers, it represents the ratio of urban employees to pensioners

Data source Statistical Bulletin of Human Resource and Social Security Undertaking Development over the years and *China Labor Statistical Yearbook* over the years

References

Abowd, John M., Francis Kramarz, David N. Margolis, Thomas Philippon, Minimum Wages and Employment in France and the United States, *CEPR Discussion Papers*, No. 2159, 2009.

Angrist, Joshua D. And Alan B. Krueger, Does Compulsory School Attendance Affect Schooling and Earnings?, *The Quarterly Journal of Economics*, 1991, 106 (4), pp. 979–1014.

Ashenfelter, Orley and Alan Krueger, Estimates of the Economic Return to Schooling from a New Sample of Twins, *The American E-conomic Review*, 1994, 84 (5), pp. 1157–1173.

Bell, Linda A., the Impact of Minimum Wages in Mexico and Colombia, *Journal of Labor Economics*, 1997, Vol. 15, No. 3, pp. S102–S135.

Cai Fang, Wang Meiyan: Why Labor Migration has Not Narrowed the Urban-Rural Income Gap, *Economic Perspectives*, 8th Issue, 2009.

Card, David and Alan B. Krueger, Minimum Wages and Employment: A Case Study of the Fast Food Industry in New Jersey and Pennsylvania, *NBER Working Paper*, No. 4509, 1993.

Du Yang, Wang Meiyan, Implementation Status of Minimum Wage System and Its Effect in China, *Journal of Graduate School of Chinese Academy of Social Sciences*, 6th Issue, 2008.

Fields, Gary and Ravi Kanbur, Minimum Wages and Poverty, *Working Paper*, WP 2005–18, Department of Applied Economics and Management Cornell University, Ithaca, 2005.

Fu Kangsheng, Economic Analysis on the Implementation of Minimum Wage System, *Jianghuai Tribune*, 6th Issue, 1995.

Ge Jing, Wang Zhen, Evolution of International Social Security System and Its Enlightenment on China, *Social Science Front*, 10th Issue, 2014.

Ge Zhijun, Xing Chengju, Targeted Poverty Alleviation: Connotation, Dilemmas in the Practice and Explanation of Reasons—based on the Survey of Two Villages in Yinchuan, Ningxia, *Social Sciences in Guizhou*, 5th Issue, 2015.

Gong Weicai, Xue Xingli, Evolution of Western Social Security Concept and Its Enlightenment—Government Function in Social Security System, *Studies on the Socialism with Chinese Characteristics*, 4th Issue, 2011.

Gu Shengzu, Xu Jin, Zheng Lingyun, Population Migration, Urbanization and Boundary Points in Western Exploitation in America, *Chinese Journal of Population Science*, 1st Issue, 2002.

Hussmanns, R., Measuring the Informal Economy: From Employment in the Informal Sector to Informal Employment, *Policy Integration Department Working Papers* No. 53, ILO, 2005.

Jiang Yongmu, Zhang Xiaolei, Shared Development and Building of A Moderately Prosperous Society in All Respects, *Leading Journal of Ideological & Theoretical Education*, 3rd Issue, 2016.

Li Qiang, "T-shaped" Social Structure and "Structural Strain", *Sociological Studies*, 2nd Issue, 2005.

Liu Ruiming, Zhao Renjie, Western Development: Growth Driver or Policy Trap—Research Based on PSM-DID Method, *China Industrial Economics*, 6th Issue, 2015.

Liu Shenglong, Wang Yahua, Hu Angang, Effect of Western Development and Regional Economic Convergence in China, *Economic Research Journal*, 9th Issue, 2009.

Luo Xiaolan, Analysis on Employment Effect of Rural Migrant Workers in Compliance with Minimum Wage Standard in China, *Journal of Finance and Economics*, 11th Issue, 2007.

Ma Xiaohong, Duan Chengrong, Guo Jing, Comparative Study of Four Categories of Floating Population, *Chinese Journal of Population Science*, 5th Issue, 2014.

Marshall, *Principles of Economics*, the Commercial Press, 1981 Edition.

Mincer, J. A., Schooling, Experience, and Earnings, NBER, http://papers.nber.Org/books/minc74-1, 1974.

Neumark, David, the Employment Effects of Recent Minimum Wage Increase: Evidence from A pre-specified Research Design, *NBER Working Paper*, No. 7171, 1999.

Norton, A., Conway, T., and Foster, M., Social Protection Concepts and Approaches: Implications for Policy and Practice in International Development, London: Overseas Development Institute, *Working Paper 143*, 2001.

Park, A., Wang, S., and Wu, G., Regional Poverty Targeting in China, *Journal of Public Economics*, Vol. 86, 2002.

Ping Xinqiao, Labor Relations in Private Enterprises, Peking University China's economy Research Center, N0. C2005001, 2005.

Qiao Xinsheng, Why We need Minimum Wage System, *Jiangnan Times*, Sept. 20, 2006.

Qin Hui, From Traditional Non-Governmental Public Welfare Organization to Modern "Third Sector"—Some Issues in Comparing the History of Chinese and Western Public Welfare Undertakings, published in *The Discussions on Ten Traditional Issues*, Fudan University Press, 2004 Edition.

Sala-I-Martin, Xavier X., I Just Ran Two Million Regressions, *The American Economic Review*, 1997, 87 (2).

She Dahuai, Liu Peiyu, Thinking Modes, Objectives and Practice Paths of Shared Development, *Social Sciences in Nanjing*, 5th Issue, 2016.

Solow, Robert M., Technical Change and the Aggregate Production Function, *The Review of Economics and Statistics*, 1957, 39 (3).

Spence, Michael, "Job Market Signaling", *Quarterly Journal of Economics*, 1973.

Sun Zhongwei, Shu Banfen, Minimum Wage Standard and Wages of Migrant Workers—Empirical Research Based on the Pearl River Delta, *Management World*, 8th Issue, 2011.

Theodore SchuHz, *Origins of Increasing Returns*, translated by Yao Zhiyong and Liu Qunyi, Peking University Press, 2001 Edition.

Wang Guogang, Urbanization: The Focus of the Transformation of Economic Development Pattern in China, *Economic Research Journal*, 12th Issue, 2010.

Wang Sangui, Guo Zihao, Discussion on the Targeted Poverty Alleviation in China, *Social Sciences in Guizhou*, 5th Issue, 2015.

Whalley, John and Xiliang Zhao, the contribution of human capital to China's Economic Growth, *NBER Working Paper 16592*, http://www.Nber.org/papers/wl6592, 2010.

Xue Zhaofeng, Inadvisability of Minimum Wage Law, *21st Century Business Herald*, Nov. 18, 2004.

Ye Jingyi, Yang Yang, Minimum Wage Standard and Income Inequality of Rural Migrant Workers—Analysis Based on Microscopic Survey Data of Rural Migrant Workers in Beijing City, *Working Paper on Development Economics Seminar*, School of Economics, Peking University, 2013.

Zhang Chewei, Changes in Rate of Return on Human Capital and Income Gap: "The Matthew Effect" and Its Policy Implications, *Economic Research Journal*, 12th Issue, 2006.

Zhang Wuchang, Minimum Wage is A Curse, *Southern Weekend*, Nov. 15, 2000.

Zhang Xiulan, Mei Zhili, Xu Yuebin, *Outline of Developmental Social Policy in China*, China Labor and Social Security Publishing House, 2007 Edition.

Zhao Manhua, Research on Scientific Connotation and Realization Mechanism of Shared Development, *On Economic Problems*, 3rd Issue, 2016.

Zheng Zhenzhen, Yang Ge, Current Status and Future Trend of the Population Flow in China, *People's Tribune*, 11th Issue, 2013.

Chapter 6
Basic Conclusion and Policy Implications

Socialism is a dynamic process no matter from its theory or practice, a process developed continuously with era. In the development history of the theory of socialism, income distribution is also a dynamic, continuously developed process advancing with times. The practice of socialism with Chinese characteristics has made new explorations of basic distribution system under the guidance of basic principles of Marxism, which become important components of socialist political economics with Chinese characteristics. We firstly review the theories of Marxist politics and western economics concerning income distribution and distribution system respectively. And discuss primary distribution system and redistribution system of China's national income on this basis. Finally, we discuss and explain new concepts and new ideas of shared development. Through the above-mentioned researches, our basic conclusion includes the following parts:

Firstly, current status of income distribution in China basically embodies the distribution principle at primary stage of socialism. Current status of income distribution in China, including labor remuneration, basically embodies the distribution principle at primary stage of socialism, i.e. distribution according to work remains the predominant mode and coexists with various other modes. After the Third Plenary Session of the Eleventh Central Committee of the CPC, "getting an equal share regardless of the work done" was abandoned, distribution was made according to labor quantity and quality, than distribution according to work was linked with labor productivity, promoted the increase in labor productivity. Since public ownership is dominant and coexists with different economic sectors, multiple distribution modes have also been derived, distribution according to work remains the predominant mode and coexists with various other modes. While considering material incentives, the relationship between labor productivity and wage should also be noticed, at the beginning of the 1990s, wage increased too rapidly, eroded profit, this was unfavorable to the expansion of reproduction and also pushed inflation. Thus, increase in labor remuneration is restricted by labor productivity, in other words, the level of labor remuneration reflects the level of labor productivity, they are mutually dependent. It's difficult to increase labor remuneration without increase in labor productivity.

C. Pei et al., *The Basic Income Distribution System of China*, China Governance System Research Series, https://doi.org/10.1007/978-981-15-3461-4_6

With the deepening of economic system reform, market degree of labor market and factor market increases gradually, labor productivity and labor remuneration are more closely related, labor productivity becomes a main factor to determine labor remuneration. That is to say, the difference in labor productivity will inevitably lead to the difference in labor remuneration. For the income distribution in China at this stage, although large income gap still exists, yet from another perspective, this includes difference in labor productivity. The income gaps between urban and rural areas, between regions in China, reflect the difference in labor productivity between different groups to certain degree. Industry is concentrated in cities and eastern coastal areas, labor productivity of industry higher than agriculture and service sector is an objective reality, and reflected in income gap, i.e. it is manifested as the difference between urban and rural areas, between regions. In other words, income gap contains the difference in labor productivity, this reflects the dominant position of labor productivity in distribution.

Secondly, objective existence of the primary stage of socialism requires two-step strategy and capital accumulation. Before reform and opening up, outcome justice at low income level cannot give full play to labor enthusiasm, is unfavorable to economic growth. Before reform and opening up, "distribution according to work" was a temporary distribution mode, "distribution according to needs" should be implemented immediately once conditions are ready. In order to avoid intensifying bourgeois right in the process of distribution according to work, equalitarianism became a symbol of distribution according to work. Such outcome justice oriented distribution mode decreased the enthusiasm of workers. In collective labor of "swarming for headlong mass action", "the same outcome regardless of doing more or less, well or badly" "hitchhiking" became a common phenomenon. In such a distribution mode, it's difficult to increase labor productivity, leading to slow economic growth, and even stagnation.

The focus of work was shifted to economic construction at the Third Plenary Session of the Eleventh Central Committee of the CPC. Promoting economic growth, increasing resident income became an overriding consideration. Two-step strategy was implemented under the ultimate goal of common prosperity, let some people and some regions become rich first, then the rich ones will help others to become rich together, and finally achieve common prosperity. In the principle of distribution according to work, increasing labor productivity becomes a breakthrough point to increase resident income, in the meantime, higher labor productivity also becomes one of the drivers of economic growth. Restricted by the level of productive forces of China at that time, in case labor productivity is a bit low, it's more practical to let regions and persons increase income by legal means if conditions permit. And it is necessary to let some persons and some regions become rich first within a period of time.

On the other side, capital accumulation also becomes an objective requirement at the primary stage of socialism. When reform and opening up was implemented, China was a developing country at low income stage, and a great agricultural country. There were rich labor force and scarce capital from the perspective of factor endowment. Although labor intensive industry is a leading industry of China after reform and opening up, but this still requires capital support. Though demographic dividend is an indispensable factor in the economic surge process of China, yet capital is also important for economic growth. At the same time, from the perspective of economic development experience, capital accumulation is one of the necessary links at early stage of economic development. Considering the development level at the primary stage of socialism in China, it is somewhat rational to accelerate capital accumulation, expand investment capacity, restrict the increase in consumption level and wage level temporarily, so as to accelerate the development in a period of time.

Thirdly, at a new stage of economic development, it's required to increase labor remuneration and highlight the integrity of efficiency and equity. At a new historical development stage, especially when economy enters a new normal, experiences economic structure adjustment and growth driver transition, the contribution role of innovations and human capital to growth becomes prominent, so increasing labor remuneration becomes an inevitable requirement, and the increase in labor productivity makes increase in labor remuneration possible. As a whole, proportion of labor remuneration in GDP is a bit low in China. In the period of 1992–1999, proportion of labor remuneration in GDP was about 52%, the proportion of labor remuneration decreased continuously after 2000, reached the lowest point 47.30% in 2011. By subject, labor remuneration of government sector increases significantly; while labor remuneration of business sector mainly shows downtrend; labor remuneration of household sector basically remains unchanged. This shows relatively slow growth of labor remuneration in the capital accumulation process of business sector. Enterprises may realize capital accumulation when growth rate of labor productivity is higher than the growth rate of labor remuneration. Meanwhile, oversupply is common in labor market, especially huge supply of migrant worker group, so labor remuneration increases slowly, the wages of rural migrant workers hardly increased before 2003. However, with continuous transition of China's population structure, demographic dividend disappears gradually, economic development enters a new stage. The relationship between labor supply and demand changes, oversupply is no longer a normal state, this promotes the increase in labor remuneration. In addition, relatively abundant capital accumulation, capital investment, introduction of machines and technological innovations promote the increase in labor productivity, and then increase in labor remuneration. From the perspective of international comparison, proportion of labor remuneration in China's GDP is lower than the level in developed countries, and even lower than the level of USA, Japan and UK at the stages similar to current development stage of China. This shows upside potential of labor remuneration in China.

New normal of economy means efficiency and fairness as two aspects of an integral whole, rather than opposite, their complementarity and compatibility are enhanced greatly. Income distribution has been improved since 2009. Resident income gap becomes narrowed continuously, the income gap within urban area, within rural area, between urban and rural areas, between regions and between industries decrease to different degrees. From the perspective of macro distribution pattern, in the period of 2009–2012, the proportion of government sector still increases, but due to significant decrease in the proportion of business sector, the proportion of household sector increases correspondingly. From the perspective of interest distribution direction in redistribution process, household sector was changed from the injured party in redistribution to beneficiary party in 2011, although the beneficial proportion is very small compared with government sector. New normal of economy requires attention to fairness while emphasizing efficiency to promote continuous and steady economic development, especially when human capital becomes the source of economic growth, fairness and efficiency have stronger integrity, complementarity and compatibility. Equal access to basic public services could reduce loss of efficiency. Because large basic education supply gap will increase unemployment risk by affecting human capital accumulation of labor; hinder economic development by affecting the stock of human capital of economically active population; hinder the expansion of middle-income group through labor productivity structure. Emphasizing fairness, and promoting equal access to basic public services will break up the difference in education supply, improve educational level and human capital in backward regions, so as to provide guarantee for the increase in labor productivity and economic growth.

On the other hand, eliminating absolute poverty is an important embodiment of common prosperity. At the same time, realizing social solidarity, enhancing society cohesion through social security system is also something inherent in common prosperity. Although with rapid economic development in China, poor population decreases greatly, comprehensive poverty alleviation still faces many difficulties. Although China's social security system has realized full coverage, yet fragmentation reduces the fairness of social security; overprotection, historical debt and aging reduce the sustainability of social security.

China is in a critical period to complete the building of a moderately prosperous society in all respects, needs to keep continuous and steady economic growth. By adding supply of essential public services, we could realize equal access to basic public services, eliminate poverty, realize fair and sustainable social security, narrow the gap in public service provision, distribute more benefits of economic development results to people, enhance social stability and cohesion, and provide new drivers for further economic development.

Fourthly, the proposal of shared development contains new policy implications. Although the level of economic development increases, China is still at primary stage of socialism, promoting economic development is still top priority. under the dual goals of guaranteeing development and narrowing income gap, shared development contains new concept. Firstly, shared development is necessarily a sharing not to impair the development efficiency of market economy. Secondly, shared development pays more attention to equality of opportunity, guaranteeing basic livelihood of the people and narrowing income gap.

Equality of opportunity includes starting point equity and process justice. More essential public services may be provided to realize equal access to basic public services, promote starting point equity. At present, great difference of essential public services exists between urban and rural areas of China, with respect to two important contents in essential public services, namely, education and medical care, the level in rural area lags behind that in urban area. From the perspective of current educational level of labor force, average educational level of rural migrant workers is junior high school, while that of urban workers is senior high school. Such gap is closely related to basic public supply, narrowing their gap is not only helpful to realize starting point equity, increase human capital of children from rural families, but also helpful to provide human capital accumulation for economic development in new normal state.

Unified factor market may be established to give full play to market allocation of factors, promote process justice. Since the reform and opening up, although factor market has been developed considerably, market degree is relatively high, market segmentation still exists. The most typical is urban-rural labor market segmentation caused by household registration system. Rural migrant workers commonly face discrimination in urban employment. In addition, the order of labor market should be further normalized, so that labor resources may be allocated by market, eliminating the allocation of labor force by non-market factors such as family background, power, relationship, getting in by the back door, so that ability and efforts may get desirable returns. In addition, degree of inequality in property is higher than the degree of inequality in income, the market of capital, resources and other factors of production is more monopolistic and administrative. For example, the income from public resources (such as coal) becomes personal income, peasants only obtain a small part of land demolition gains. Establishment of a unified market is helpful to break up the monopoly, weaken administrative intervention, play the role of narrowing income gap.

With respect to the guarantee of basic livelihood of the people, eliminating poverty, establishing fair and sustainable social security system, basic insurance and sustainability become the starting point of social security system under shared development. The goal and principles of China's social insurance reform were proposed in the 18th National Congress of CPC Report, "full coverage, basic insurance, multi-level, sustainable", "enhance fairness, adapt to mobility, guarantee sustainability". China's social insurance system does not play its due role in regulating income distribution. Because the design of social insurance system is oriented to population characteristics, does not emphasize solidarity between different groups, leads to good benefits for high income group, poor benefits of low income group, and even reverse redistribution. Basic insurance breaks up the difference between groups, is helpful to explore the establishment of a unified social security system based on residential identity. While enhancing social solidarity, this provides foundation to improve a unified planning and transfer connection of social security, is also more adaptive to labor mobility demand. On the other hand, basic insurance reduces insurance premium and financial expenditure greatly, enhances sustainability of social security funds. In case of basic insurance, multi-level purchase is optional, paths are offered for different groups to pay and purchase social insurance items according to their needs, so as to meet multi-level social security needs of different groups, realize unified equity and sustainability.

With respect to narrowing income gap, redistribution regulation may be strengthened to narrow income gap. From the perspective of macro distribution pattern, China's income distribution pattern is mainly determined by primary distribution, the role of redistribution is negligible. The process of promoting equality of opportunity embodies equal access to basic public services driven by redistribution, increase in labor productivity, emphasizing efficiency and normalizing market, so as to realize equal pay for equal work. This will narrow income gap in the process of primary distribution, especially eliminate unfair income gap. In the redistribution link, tax and public spending, transfer payment regulate high income and increase low income jointly to narrow the income gap. Tax is an important means to narrow income gap, but indirect tax is dominant in China's taxation, the proportion of direct tax which is helpful to narrow income gap is low. Low proportion of direct tax is firstly embodied in tax system, the tax system of progressive tax amount and regressive tax rate reduces the regulation force of income tax on high income group. Secondly, low proportion of direct tax is embodied in relatively low management capability. Fine management is required to give full play to direct tax. Insufficient supervisory capacity and collection capacity might lead to reverse income redistribution effect. Improving governing capacity will be helpful to the implementation of refined tax management, so as to increase regulation force of direct tax on income gap. Strengthening the regulation force of redistribution may be embodied in regulating high income, increasing low income and reducing poverty. Public spending and transfer payment become important means to enhance the income of low income group. The effect of public spending and transfer payment may be improved only by aiming at the groups "accurately". Starting from the idea of targeted poverty alleviation, the improvement of income redistribution policy requires "accurate identification, accurate support, accurate management and accurate evaluation". The regulation force of redistribution should be strengthened in two aspects "regulating high and increasing low" simultaneously, so as to improve the role of redistribution in narrowing income gap.

Annex: Review of the Discussions and Policies Concerning Income Distribution Since the Reform and Opening Up[1]

See Tables 1, 2, 3, 4, 5.

Table 1 The proposal of "common prosperity"

In 1978: Emancipate the Mind, Seek Truth From Facts, Unite and Look Forward	"We should allow some regions and enterprises and some workers and peasants to earn more and enjoy more benefits sooner than others, in accordance with their hard work and greater contributions to society." This will inevitably be an impressive example to their "neighbours" and other regions, ultimate goal "This will help the whole national economy to advance wave upon wave and help the people of all our nationalities to become prosperous in a comparatively short period."
The Third Plenary Session of the Twelfth Central Committee of the CPC in 1984: Decision of the CCCPC Concerning the Reform of Economic System	"Only when we allow some regions and enterprises and some workers and peasants to earn more and enjoy more benefits sooner than others, in accordance with their hard work and greater contributions to society, most of others will want to learn from them, this will help the whole national economy to advance wave upon wave and help more and more people to become prosperous."

(continued)

[1] With respect to the discussions and policies for income distribution since the reform and opening up, only primary distribution and redistribution contents that influence income distribution directly are reviewed, excluding contents that influence income distribution indirectly. For example, labor migration, rural infrastructure construction are not within the scope of review.

Table 1 (continued)

In 1992: *Southern Tour Talks by Deng Xiaoping*	"To take the road to socialism is to realize common prosperity step by step. Our plan is as follows: where conditions permit, some areas may develop faster than others; those that develop faster can help promote the progress of those that lag behind, until all become prosperous. If the rich keep getting richer and the poor poorer, polarization will emerge. The socialist system must and can avoid polarization. One way is for the areas that become prosperous first to support the poor ones by paying more taxes or turning in more profits to the state. Of course, this should not be done too soon. At present, we don't want to dampen the vitality of the developed areas or encourage the practice of having everyone "eat from the same big pot". We should study when to raise this question and how to settle it. I can imagine that the right time might be the end of this century, when our people are living a fairly comfortable life."

Table 2 Re-establishment of distribution according to work as dominant

In 1975: Opinions Concerning the Development of Industry	"Adhere to the principle of distribution according to work." "The so-called material incentives were rare in the past."
In 1978: Reconstruction of Enterprises Using Advanced Technology and Management Methods	"We should truly implement distribution according to work. This is not bourgeois." "Socialism should embody its superiority, not like now, still so poor after more than twenty years, why did way select socialism?"
In 1978: Adhere to the Principle of Distribution According to Work, *Selected Works of Deng Xiaoping* Volume 3, p. 101	The starting point, necessity of distribution according to work and how to realize distribution according to work are fully explained in the Adhere to the Principle of Distribution According to Work. Which provides theoretical basis for the implementation and promotion of distribution according to work
In 1980: Reform of the Party and State Leadership System	"We advocate distribution according to work, admit material benefits, and will strive for material benefits of all the people. Everyone should have its own material benefits, but this does not advocate everyone to be money-oriented without considering the state, collective and others. Otherwise, what's the difference between socialism and capitalism?"
The Third Plenary Session of the Twelfth Central Committee of the CPC in 1984: Decision of the CCCPC Concerning the Reform of Economic System	"The socialist principle of distribution according to work will be further implemented, a major step has been taken in this aspect, i.e. fund for enterprise employees is determined by the enterprise according to its operation conditions. …Within an enterprise, wage gap should be widened to make difference, so as to fully embody rewarding the diligent and punishing the lazy, rewarding the good and fining the bad, fully embody more pay for more work, less pay for less work, fully embody the difference between brainwork and physical labor, between complex labor and simple labor, skilled labor and unskilled labor, heavy work and non-heavy work. Particularly a bit low remuneration for brain work should be changed now. State organs and institutions should also reform wage system, the principle of reform is to link staff salaries with personal responsibility and performance closely. During the reform of wage system in enterprises, state organs and public institutions, the reform of labor system should also be quickened."

Table 3 The evolution of distribution according to work as predominant mode and coexisting with various other modes

The 13th National Congress of CPC Report in 1987: Advance Along the Road of Socialism with Chinese characteristics	"Implement multiple distribution modes and correct distribution policy in which distribution according to work is dominant. It's impossible to implement single distribution mode at the primary stage of socialism. We must adhere to such principle that, distribution according to work is dominant, other distribution modes are supplementary. In addition to the main mode of distribution according to work and individual earned income, if an enterprise issues bonds to raise money, interest will be obtained from creditor's rights; with the emerging of share economy, share dividend will appear; the income of enterprise operator includes partial risk compensation; certain number of labor force employed by privately-operated enterprise will bring non-labor income to the entrepreneur. These incomes mentioned above should be permitted as long as they are legal."
The Third Plenary Session of the Fourteenth Central Committee of the CPC in 1993: Decision of the CPC Central Committee Regarding a Number of Issues Concerning the Establishment of a Socialist Market Economy	"We should adhere to the following principle for personal income distribution: distribution according to work remains the predominant mode and coexists with various other modes, …Competitive mechanism should be introduced into individual labor remuneration of workers to break/abandon equalitarian, implement more pay for more work, enlarge the wage gap reasonably. We should still encourage some regions and some persons to become rich first through honest work and legal operation, advocate those who become rich first to drive and help others, and realize common prosperity step by step." "The state protects all legitimate incomes and properties of legal persons and residents according to law, encourages saving and investment behaviors of urban and rural residents, permits capital and other factors of production that belong to individuals to participate in income distribution."
The 15th National Congress of CPC Report in 1997: Hold High the Great Banner of Deng Xiaoping Theory for an All-Round Advancement of the Cause of Building Socialism with Chinese Characteristics into the 21st Century	"We should adhere to the system in which distribution according to work remains the predominant mode and coexists with various other modes. Combine distribution according to work with distribution according to productive factors, give priority to efficiency with due consideration to fairness, optimize allocation of resources, promote economic development and keep social stability. Protect legitimate income according to law, permit and encourage some persons to become rich first through honest work and legal operation, permit and encourage capital, technology and other factors of production to participate in income distribution." "Ban illegal income, punish those who embezzle publicly-owned property and seek profits by illegal means such as tax dodge, tax evasion and power-for-money deal, uncompromisingly according to the law. Rectify unreasonable incomes, make correction on those who get additional individual incomes relying on industry monopoly and some special conditions."

(continued)

Table 3 (continued)

The 16th National Congress of CPC Report in 2002: Build a Well-off Society in an All-Round Way and Create a New Situation in Building Socialism with Chinese Characteristics	We must respect work, knowledge, competent people and creation. This should be an important policy of the Party and state to be conscientiously implemented in society at large. We need to respect and protect all work that is good for the people and society. All work that contributes to the socialist modernization drive in China, physical or mental and simple or complicated, is glorious and should be acknowledged and respected. All investors at home or from overseas should be encouraged to carry out business activities in China's development. All legitimate income, from work or not, should be protected. It is improper to judge whether people are politically progressive or backward simply by whether they own property or how much property they own. But rather, we should judge them mainly by their political awareness, state of mind and performance, by how they have acquired and used their property, and by how they have contributed to the cause of building socialism with Chinese characteristics through their work." "We should establish the principle that labor, capital, technology, managerial expertise and other production factors participate in the distribution of income in accordance with their respective contributions, thereby improving the system under which distribution according to work is dominant and a variety of modes of distribution coexist." "We should standardize the order of income distribution, properly regulate the excessively high income of some monopoly industries and outlaw illegal gains."
The 17th National Congress of CPC Report in 2007: Hold High the Great Banner of Socialism with Chinese Characteristics and Strive for New Victories in Building A Moderately Prosperous Society in All Respects	"We will adhere to and improve the system whereby distribution according to work remains the predominant mode and coexists with various other modes. We will improve the distribution system to allow factors of production such as labor, capital, technology and managerial expertise to have a rightful share according to their respective contribution." "Conditions will be created to enable more citizens to have property income." "We will protect lawful incomes, regulate excessively high incomes and ban illegal gains." "Break business monopolies, create equal opportunities."

(continued)

Table 3 (continued)

The 18th National Congress of CPC Report in 2012: Firmly March on the Path of Socialism with Chinese Characteristics and Strive to Complete the Building of A Moderately Prosperous Society in All Respects	"We should improve the primary distribution system to allow factors of production such as labor, capital, technology and managerial expertise to have their due share of income according to their respective contribution; and we should take speedy steps to improve the mechanism of secondary distribution regulating income distribution mainly through taxation, social security, and transfer payments." "We should deepen reform of the wage and salary system in enterprises, government bodies and public institutions, promote collective bargaining on wages in enterprises, and protect income earned through work." "We should increase proprietary individual income through multiple channels." "We should improve the way in which income is distributed, protect lawful income, …and prohibit illicit income."
The Third Plenary Session of the Eighteenth Central Committee of the CPC in 2013: the Decision on Major Issues Concerning Comprehensively Deepening Reforms	"We will improve the system in which the returns for capital, knowledge, technology, managerial expertise and other production factors are determined by the market. We will open up channels for investment and lease services, optimize the mechanism of return for investors of listed companies, and protect the legitimate rights and interests of the investors, particularly the medium and small investors, so as to increase the citizens' property incomes via various channels." "We will regulate income distribution procedures and improve the regulatory systems and mechanisms and policy system for income distribution, establish an individual income and property information system, protect legitimate incomes, regulate excessively high incomes, redefine and clear away hidden incomes, outlaw illegal."

Table 4 Redistribution policy under efficiency and fairness 1—regulating income gap

The Third Plenary Session of the Twelfth Central Committee of the CPC in 1984: Decision of the CCCPC Concerning the Reform of Economic System	We put forward redistribution policy for some regions and persons while encouraging some regions and persons to become rich first under the concept of common prosperity "Provide social relief for those who are old, weak, ill or disabled, and those have no kin and cannot support themselves, support the people who are not rich actively, implement special preferential policies in some economically backward old revolutionary bases, ethnic minority communities, frontier and remote areas and other poverty-stricken areas, and provide necessary material and technical support."
The Third Plenary Session of the Fourteenth Central Committee of the CPC in 1993: Decision of the CPC Central Committee Regarding a Number of Issues Concerning the Establishment of a Socialist Market Economy	Efficiency and fairness: "embody the principle of giving priority to efficiency with due consideration to fairness." Narrowing income gap: "establish a system of declaration of individual incomes for tax payment gradually, strengthen the collection and management of individual income tax according to law, levy estate and gift tax in due time. Avoid growing income disparity due to extremely high income of a few people via distribution policy and tax regulation."
The Fifth Plenary Session of the Fourteenth Central Committee of the CPC in 1995: Proposal of the CPC Central Committee for the Ninth Five-Year Plan for National Economic and Social Development and the Long-Range Objectives to the Year 2010	"We should earnestly implement national poverty alleviation plan and policy measures, intensify poverty alleviation work, basically solve the problem of food and clothing of seventy million population still in poverty by 2000. Continue to add, manage and use poverty alleviation funds, mobilize the whole society extensively to care and support poverty alleviation efforts. Solve the problems of urban low income residents and rural poor population who have difficulties in providing for themselves earnestly."
The 15th National Congress of CPC Report in 1997: Hold High the Great Banner of Deng Xiaoping Theory for an All-Round Advancement of the Cause of Building Socialism with Chinese Characteristics into the 21st Century	Efficiency and fairness: "we should give priority to efficiency with due consideration to fairness, optimize allocation of resources, promote economic development and keep social stability." Narrowing income gap: "regulate extremely high income, improve individual income tax system, levy estate tax and other new types of tax. Normalize income distribution, enable income gap to be reasonable, prevent growing income disparity." "We should implement policies to guarantee basic living of urban residents in difficulty. The state will take allaround measures to intensify poverty alleviation, basically solve the problem of food and clothing of rural poor population by the end of this century." Macro distribution pattern: "we should deal with the distribution relationship between state, enterprises and individuals and between central and local governments properly, increase the proportion of government revenue in Gross National Product and the proportion of central government revenue in national government revenue gradually, adapt to structural changes of ownership and the transformation of government functions, adjust revenue and expenditure structure, establish stable and balanced national finance."

(continued)

Table 4 (continued)

16th National Congress of CPC Report in 2002: Build a Well-off Society in an All-Round Way and Create a New Situation in Building Socialism with Chinese Characteristics	Efficiency and fairness: "We should give priority to efficiency with due consideration to fairness, earnestly implementing the distribution policy while advocating the spirit of devotion and guarding against an excessive disparity in income while opposing equalitarianism. In primary distribution, we should pay more attention to efficiency, bringing the market forces into play and encouraging part of the people to become rich first through honest labor and lawful operations. In redistribution, we should pay more attention to fairness and strengthen the function of the government in regulating income distribution to narrow the gap if it is too wide." Narrowing income gap: "Bearing in mind the objective of common prosperity, we should try to raise the proportion of the middle-income group and increase the income of the low-income group." "We should intensify our efforts to fight poverty through development, build on the achievements we have scored in this regard, strive to accomplish the task of providing adequate food and clothing for the impoverished rural population and gradually enable them to lead a well-off life."
The Third Plenary Session of the Sixteenth Central Committee of the CPC in 2003: Decision of the CCCPC on Some Major Issues Concerning the Improvement of Socialist Market Economy System	Narrowing income gap: "we should deepen rural tax and fee reform. Rural tax and fee reform is a great move on alleviating peasants' burden and deepening rural reform. We should improve the policies for rural tax and fee reform pilot, cancel tax on special agricultural products, quicken comprehensive coordinated reforms of county and township government institutions. And rural compulsory education system etc. We should reduce agricultural tax rate gradually, reduce peasants' burden effectively based on pilot work."
The Fifth Plenary Session of the Sixteenth Central Committee of the CPC in 2005: CPC Central Committee Recommendations for the 11th Five-Year Plan for Economic and Social Development	Narrowing income gap: "we should make vigorous efforts to raise the income of low-income groups level, expand the proportion of middle-income earners gradually, regulate extremely high income effectively, and normalize personal income distribution order, make efforts to mitigate widening trend of income distribution gap between regions and between social members of sectors." "increase minimum living security and minimum wage standard gradually on the basis of economic development, solve housing, medical care and child education difficulties of low income earners earnestly."
The Sixth Plenary Session of the Sixteenth Central Committee of the CPC in 2006: Decision of the CPC Central Committee on Some Major Issues Regarding the Building of a Harmonious Socialist Society	Narrowing income gap: "we should continue to promote Western Development, revitalize old industrial bases in Northeast China, promote rising of central region, encourage initiative development of Eastern Region, we should form regional industry structure of reasonable work division, distinct characteristics and complementary advantages, promote joint development of all regions. Strengthen the support for underdeveloped areas and depressed areas. We should use central finance transfer payment funds mainly in central and western regions, improve infrastructure and education, health, culture and other public service facilities in central and western regions as soon as possible, and narrow essential public service gap between regions gradually. Strengthen transfer payment to old revolutionary base areas, minority areas, border areas, poverty-stricken areas and main grain producing areas, mineral resource development areas, areas of heavy ecological protection tasks, and enhance our support for minorities with less population." "Strengthen assistance for poverty-stricken population, improve the systems for urban minimum living security, rural five guarantees supporting, poor households assistance, assistance for victims of natural calamity, assistance for urban vagrants and beggars etc."

(continued)

Table 4 (continued)

The 17th National Congress of CPC Report in 2007: Hold High the Great Banner of Socialism with Chinese Characteristics and Strive for New Victories in Building A Moderately Prosperous Society in All Respects	Efficiency and fairness: "A proper balance will be struck between efficiency and equity in both primary distribution and redistribution, with particular emphasis on equity in redistribution." Narrowing income gap: "we should make vigorous efforts to raise the income of low-income groups, increase poverty-alleviation aid and minimum wage gradually", "We will protect lawful incomes, regulate excessively high incomes and ban illegal gains. We will increase transfer payments, intensify the regulation of incomes through taxation, break business monopolies, create equal opportunities, and overhaul income distribution practices with a view to gradually reversing the growing income disparity." Macro distribution pattern: "We will gradually increase the share of personal income in the distribution of national income, and raise that of work remuneration in primary distribution."
The Fifth Plenary Session of the Seventeenth Central Committee in 2010: Proposal of the CPC Central Committee for Formulating the Twelfth Five-Year Plan	Narrowing income gap: "we should increase minimum wage standard gradually, guarantee normal growth and payment of staff salaries. Normalize distribution order, enhance the regulating effect of tax on income distribution, regulate extremely high income effectively, make efforts to reverse the yawning income gap between urban and rural areas, between regions, between industries and between members of society. Improve public servant wage system, deepen income distribution system reform of public institutions."
The 18th National Congress of CPC Report in 2012: Firmly March on the Path of Socialism with Chinese Characteristics and Strive to Complete the Building of A Moderately Prosperous Society in All Respects	Efficiency and fairness: "A proper balance should be struck between efficiency and fairness in both primary and secondary distribution, with particular emphasis on fairness in secondary distribution. We should improve the primary distribution system to allow factors of production such as labor, capital, technology and managerial expertise to have their due share of income according to their respective contribution." Narrowing income gap: "we should take speedy steps to improve the mechanism of redistribution regulating income distribution mainly through taxation, social security, and transfer payments." Macro distribution pattern: "To ensure that the people share in the fruits of development, we must deepen reform of the income distribution system, and increase individual income in step with economic development and work remuneration in step with improvement in labor productivity, and we should raise the share of individual income in the distribution of national income and increase the share of work remuneration in primary distribution."
The Fifth Plenary Session of the Eighteenth Central Committee of the CPC in 2015: Recommendations for the 13th Five-Year Plan for Economic and Social Development	Narrowing income gap: "all rural residents living below the current poverty line will be lifted out of poverty, and poverty will be eliminated in all poor counties and regions." "We will give more transfer payment to old revolutionary base areas, ethnic autonomous areas, border areas and poverty-stricken areas. Provide more support for specific groups in special difficulties." "We will take targeted measures to alleviate and eliminate poverty in light of local conditions, increase actual effect of poverty alleviation." "We will narrow the income gap, increase the proportion of middle-income population." "Implement policies favorable to narrow income gap, increase the income of low-income workers obviously, expand the proportion of middle-income earners." Macro distribution pattern: "increase individual income in step with economic development and work remuneration in step with improvement in labor productivity, increase urban and rural resident income continuously. Adjust the pattern of national income distribution, normalize primary distribution, intensify the regulation effect of redistribution."

Table 5 Redistribution policy under efficiency and fairness 2-equal access to basic public services

The Third Plenary Session of the Fourteenth Central Committee of the CPC in 1993: Decision of the CPC Central Committee Regarding a Number of Issues Concerning the Establishment of a Socialist Market Economy	Social security: "establish multi-level social security system", "social security system includes social insurance, social relief, social welfare, veteran benefit and placement, social mutual aid, personal savings accumulation guarantee. Social security policies should be unified, and management should be legalized. Social security level should adapt to development level of social productive forces and affordability in all aspects of China. Social security methods of urban and rural residents should be differentiated. We advocate social mutual aid. Develop commercial insurance industry, as a supplement to social insurance." Pension and unemployment insurance: "we should improve enterprise pension and unemployment insurance system". Urban employees' pension and medical insurance premiums should be assumed jointly by organizations and individuals, we should combine social pooling with individual accounts. Further improve unemployment insurance system, insurance premium should be paid by enterprises unifiedly according to certain proportion of total staff wages. Generally establish enterprise on-job injury insurance system. Family security should be dominant for peasants' pension, in combination with community support. Personal savings accumulation pension insurance may also be implemented according to the will of peasants if conditions permit. Rural cooperative medical service system should be developed and improved
The Fifth Plenary Session of the Fourteenth Central Committee of the CPC in 1995: Proposal of the CPC Central Committee for the Ninth Five-Year Plan for National Economic and Social Development and the Long-Range Objectives to the Year 2010	Social security: "during the 'Ninth Five-Year Plan', we should quicken the reform of pension, unemployment and medical insurance systems, initially form multi-level social security system that combines social insurance, social relief, social welfare, veteran benefit and placement, social mutual aid and personal savings accumulation guarantee. We should formulate corresponding policies, protect legal rights and interests of women, minors and the aged, the disabled and other special social groups earnestly."
The 15th National Congress of CPC Report in 1997: Hold High the Great Banner of Deng Xiaoping Theory for an All-Round Advancement of the Cause of Building Socialism with Chinese Characteristics into the 21st Century	Social security: "establish social security system, implement pension, medical insurance systems that combine social pooling and individual accounts, improve unemployment insurance and social relief system, provide the most fundamental social security. Establish urban housing provident fund, quicken the reform of housing system."
The 16th National Congress of CPC Report in 2002: Build a Well-off Society in an All-Round Way and Create a New Situation in Building Socialism with Chinese Characteristics	Social security: "Establishing and improving a social security system compatible with the level of economic development constitutes an important guarantee for social stability and long-term peace and order in the country. We should stick to and improve the basic old-age pension and medical insurance systems for urban workers, combining socially pooled funds with personal contributions. We should improve the systems of unemployment insurance and subsistence allowances for urban residents. We should try various channels to raise and accumulate social security funds. Reasonable standards for social security benefits should be set in light of local conditions. We should develop social relief and welfare programs in urban and rural areas. Wherever conditions permit, we should try to establish systems of old-age pensions, medical insurance and subsistence allowances in rural areas." "Further efforts should be made to develop public service facilities, better people's living environment and expand community services in order to make life easier for people. We should establish a medical service and health care system that meets the requirements of the new situation. We should improve medical and health conditions in rural areas and the medical and health care for urban and rural residents."

(continued)

Table 5 (continued)

The Third Plenary Session of the Sixteenth Central Committee of the CPC in 2003: Decision of the CCCPC on Some Major Issues Concerning the Improvement of Socialist Market Economy System	Social security: "we should quicken the construction of social security system corresponding to the level of economic development. Improve basic pension insurance system for enterprise employees, persist in the combination of social pooling and individual accounts, provide sufficient funding for personal accounts gradually. Include workers employed in urban areas in basic pension insurance. Establish and consummate pension insurance adjustment fund at provincial level, implement pooling at provincial level gradually based on perfect pooling at city level, implement national pooling of the fundamental part of basic pension when conditions permit. Improve unemployment insurance system, enable basic life security of laid-off workers from state-owned enterprises to be in line with unemployment insurance. Continue to improve synchronized reform of basic medical insurance system for urban employees, health care and pharmaceutical production and distribution system, expand the coverage of basic medical insurance, improve social medical assistance and multi-level medical security system. Continue to promote work-related injury and maternity insurance of employees. Explore social security system reform of government organs and institutions actively. Improve minimum living standard security system of urban residents, determine guarantee standard and mode reasonably. Adopt multiple methods including transfer of some state-owned assets to enrich social security fund according to law. Intensify the collection of social security fund, expand collection coverage, normalize fund supervision, ensure fund security. Encourage enterprises to establish supplementary insurance if conditions permit, develop commercial pension, medical insurance actively. Family should be dominant in rural pension security, which should be combined with community security and national relief. Rural minimum living standard security system should be explored and established where conditions permit." Education: "we should deepen education system reform. …Promote education innovation, optimize education structure, reform training mode, improve education quality, develop an education system corresponding to economic and social development requirements. Consolidate and improve rural compulsory education management system in which management by government at county level is dominant. Implement full employment and teacher qualifications access system. Improve and normalize the education investment system in which government investment is dominant, funds are raised through multiple channels, form joint development pattern of public schools and private schools. Improve the system of subsidizing students from poor households by state and society." Medical care: "we should deepen public health system reform. Strengthen government function of public health management, establish a medical and health system corresponding to socialist market economy system. Strengthen the construction of public health facilities, fully utilize, integrate existing resources, establish and consummate disease information network system, disease prevention and control system and medical rescue system, increase public health service level and response capability to emergency public health events. Quicken urban medical and health system reform. Improve rural health and medical conditions, establish new rural cooperative medical system to provide medical assistance for poor peasants actively. Give play to the advantages of integrated traditional Chinese and western medicine. Keep environmental sanitation, set up public health awareness. Improve health supervision system, ensure safety of food, drugs and medical care of the people."
The Fifth Plenary Session of the Sixteenth Central Committee of the CPC in 2005: CPC Central Committee Recommendations for the 11th Five-Year Plan for Economic and Social Development	"We should develop rural public utilities vigorously. Quicken the development of rural culture education undertakings, popularize and consolidate rural nine-year compulsory education, exempt rural students from miscellaneous expenses, provide textbook free of charge and subsidy for boarding and living cost of students from poor family. Strengthen the construction of rural public health and basic medical service system, establish new rural cooperative medical system, strengthen the prevention and control of zoonotic diseases. Implement reward and support system for rural households subject to family planning and 'Fewer children equals faster prosperity' poverty alleviation project. Develop distance learning and broadcast TV 'to every village'. Increase investment in rural infrastructure construction, quicken rural road construction, develop rural communication, continue to improve rural power grid, solve rural drinking water difficulties and safety issues gradually. Popularize rural biogas vigorously, and develop clean energy suitable for rural features actively."
The Sixth Plenary Session of the Sixteenth Central Committee of the CPC in 2006: Decision of the CPC Central Committee on Some Major Issues Regarding the Building of a Harmonious Socialist Society	Essential public services: "improve public finance system, realize equal access to basic public services gradually. Improve public finance system, adjust revenue and expenditure structure, invest more financial fund into public service field, increase fiscal investment in education, health, culture, employment and reemployment service, social security, eco-environment, public infrastructure, public security etc."

(continued)

Table 5 (continued)

The 17th National Congress of CPC Report in 2007: Hold High the Great Banner of Socialism with Chinese Characteristics and Strive for New Victories in Building A Moderately Prosperous Society in All Respects	Essential public services: "Accelerate the development of social programs and improve every aspect of the people's well-being. The modern system of national education will be further improved, a basic system for lifelong education will be in place, the educational attainment of the whole nation will rise to a much higher level, and the training of innovative personnel will be improved markedly. Employment will be further expanded. A basic system of social security will cover both urban and rural residents so that everyone is assured of basic living standards. A reasonable and orderly pattern of income distribution will be basically in place, with middle-income people making up the majority and absolute poverty basically eliminated. Everyone will have access to basic medical and health services. The system of social management will be further improved." Education: "Give priority to education and turn China into a country rich in human resources. Education is the cornerstone of national rejuvenation, and equal access to education provides an important underpinning for social equity. …We will optimize the educational structure, promote balanced development of compulsory education, move faster toward universal access to senior secondary education, vigorously develop vocational education, and improve the quality of higher education. We will also attach importance to pre-school education and care about special education. …We will continue to run education on a nonprofit basis, increase government spending on education, regulate the collection of education-related fees, support the development of education in poverty-stricken and ethnic autonomous areas, improve the system of financial aid to students, and ensure that children from poor families and of rural migrant workers in cities enjoy equal access to compulsory education as other children. We will build up the ranks of teachers, with the emphasis on improving the quality of teachers in rural areas. We will encourage and regulate educational programs run by nongovernmental sectors. Distance learning and continuing education will be promoted to make ours a society in which every citizen is committed to learning and pursues lifelong learning." Social insurance: "Accelerate the establishment of a social security system covering both urban and rural residents and guarantee their basic living conditions. …We will step up the building of a sound social security system that is based on social insurance, assistance and welfare, with basic old-age pension, basic medical care and subsistence allowances as its backbone, and supplemented by charity and commercial insurance. We will promote reform of basic old-age insurance systems in enterprises, Party and government organs and public institutions and explore ways to set up an old-age insurance system in rural areas. We will promote the development of basic medical insurance systems for urban workers and residents and a new type of cooperative medical care system in rural areas. We will improve the system of subsistence allowances for both urban and rural residents and gradually increase such allowances. We will improve the systems of unemployment, workers' compensation and maternity insurances. We will upgrade management of social security funds to higher-level authorities and work out unified methods for transferring social security accounts nationwide. We will provide more social security funds through various means and strengthen their oversight and management to maintain and increase their value. We will improve social assistance. We will do a good job providing special assistance to families of martyrs and servicemen and helping demobilized military personnel return to civilian life. We will promote programs for the disabled in a humanitarian spirit. We will develop more programs for the elderly. We will intensify our efforts in disaster prevention and reduction. We will improve the low-rent housing system and speed up resolution of the housing difficulties of low-income families in urban areas." Health care: "Establish a basic medical and health care system and improve the health of the whole nation. …We must maintain the public welfare nature of public medical and health care services, always put disease prevention first, center on rural areas and attach equal importance to traditional Chinese medicine and Western medicine. We will separate government administration from medical institutions, management from operation, medical care from pharmaceuticals, and for-profit from nonprofit operations. We will increase government responsibilities and spending, improve the national health policy, and encourage greater participation of nongovernmental sectors so as to develop systems of public health services, medical services, medical security and medicine supply to provide both urban and rural residents with safe, effective, convenient and affordable medical and health services. We will improve the system to prevent and control the outbreak of major diseases and enhance our capacity to respond to public health emergencies. We will improve the three-tier rural health care network spanning the county, township and village and the urban community-based health care system, and deepen reform of public hospitals. We will set up a national system for basic pharmaceuticals to ensure their supply. We will support the development of traditional Chinese medicine and the folk medicines of ethnic minorities. We will work harder to improve the professional ethics and style of work of health workers and the quality of medical services. We must ensure food and drug safety."

(continued)

Table 5 (continued)

The Third Plenary Session of the Seventeenth Central Committee of the CPC in 2008: Decision of CPC Central Committee on A Number of Important Issues concerning the Rural Reform and Development	"We should make a unified planning of urban and rural infrastructure construction and public services, improve financial support in an all-round way to guarantee the level of rural public utilities, establish urban and rural unified public service system gradually. Make a unified planning of urban and rural labor employment, quicken the construction of unified urban and rural human resource market, guide peasants in outgoing employment orderly, encourage peasants to engage in nearby transfer employment, support rural migrant workers back home to run business. Protect the rights and interests of rural migrant workers, enable rural migrant workers to enjoy equivalent benefits as urban residents in aspects of labor remuneration, child schooling, public health, house rent and purchase etc. gradually, improve rural migrant workers labor conditions, guarantee production safety, expand the coverage of work-related injuries, medical care, pension insurance for rural migrant workers, formulate and implement pension insurance relationship transfer and renewal methods for rural migrant workers as soon as possible. Unify urban and rural social administration, promote the reform of household registration system, relax restrictions of permanent residency conditions in medium-and small-sized cities, enable peasants who have stable employment and residence in urban areas to be transformed to urban residents orderly. We should promote innovations in floating population service and management system. Expand county development autonomy, increase general transfer payment for counties, promote matching of financial resources with duties and responsibilities, enhance economic vitality and strength in counties."
The 18th National Congress of CPC Report in 2012: Firmly March on the Path of Socialism with Chinese Characteristics and Strive to Complete the Building of A Moderately Prosperous Society in All Respects	Essential public services: "Equal access to basic public services should be generally achieved. The educational level of the entire population should be significantly raised and training of innovative professionals markedly improved. China should have a large pool of competent professionals and be rich in human resources, and it should basically modernize its education. There should be more employment opportunities. Income gaps should be narrowed, middle-income groups should keep growing, and the number of people living below the poverty line should drop by a large margin. Social security should cover all the people. Everyone should have access to basic medical and public health services. The system of housing for low-income groups should take shape, and there should be social harmony and stability." Education: "Work hard to run education to the satisfaction of the people. …We should develop preschool education, promote balanced development of nine-year compulsory education, make senior secondary education basically universal, accelerate development of modern vocational education, and bring out the full potential for development of higher education. We should actively develop continuing education, improve the system of lifelong education, and build a learning society. We should vigorously promote fairness in education, and ensure balanced allocation of educational resources with a focus on rural, remote, poor and ethnic minority areas. We should support special education, increase subsidies to students from poor families, and ensure that children of rural migrant workers in cities have equal access to education. All this is designed to help all children gain required knowledge and skills. We should encourage and guide nongovernmental entities to run educational programs. We should strengthen the ranks of teachers, and enhance their work ethics and professional competence as well as their sense of honor and responsibility as teachers." Social security: "to promote the construction of urban and rural social security system unifiedly, we should institute a complete, multi-tiered and sustainable system for providing basic social security for both the urban and rural population, with emphasis on making the system more equitable and sustainable and ensuring the smooth transfer of social security accounts between localities. We should reform and improve the social insurance system for enterprises as well as government bodies and public institutions, integrate the basic old-age insurance and basic medical insurance systems for non-working urban residents and the rural population, provide sufficient funding for personal accounts for old-age insurance in a phased way, place basic pensions under unified national planning, and establish mechanisms for setting standards on social security benefits and regularly adjusting them that give due consideration to the interests of people from all walks of life. We should widen channels for raising money for social security funds, introduce a system to manage investment operations of social insurance funds, and ensure that these funds are safe and appreciate over time. We should improve the social assistance system and the social welfare system, support the development of charities, and ensure preferential treatment to entitled groups. We should put in place a housing system that combines market supply and government support, strengthen construction and management of low-income housing, and better meet poor families' basic housing needs." Health care: "Improve people's health. …We should improve the medical insurance system that covers the whole population, establish a mechanism to provide insurance and aid in treating major and very serious diseases, and improve mechanisms for handling public health emergencies and for preventing and controlling major diseases. We should consolidate the system for using basic drugs. We should improve the rural medical and health service network at county, township and village levels and the system of urban community health services, deepen reform of public hospitals, and encourage the development of private hospitals. We should support the development of traditional Chinese medicine and the traditional medicine of ethnic minorities. We should ensure that medical personnel provide better services and improve their work ethics. We should reform and improve institutions and mechanisms for managing and supervising food and drug safety."

(continued)

Table 5 (continued)

The Second Plenary Session of the Eighteenth Central Committee of the CPC in 2013: the Decision on Major Issues Concerning Comprehensively Deepening Reforms	Essential public services: "We must deepen social structural reform by centering on safeguarding and improving the people's wellbeing and promoting social fairness and justice. We should reform the income distribution system and promote common prosperity. We should promote system innovation in the social sector, promote equal access to basic public services, and step up efforts to form a scientific and effective social management system so that our society is full of vigor, but also harmonious and orderly." "We will make overall plans for developing urban and rural infrastructure and communities, and promote equitable access to basic public services in urban and rural areas." Education: "Deepening the comprehensive reforms in the area of education. …We will vigorously promote educational equality, improve the financial assistance system for students from families with financial difficulties, and establish an effective mechanism to expand the coverage of high-quality education resources by means of information technology, so as to gradually narrow the gaps between different regions, between urban and rural areas and between different schools. We will make a balanced allocation of compulsory education resources between urban and rural areas, set unified standards for the construction of public schools, exchange principals and teachers among different public schools, and abolish the practice of establishing key schools or classes, so as to overcome the problem caused by choosing schools and reduce the academic burden on students. We will quicken steps in the development of a modern vocational education system, deepen the integration of production and education and cooperation between schools and enterprises, and train high-caliber workers and technical talents. We will make innovations in the mechanism of higher learning institutions that trains talents, encouraging them to strive for specialty and excellence. We will boost the reform and development of pre-school, special and continued education. …We will further push ahead with the separation of government administration, school management and educational evaluation, delegate greater power to provincial governments in making their overall educational development plans and to schools to make their own decisions about school affairs, and improve the internal governance structure of the schools. We will strengthen the state's function in supervising education, and entrust social organizations to carry out evaluation and monitoring of education. We will improve the systems of government subsidies, government services purchase, student loans, scholarships and incentive for donation to education, and encourage social funds to be channeled into education." Social security: "Instituting a fairer and more sustainable social security system. We will adhere to the basic old-age insurance system that combines social pools with individual accounts, improve the individual accounts system, complete the incentive mechanism in which those who contribute more will get more, guarantee the rights and interests of the insured, place basic old-age pension under unified national planning, and uphold the principle of balance based on actuarial mathematics. We will push forward the reform of the old-age insurance system for government organs and public institutions. We will integrate the basic old-age insurance and medical care insurance systems for urban and rural residents, and expedite the balanced development of the minimum living allowance system in both urban and rural areas. We will establish and improve a social security benefits calculation and regular adjustment mechanism that gives appropriate consideration to various groups. We will improve policies on the transfer and continuation of social insurance, extend insurance coverage to more groups of people, and reduce the social insurance premiums appropriately and in a timely manner. We will study and work out a policy to progressively raise the retirement age. We will speed up the improvement of a social security management system and service network. We will improve a housing security and supply system consistent with our national conditions, create an open and standard housing provident fund system, and improve the regulations on the withdrawal, use and supervision of the provident fund. …We will respond actively to the aging of the population, quicken steps in the establishment of a social endowment service system and development of the service industry for the elderly. We will improve the caring service system for children, women and seniors left behind in the rural areas and a classified security system to protect the rights and interests of the disabled and children in difficulties." Health care: "Deepening reform in medicine and health care. We will proceed with a comprehensive reform in medical security, medical care, public health, and the medicine supply and regulatory system. We will deepen the comprehensive reform of grass-roots medical and healthcare institutions, and improve the network of urban and rural basic medical and healthcare services. We will accelerate the reform of public hospitals, ensure the government shoulders its responsibilities in this regard, and set up a scientific medical treatment assessment mechanism and a personnel training and salary system suited to the characteristics of this sector. We will improve the rational modes of graded diagnosis and treatment, establishing a service contract between community doctors and residents. We will make full use of information means to promote the downward flow of high-quality medical sources, and strengthen the regional integration of public medical service resources. We will abolish the practice of raising medicine prices to make up for the shortfall in hospital funds, rationalize the prices of medical services and medicines, and establish an appropriate compensation mechanism. We will reform the methods of insurance payouts, and extend the medical insurance system to all the people. We will speed up the completion of the medical insurance and medical assistance system against fatal and serious diseases. We will improve the policies and mechanisms for the development of traditional Chinese medicine. We will encourage private funds to flow to medical services, first supporting them to flow to not-for-profit medical institutions. We will allow private funds to invest directly in services that are short of resources or are to meet diverse demands, and to participate in the reform and restructuring of public hospitals in various forms. We will allow doctors to work for more than one hospital, and allow private medical institutions to be included in designated medical insurance institutions."

(continued)

Table 5 (continued)

The Fifth Plenary Session of the Eighteenth Central Committee of the CPC in 2015: Recommendations for the 13th Five-Year Plan for Economic and Social Development	Essential public services: "employment, education, culture, social security, medical care, housing and other public service systems should be more complete, the level of equal access to basic public services should be enhanced steadily." "Persist in inclusive, basic insurance, equal access, sustainable direction, firstly solve the most direct, most realistic issues of interests most concerned by people, enhance government responsibilities, increase public service co-construction capability and sharing level." "Strengthen compulsory education, employment service, social security, basic medical care and public health, public culture, environmental protection and other essential public services, make efforts to realize full coverage." "Promote balanced allocation of urban and rural public resources, improve long-acting mechanism of the investment in rural infrastructure, put development priorities of social undertakings in rural areas and the cities and towns that accept more agricultural transfer population, promote the extension of urban public services to rural areas. Increase new socialist rural construction level, carry out rural living environment improvement initiative, provide more protection for traditional village houses and towns and villages with rich historical and cultural heritage, construct beautiful and livable villages." Education: "improve education quality. …Promote balanced development of compulsory education, improve teaching quality in an all-round way. Popularize education at senior high school stage, exempt secondary vocational education from miscellaneous expenses in a classified way step by step, firstly exempt archived students of poor families from miscellaneous expenses in ordinary senior high school. We should develop preschool education, encourage inclusive kindergarten development. Improve aid modes, cover all students from poor families. Promote equal access to education. We should accelerate standardized construction of urban and rural public schools for compulsory education, strengthen team building of teachers especially rural teachers, promote communication between urban and rural teachers. Do a good job in special education. …Implement and deepen examination and enrollment system reform and education and teaching reform. Create individual study account and credit accumulation system, clear the paths to further education and lifelong learning. Promote education informatization, develop distance learning, expand the coverage of high quality educational resources. Improve educational supervision, strengthen social supervision. Support and normalize the development of private education, encourage social forces and private capital to provide diversified education services." Social security: "implement full coverage program, basically realize full coverage of statutory personnel. Persist in actuarial balance, and improve financing mechanism, differentiate the responsibilities of government, enterprise, individual etc. Reduce social insurance fee rate properly. Improve social insurance system Improve staff pension insurance individual account system, complete the more-pay-more-gain incentive system. Realize national pooling of basic staff pension, establish reasonable adjustment mechanism for basic pension. Broaden the investment channels of social security fund, strengthen risk management, increase rate of return on investment. Increase the proportion of state-owned capital gains paid to public finance gradually, transfer partial state-owned capital to enrich social security fund. Promulgate progressively delayed retirement age policy. We should develop occupational pension, enterprise pension, commercial pension insurance Improve stable, sustainable financing and reimbursement rate adjustment mechanism for medical insurance, discuss to implement medical insurance payment and participation policy for employees and retirees. Implement critical illness insurance system for urban and rural residents comprehensively. Reform medical insurance payment mode, give play to cost control function of medical insurance. Improve individual accounts, carry out unified planning of outpatient expenditure. We should realize direct settlement of inpatient cost of interprovincial nonlocal retirees. Integrate medical insurance policy and handling management of urban and rural residents. Encourage the development of supplemental medical insurance and commercial health insurance. Encourage commercial insurance companies to participate in the handling of medical insurance. Consolidate maternity insurance and basic medical insurance for implementation. Carry out unified planning of assistance system, strengthen policy connections, promote institutional integration, ensure basic living of poverty-stricken population." Health care: "we should deepen the reform of medical and health care system, link medical care, medical insurance and medicine together, promote separation of medicine and pharmacy, implement hierarchical diagnosis and treatment, establish basic health care system and modern hospital management system covering urban and rural areas. Fully promote integrated reform of public hospitals, adhere to public welfare attribute, break down profit-seeking mechanism, establish human resource salary system in compliance with the features of medical industry. Optimize the layout of medical and health institutions, improve medical service system of linked upper and lower parts, which are connected and complementary, improve medical service mode at community level, develop remote medical care. Promote the flow of medical resources to community level, rural areas, improve the ability of general practitioners, family doctors, medical services in urgently need fields, electronic health archives and so on. Encourage social forces to enter health service industry, promote equivalent treatment of non-profit private hospitals and public hospitals. Strengthen medical care quality supervision, improve dispute mediation mechanism, build harmonious doctor-patient relationship."

Postscript

This book is one of the research results of "Innovation Think-Tank", Institute of Economics, Chinese Academy of Social Sciences. Pei Changhong (head of the Institute of Economics, Chinese Academy of Social Sciences, researcher) is responsible for design, final compilation and edit of the whole book, and he writes Chap. 6; Wang Zhen (Director of Microeconomics Research Office, Institute of Economics, Chinese Academy of Social Sciences, researcher) writes Chap. 1, Chap. 4, Sects. 3 and 4 of Chap. 5; Sun Jingfang (associate researcher of Development Economics Research Office, Institute of Economics, Chinese Academy of Social Sciences) writes Chaps. 2 and 3, Sects. 1 and 2 of Chap. 5, and is responsible for tabulation in the Annex. I express my gratitude to Comrades Lu Hua and Xie Qian in the Scientific Research Office, Institute of Economics, Chinese Academy of Social Sciences who provided great convenience and assistance in the writing process of this book. And I appreciate China Social Science Press for willing to publish this book, I also appreciate editors Wang Yin and Wang Heng for their careful and meticulous work.

The Author
Sept. 26, 2016

C. Pei et al., *The Basic Income Distribution System of China*, China Governance System Research Series, https://doi.org/10.1007/978-981-15-3461-4

Bibliography

Karl Marx and Frederick Engels, Volume 4, People's Publishing House, 1958 Edition.
Li Qiang, Wang Hao, Four Worlds of Social Hierarchy in China, *Social Science Front*, 9th Issue, 2014.
Marshall, *Principles of Economics*, the Commercial Press, 1981 Edition.
Simon Kuznets, *Economic Growth of Nations*, the Commercial Press, 1999 Edition.
Social Security Research Group of the Institute of Economics, Chinese Academy of Social Sciences, Transition Path of Multi-Track Social Security Pension System, *Economic Research Journal*, 12th Issue, 2013.
Wei Zhong, Wang Zhen, Deng Quheng, *China Income Distribution and Its Policy Thinking*, Guangdong Economic Press, 2015 Edition.
William Petty, *Political Anatomy of Ireland*, the Commercial Press, 1974 Edition.
Zhang Wenmin, Comment on the Discussions of Distribution According to Work Since the Establishment of China, *Economic Science*, 5th Issue, 1985.

C. Pei et al., *The Basic Income Distribution System of China*, China Governance System Research Series, https://doi.org/10.1007/978-981-15-3461-4

The manufacturer's authorised representative in the EU is Springer Nature Customer Service Centre GmbH, Europaplatz 3, 69115 Heidelberg, Germany. If you have any concerns regarding our products, please contact ProductSafety@springernature.com

Printed and bound by CPI Group (UK) Ltd, Croydon, CR0 4YY
05/10/2026
02228121-0009